PENGUI
TIM

Protima Bedi was born in Delh
Bombay in the late sixties anc
film actor Kabir Bedi in 1969, and had two children, Pooja and Siddharth. She separated from Kabir in 1978. Protima started learning odissi dance in 1975 and within a few years, became an accomplished dancer. In 1989, she established Nrityagram, a dance village on the outskirts of Bangalore. Protima died in 1998.

Pooja Bedi Ebrahim was born in Bombay in 1970. She has been a successful film and theatre actress and a model and now designs bedroom accessories. She is currently working on a book on pregnancy. Pooja lives in Bombay with her husband and daughter.

PENGUIN BOOKS
TIMEPASS

Protima Bedi was born in Delhi in 1949. A prominent model in Bombay in the late sixties and early seventies, she married the film actor Kabir Bedi in 1969 and had two children—Pooja and Siddharth. She separated from Kabir in 1978. Protima started learning odissi dance in 1975 and within a few years became an accomplished dancer. In 1989, she established Nrityagram, a dance village on the outskirts of Bangalore. Protima died in 1998.

Pooja Bedi Ebrahim was born in Bombay in 1970. She has been a successful film and theatre actress and a model, and now designs body wear accessories. She is currently working on a book on pregnancy. Pooja lives in Bombay with her husband and daughter.

timepass

the memoirs of
Protima Bedi

with Pooja Bedi Ebrahim

PENGUIN BOOKS
An imprint of Penguin Random House

PENGUIN BOOKS

USA | Canada | UK | Ireland | Australia
New Zealand | India | South Africa | China

Penguin Books is part of the Penguin Random House group of companies whose addresses can be found at global.penguinrandomhouse.com

Published by Penguin Random House India Pvt. Ltd
7th Floor, Infinity Tower C, DLF Cyber City,
Gurgaon 122 002, Haryana, India

First published in Viking by Penguin Books India 1999
Published in Penguin Books 2000

15 14 13 12 11 10 9 8

ISBN 9780140288803

Typeset in PalmSprings by SŪRYA, New Delhi

Printed at Repro Knowledgecast Limited, India

www.penguin.co.in

contents

editor's introduction

Passion, compassion, laughter. I couldn't describe Protima Bedi better. As a mother she was phenomenal. She brought joy into our lives with her constant need to be different and creative. She was determined never to lead an ordinary life.

Almost everything about our childhood was unique and full of fun. Siddharth and I were taught the alphabet on sandy beaches, not on slate or paper. We dined on top of our car, in gardens, on the beach, in a tent in our living room, even in our bathtubs! Rarely was it the normal dining room scenario. Our bedroom was ever changing. One day there would be a lake in it for her 'water babies'—a round blue satin mattress on a dark blue carpet, and a wall-to-wall poster of Swiss mountains. Another day there would be bunk beds for her precious 'army children' (when we were studying at the military boarding school in Sanawar). Our birthdays were celebrated wherever we wanted. Siddharth once cut his cake in the clowns' tent at a circus, and because I wanted snow on one of my birthdays (in the month of

May), she took us all the way up to Rohtang Pass.

She would come to our school with a hang-dog expression and say to the teachers, 'Their nani is very ill,' and whisk us away to Alibaug, Powai, Lonavla or Panchgani in her crazy car which she had got us and all her friends to paint with funky motifs—flowers, stars, hearts and scarlet lips. We'd go tenting in the middle of nowhere, just the three of us, carrying canned food and cold drinks. This kidnapping routine became so frequent that whenever she entered the classroom, Siddharth and I would groan, 'Oh, no! Not again!' Needless to say, our attendance was never very impressive. And if she caught us doing homework, she would shriek, 'Why are you bringing work home from school? This is *my* time with you! Do I give you work from home to take to school?'

I remember the time when our school issued forms on which we were required to state our religion. It confused me. What was I? My mom was half Bengali, half Haryanvi. My dad was half British with traces of German and French blood, his mother had become a Buddhist nun, and on his father's side he was the eighteenth descendent of Guru Nanak. So what did that make me?

'Indian,' Mom said. 'You will write Indian. And if they have a problem with that let them come and talk to me. They have no business asking you your religion. How is that the basis for an educational qualification?'

She was never the conventional mother. She was a friend who kept no secrets from us and did not expect us to keep any from her. When she streaked, I was barely five years old. I was very upset and told her, 'All the children in my school say that their mummies said you ran nanga.' She kept quiet for a minute, then slowly, and very intensely, she said to me, 'This is *my* life. No one has the right to tell me how to live it or to question what I do. When you grow up, you will make your own choices. It will be your life and you will live it your way. I will never interfere.

It must be awful for these people to have such boring lives that all they can do to make them interesting is to talk about somebody else's life. I'm glad I provided them with timepass conversation.'

Many 'uncles' drifted in and out of our lives, mostly showering us with gifts and chocolates. Mom always made sure we were included in everything, so we would accompany her on many of her dinner dates (especially if she thought the man might be the lecherous kind). We danced around midnight bonfires with her and her friends, went to parties and to discotheques. (I'm told that I was put in a basket and taken off to the disco when I was barely two months old.)

When Pandit Jasraj entered her life, she was infused, much to our chagrin, with a passion for classical music. At six every morning we would hear the gentle strains of the taanpura, and then this awful 'Aaaaaaaa'. We would suffer it for ten minutes or so, and when we could not bear it any longer, we would pounce on her and gag her. We named her Cacofonix, after that awful bard in the Asterix comics. Even in our letters we used to lovingly refer to her as Caco.

When she started her dance practice, she would go thump, thump, thump—at six in the morning again—to some badly taped music. We would bury our heads under our pillows and wait for Asrani, who lived in the flat below us, to stop her. He would arrive, grumpy, his arms flailing, and complain, 'My ceiling is cracking, my lights and fans are shaking . . . My wife has got a splitting headache!' We would laugh when he left and tease her mercilessly.

But nothing got her spirits down for long. No matter how tiring or unsuccessful her day may have been, she would forget it all at the sight of a beautiful sunset, smiles on our faces, or even a cheery wave from the batli bai (the woman who came collecting empty bottles).

She would laugh at herself often, especially when she recognized a pettiness of mind and soul. She was amused by how seriously people took themselves and marvelled at their preoccupation with a 'respectable' place in society. 'The world isn't just what you see outside your window,' she would tell us. 'It's so much larger, so much grander. We are just microscopic specks in the whole big scheme of things in this universe! How bogged down we get by rules, by what society wants and what people say, when in fact it's all just timepass. Enjoy the moment, even the grief. Celebrate the joy of being alive. It's so very, very easy to be happy.'

This is not to say that she lived in a permanent state of euphoria. She was human. But whatever she did—living, loving, leaving, creating—she did with passion and conviction: 'Lead, follow or get out of your own way. To put it simply, shit or get off the pot. Be productive. And if you're doing something, do it well or don't do it at all.'

Putting her memoirs together, I was surprised by how often she felt that she could have done more for Siddharth and me. How? Giving birth to children does not mean that your life is over, that you must give up on your dreams, ambitions and sense of self. Mom believed this too, and would often joke, 'Give birth to children and they never forgive you for it.' There was no reason for her to have felt that she had failed as a mother. In an age when parenting is so mechanical, mundane and almost devoid of laughter and sharing, I thank God for having given me a mother like her. Her spirit, creativity, boundless energy and unconditional love brought joy into Siddharth's life and mine. We were fortunate to have had a mother with an incredibly open mind and the desire to share herself every step of the way.

The two things she never got over were Siddharth's suicide and an ugly experience I had with Mario Kropf, the man she had a very long and serious relationship with. When I was fifteen, Mario made sexual advances towards me. I told my mother (who was abroad at the time) all about it and left for boarding school. She wrote saying, 'Mario and my relationship is too deep to let something as shallow as this affect it.' Of course I was hurt and felt let down. When I returned she told me that it was rotten of me to have made up such stories, that it was my devious way of getting rid of Mario because I had never liked him. I was aghast. The man had denied everything when she had asked him about it. I confronted him, and then all hell broke loose. He admitted the truth to Mom sometime later and that marked the beginning of the end of their relationship. She never forgave herself for not believing me, for being blinkered and selfish.

The birth of Aalia was a momentous event for my mother. She was right there beside me in the labour room (along with my husband Farhan, my stepmother Nikki and my best friend Sonia). She would croon to her grandchild and hold her tight to her bosom. Aalia's birth had rekindled a spark that had died after Siddharth's suicide. She would creep into my room early in the morning and carry newborn Aalia off to sing to her, photograph her and play with her.

When Aalia was four months old, I took her to Nrityagram for ten days. The girls there said that they hadn't seen Mom so happy in a long time. Every morning I would wake up to find grandmother and granddaughter clinging to each other and swinging on the jhula outside the room. Aalia brought back hope into Mom's life. Despite her doctor's warning, she announced her comeback as a dancer. She was going to dance solo on stage after a gap of seven years. Little Aalia was the chief guest at the programme and lit the inaugural lamp. It turned out to be Mom's last public performance.

I have yet to meet someone more loving and generous than my mom. She wanted nothing for herself. She never bought herself fancy clothes or jewellery. Despite the fact that she was hurt because my dad had shelled out so little for our upkeep ('He buys Italian wine glasses—$100 a stem! Twelve of them! Just imagine, one glass will pay for your upkeep for a whole month!'), she took enormous pleasure in helping him financially.

She helped him obtain land in Bangalore and gave him a loan to start a business with his brother Ranga. When he married Nikki, she gave them her flat to stay in.

I know that she never stopped loving my dad. He was to her the ultimate man in her life—the father of her children, the person she would grow old with—and nothing shook her belief in that.

My mother was an amazing human being, full of tenacity, courage, zest, curiosity, laughter and kindness. And going by Ralph Waldo Emerson's definition of success, she was the most successful person I have ever known:

'To laugh often and much; to win the respect of intelligent people and the affection of children; to earn the appreciation of honest critics and endure the betrayal of false friends; to appreciate beauty; to find the best in others; to leave the world a bit better, whether by a healthy child, a garden path or a redeemed social condition; to know that even one life has breathed easier because you have lived. This is to have succeeded.'

o

For as long as I can remember, my mother had been keen to write her memoirs. Her journals date back to 1969 and continue till a few months before her death. She had, in fact, started writing her autobiography about a year prior to her death. When she died, she left behind, in addition to her unfinished manuscript, a note on how her book was to be structured, letters that she had selected as sources, and thousands of pages with her recollections, confessions and thoughts on life, relationships, religion, society and politics.

Timepass draws from all these sources. I have spliced together sections from her journals, letters and the fragment of her autobiography to cover every aspect of her life. References at the back of the book give a detailed list of the sources from which the different sections have been derived. Wherever editorial interpolations and explanations have become necessary to provide the context for certain events or the connections between them, these have been set in italics and within square brackets.

There is a lot that has not been included in these memoirs because she did not record it. Some of it deserves mention: her unshakable belief in her dream project, Nrityagram, even when she had dissociated herself from it; her great faith in and love for her protégée Surupa Sen (she even willed a fixed amount of money to be paid to Surupa every month for her dance training); her dependence on Lynne Fernandez, who now runs Nrityagram; the way she pushed her students into the limelight and sat back in the shadows ('They're far better dancers than me,' she'd say, which was highly unusual in the competitive, guru-is-best world of dance).

Since my mother had herself selected and arranged much of the material for her autobiography, putting this book together was not as difficult a task as it would otherwise have been. While this is not the book she would have written—for she was a perfectionist and would have ensured a finished manuscript, had she the time—it is as close to the kind of book that I imagine she would have wanted on her life. By finally making it happen, I am paying the best tribute I can to a wonderful mother and a very special human being.

POOJA BEDI EBRAHIM

introduction

I am told that I was born in Delhi, in October 1949. I say 'I was told' and not 'I was' because I am afraid of putting anything down as definite anymore. Nothing is quite the same if you look at it from another point of view, and by God, there are so many points of view, all valid in themselves. So, the question is, where do I position myself to tell my story?

It would be the easiest thing in the world to tell it straight, from my point of view alone. It is easy to say that the world took advantage of me—that my husband was a bastard to have left me with two children, and to have married again without batting a bloody eyelid; that a powerful barrister-turned lawyer seduced me; that my position throughout my marital life was that of a handmaiden. It is always easy to present yourself as a martyr. But the reality of life is too complex, and I am not interested in painting for the uninitiated who only understand black and white, the colours of small-mindedness, pettiness and idiocy.

I could not—and I would not—be a Sita to my husband, nor

a Radha to my lovers. And I doubt if I have been a Yashoda to my children. In other words, as far as the world is concerned, I have been a total flop. A flop as a wife, mistress, mother, daughter, sister, friend. A flop as a woman. And, of course, I have also been a flop as a social being, for I have broken every single rule that our society has so carefully constructed and upheld for over 2000 years. I have known no barriers. I have done precisely what I bloody well felt like doing and never given a damn. I have flaunted my youth, my sex, my intelligence, and I have done it shamelessly. I have loved many, been loved by some (though I couldn't tell you whom I loved the most, or who loved me the most).

People have reacted to me in all kinds of ways. I have been ostracized from polite society from time to time, I have been humiliated, taunted, jeered at, laughed at, shrugged off. And through it all the press has never tired of writing about my antics. At times I have been eulogized; women have flocked to me with their problems, young people have hailed me as their ideal. My children worship me, all my lovers are loyal to me, I am my ex-husband's 'best friend' and his wife is like a sister to me. My students and dance audiences respect me, and my servants swear by me. Why? I wish I knew. I wish I had answers to everything. There is nothing, really, that I truly know. And yet I do know enough to be able to say with total conviction that it is easy to be happy—so very, very easy.

Most people would say that I have achieved a lot in life. But I know that I have done nothing. I have merely let life live me. You have only to ready yourself, to allow things to happen as they should. The greatest favour you can do yourself is to 'get out of your own way'.

And if there is any regret, it is only that I did not do enough in my youth. The body had matured, but the mind had not. I wish we could all be born old and wise and die young and innocent.

my first death

I should start with Urvashi, but I may as well start at the very beginning. After a few mistakes, Brahma, the Creator, managed to get things going fairly smoothly, and soon the political order was firmly established in heaven. At the top were Brahma, Vishnu and Mahesh—Creator, Preserver and Destroyer. They were the Trinity, and they were all men. They were self-born, pure energy, and no one could know or reach them. Directly below them were the great sages, the rishis. They were pure knowledge. They knew everything but never told. Below them were reachable beings—gods and goddesses of all kinds, in charge of just about everything. All-powerful and immortal, they were not humans but they had feelings. Most of the goddesses sat at the divine lotus-feet of their husbands.

Between this god-world and the mortal world was Gandharvalok, populated with demi-gods and the apsaras—celestial dancers of exceeding beauty and extraordinary powers. The apsaras were adept at many skills and except for enjoyment, had no other feelings. They were the robots.

My story begins in the court of Indra, the king of the god-world. He was such a show-off that he was made the god of thunder and lightning. He was physically attracted not only to his wife, but to a whole horde of beauteous women. He had no concept of love. It was in Indra's court that the apsaras were to be found. Mind you, it was not a private harem, and he did not keep them all to himself. They were there to entertain other gods as well, for they were utterly beautiful, highly skilled in the arts of dancing, singing, and love-making. They were not born and they did not die, and though under the direct command of the gods, they had some sort of free will.

Urvashi was the first among the apsaras, the brightest jewel in Indra's court.

Sometimes when a mortal king or sage got too powerful or seemed to know too much, an apsara would be sent to corrupt and distract him and bring him to his doom (and Urvashi usually succeeded where the other apsaras failed). Nothing upsets the gods more than when mortals start realizing their own power. Which is why they invented Death—in truth only a kind of anaesthesia, but the mortals fear it as 'the end'—and gave humans the gift of the nine fabulous emotions, toys to keep them pointlessly busy all their lives. The only emotion which could bring mortals in contact with their inner selves was love. In love you realize that you are part of it all, that you are God, that you are the universe. Naturally, love is a great threat to the gods.

Urvashi too fell in love.

One day, the gods Mitra and Varun, displeased with Urvashi, cursed her. She lost all her powers and was forced to descend to earth as a mere mortal. It was while she was on earth that she saw and fell in love with the mighty king Pururavas. Fortunately for her, Pururavas reciprocated her feelings and they lived in bliss. Being an apsara, Urvashi was aware that the curse would one day be lifted and then she would have to return to

Gandharvalok. If she returned, she would become a beauteous robot again, incapable of feeling any emotion. But she had known love, and would not give it up now. The only way to fight that terrible future, she felt, was to make Pururavas aware of the great scheme of things. He too could be a god, and she a goddess.

Urvashi spent many nights in great turmoil. The thought of being parted from her beloved was too painful. She finally made her decision. One evening she told Pururavas all about the big scheme; about his own potential, about the gods, the demons, the Trinity. In short, she spilled the beans.

But the gods are great eavesdroppers, they have eyes everywhere. Indra was furious. He threw his lightning bolt at the earth, and the sky was ablaze. He roared mighty thunder. The universe trembled. There were tidal waves and volcanic eruptions on earth. All was night. Petrified of being taken back to Gandharvalok, of being parted from her beloved Pururavas, Urvashi made yet another bold decision. She committed suicide.

Once you die as a mortal, you enter the endless karmic cycle. A few million lifetimes have since passed, as Urvashi lives and dies, and lives and dies, playing out the same story in different bodies, sometimes realizing her true nature, but mostly without the knowledge of who she is and why.

In each lifetime she finds herself the property of an earthly Indra, being used as an apsara, and always she yearns to unite with her Pururavas and to know her true self.

O

On 12 October 1949 a second child was born to Laxmichand and Reba Gupta, and all hell broke loose. Yet another daughter. It was a disaster.

Laxmichand was the only son of a 'respectable' middle-class Gupta family in Haryana—a state where, as is often said, the only culture is agriculture (this is not a poor joke, it is the truth). The Guptas were ridiculously traditional in a hypocritical way; staunch upholders of India's ancient traditions. Perhaps they seriously believed that but for them the fabric of Indian society would fall apart. Then fate played a nasty trick on the pure, god-fearing Gupta family: Laxmichand fell head over heels in love with a black Bengali girl. To make matters worse, the girl had no family to speak of, or none that she wanted to speak of anyway. A great battle ensued in the Gupta household. Young Laxmichand was thrown out of the house, for he insisted on marrying the black Bengali.

Laxmichand moved with his wife to Delhi, where he joined an iron and steel company, and worked like a dog trying to redeem himself. He had to prove to his family that he could do without them. And he did it very well. He realized how fascinated his colleagues were by the unusual beauty of his young, dusky wife, so he encouraged her to smile more than she should have, to drink so that she could lose her inhibitions as a traditional Hindu wife. In time she became rather good at the game (I remember the looks she gave some of the men, the self-conscious flirting, and at the time I hated it). So, with a little help from his wife, the hardworking Laxmichand Gupta reaped the rewards.

But at the same time, there was a very dark, thick line that Laxmichand had drawn at the threshold, and he meant his wife to see it: this far, because it suits me, and no further, because it does not. Reba was not perceptive enough, so she did not always understand the meaning of that line, and sometimes she just plain forgot.

In 1947, Reba produced their first child, Monika. As often happens, the arrival of the child caused the aggrieved parents to relent. Laxmichand's family softened and they cuddled the baby and cooed over her. But the black Bengali woman was pointedly ignored. It was their son's child, she was only the necessary womb. They didn't have to be nice to her, and they weren't. Two years later, she produced a spitting image of Laxmichand in yet another daughter, Protima (that's me). There was a big hue and cry at this birth. Another girl! 'What rotten luck!' they said. 'That Bengali witch is good for nothing! Two girls!' they wailed.

If you were a girl but the firstborn, it was not so bad. But to be a secondborn and a girl was a disaster. They hated me.

A year and half later, the desired boy was born, and two years after him, the fourth child, another girl. So, as I saw it, Monika, the firstborn, was loved by all. Bipin, the only boy, was naturally adored by all. Ashita, the youngest, was cuddled by all. That left the secondborn, and a girl at that, nowhere. I became a very lonely child. My mother, aunts and sisters swear that I was not neglected and that it is a figment of my imagination. They could be right, but, as I have told them, what is important is that I *had* felt the neglect. And feeling left out, I had suffered immensely all through my childhood. Obviously, I was the only one to blame for it, but that didn't make the hurt any less. In my mind, I was alone throughout my childhood. Terribly alone and full of complexes. Now I laugh at the memory of those days and wish that I had a bigger head at that time to understand more than I did. I had no cause to be as unhappy as I was—I had my books, I had a comfortable home and a great education. My father was reasonably rich and by normal standards my parents were not too bad. But then there are always those abstract things which make you unhappy at that age.

In 1953, we shifted to Goa, where my father had leased manganese ore mines from the Portuguese government. Father had moved up considerably in life and we were living in a large bungalow surrounded by many trees. Beautiful mother and tubby father socialized a lot and had no time for the four of us. We spent our days collecting cashew-nuts from the trees in our garden and listening to ghost stories told to us by Mary, our Goan ayah who didn't wear panties.

I was the tomboy of the family. There was nothing, I felt, that

I could not do. Once, standing on a rock at the edge of a stream, I had boasted that I could take a flying leap and cross the fifteen-odd feet of water if I really wanted to. When Monika defied me, I leapt, and landed four feet away on a huge rock and split open my right knee. I was barely five then. The scar is still there, four inches long, one inch wide.

Nothing much happened in Goa till I was seven years old. That was the time I died and was reborn. Seven is a mystical number. It had to be then. Father had bought a big box of Brooklax tablets which tasted like chocolates. There was also a box of real chocolates. Clever Monika gave the Brooklax tablets to me and kept the real chocolates for herself. I ate the boxful—twenty-four big tablets of purgatives. My stomach collapsed. When there was almost no fluid left inside, I passed blood. It was late afternoon, my father was away at the mines and my mother and the servants were napping. It was a large house, and I lay alone in the linen room, cold, life slowly leaking out of me. Because I was such a tomboy no one worried about where I was till late after tea-time. When they finally found me, I was dead. Nothing striking; just an ordinary seven-year-old dead in an ordinary, orthodox household.

The mines were closed. The doctor wrote out my death certificate. My body was washed and prepared for the pyre. The family was gathered around, weeping and wailing, and the workers from the mines stood respectfully at a distance, silently mourning. Above them all hovered the divine apsara Urvashi, caught in the cruel web of karma. She had recently passed out of one body and was in search of another.

'Here's my chance,' said Urvashi to herself, 'to hide from the gods and the demons again. This time they will not know where I have been born. This time I will trick them.

Yamraj had not yet arrived, and he could be easily fooled. Urvashi descended into her new abode. I was reborn.

the early years

When I was about nine years old, I was sent off to stay with my father's relatives in a village in the Karnal district of Haryana. I don't exactly know why I was sent there, but I suspect my father was in a financial mess and had just moved house and home to Bombay. These few months from my childhood are the most vivid in my memory. I remember the toilet was upstairs, on the terrace, and we had to carry sticks and stones with us to chase away the big monkeys that abounded there. I remember the mud walls, the community baths, and the mud floor plastered with cowdung.

There were a great many people in that large house, and among them was a cousin, a horrible, pathetic boy, dark and ugly. He must have been barely fifteen. He would take me to the terrace alone or come to my bed at night and put his hands under my dress, groping and clawing. One night he climbed into my bed, dug his hand into my panties and oiled me there. I didn't quite understand what he was doing. I was terrified as he put one hand on my mouth and climbed on top of me. He raped me. I remember the shock and the pain. I remember how frightened I was. I was so ashamed of what had been done to me that I kept quiet.

The following night I pretended to be afraid of sleeping on my own and made a fuss about wanting to sleep with one of my cousin sisters, but no one paid me any heed. I had to sleep alone in my bed and that cousin repeated what he had done to me the previous night. This happened over and over again, almost every night. I was overcome with disgust and loathing and a dreadful fear. I hated the sight of my cousin brother, I didn't dare look at him. I didn't dare tell his mother. I didn't dare do anything. I was really quite a mouse then.

I became a little withdrawn and kept mostly to myself. I would climb onto the mango tree in the backyard and spend hours up there, watching the goings on of the world. When I wasn't on that tree, I was busy collecting cowdung and making flat chapattis out of it. My head was full of lice and my right foot had a perpetual eczema. In the paathshala, the local school, I was the quietest child, diligently writing big black Hindi alphabets on my white slate. People generally let me be. I was, after all, the most intelligent child in the village, the bright, city-bred daughter of my aunt's rich brother.

My aunt owned a temple in the village and on certain festive days people would gather there and sing bhajans, playing the cymbals, gongs and dholaks. On one of these occasions, an old lady, obviously a widow, sprang up from the seated crowd and broke into a dance. Her arms outstretched, she whirled like a dervish. She kept dancing till she was in a swoon. I was sitting next to her, clapping my hands to the chants of 'Krishna-Krishna, Hare-Hare', and I saw an expression of complete ecstasy on her face. There were tears rolling down her cheeks but she seemed unaware of this, for her face was radiant. She was absorbed in something beyond time, oblivious to us all. I turned to stone, my hands froze, my mind was still. I too was lost. She was carrying me away with her, to wherever it was that she was going. Perhaps that is where my fascination with dance began; or perhaps it began before that, when I was reborn as an incarnation of Urvashi, the queen of the apsaras.

O

Back with my family in Bombay, I remained withdrawn, immersed in my books most of the time. I was sent with my sisters to Kimmens, a convent in Panchgani. I hated boarding school in the beginning. I used to wet my bed at night (an affliction that I have continued to suffer from as an adult; I still wet my bed some nights) and the nuns would make me carry the wet mattress on my shoulder and walk through the corridors in the morning. It was humiliating, but I got used to it after a while, and perhaps that acceptance drained me of any capacity for real personal hate for the rest of my days.

I did quite well at school. I always came first or second in class and my father, in rare moments of softness, would say with great pride, 'She will be a very famous lawyer.' I had always known that I would not. My interests lay elsewhere, in dance and painting. But no one at home took any particular interest in my hobbies, or even in me. I was thin, black and cranky, and therefore the ugly duckling in the family. They called me 'Kali'. 'Who will marry you?' they would taunt. I used to gaze at myself in the mirror and wonder why God had made me so ugly. The nose was fat and flat. My big eyes, which are now considered beautiful, looked at that time like frog's eyes. Thick lips were never thought sexy then; only Africans had such unfortunate lips.

I took refuge in my books, but I could never forget my 'ugly' body. I wished I was beautiful, like my sister Monika. She was slim but healthy and had big boobs. And of course she was fair.

Naturally, she had many admiring boyfriends, and I would often carry her letters to them. I was in awe of Monika. My greatest ambition at that time was to marry and have ten children.

I became obsessed with my physical appearance. I dreamed of being a woman whom men would desire and marry, and this found expression, when I was ten or eleven, in secret cabaret routines that I did in front of the mirror in our bedroom. It was serious business. It was art: striptease to Bach. We had one record of Western classical music and a temperamental old record player which often gave us electric shocks, so that we had to use a wooden stick to start it. I would lock the bedroom door and put on my mother's bra, stolen from the clothes line, with great wads of cotton stuffed into the cups. Then I'd pull on a tight shirt and a skirt and pose in front of the full-length mirror, my chest thrust out. The profile was important. The voluptuous breasts (fake as they were) were absolutely essential to get the right contours for the pose.

Then the music would begin and I would start swaying gently. I took my clothes off, as artistically as I could, except the bra stuffed with cotton. But this removal of garments was done with 'Art' in mind, with proud expression on the face and grace in the body. The routine could not, under any circumstances, be vulgar. My arms fluttered over my head, my slender girlish hips gyrated, my fake breasts heaved and shook a little, and a strange thrill ran through my whole body. All the time my eyes remained on my image in the mirror. As the music rose to a crescendo, my movements became more dramatic, and the finale was always orgasmic—semi-orgasmic, actually—and achieved with consummate class. I was mesmerized.

'This is what I'll do when I run away from home,' I decided, 'this is how I shall make my living!' I would raise the striptease act to the level of a glorious art. I would perfect the technique, and by the time my boobs had sprouted, I would be ready to dazzle the world. But this wait, for the boobs to sprout, took away most of the dynamism in my act. After all, what could be more ridiculous than a striptease by a girl without breasts? What frustration! Why didn't the damned boobs sprout quickly? What a waste of talent!

It was when I was standing breathless and sweaty and fulfilled before the mirror one day, having just demonstrated the highest of arts to myself, that I saw them, my mother and my elder sister. They had climbed onto the thin ledge under the window to watch me. They were giggling and laughing. I was filled with a great sense of shame and outrage. They had seen the stuffed bra on me, seen my complete transformation! They had seen my classy orgasm! I cried for days and never danced again at home. What a loss to the world of cabaret. I had wanted to take striptease to mystical levels. I had disrobed myself to the music of Bach and Debussy. I had glimpsed the possibility of a major transformation in the dance world! My mother and sister had robbed the world of greatness. I wept for myself. I wept for the world.

It was a while before I dared to dance again. On Saturday nights, the senior girls in our boarding school were allowed to play the gramophone and dance in the recreation room. Only the Anglo-Indian girls dared to get up and jive together. Dolly was always the 'man' who led and Priscilla was the sexy girl. There were others like Deveea, Mavis, Joy and her sister who also had no shame. I remember some of the girls turning their faces away from time to time out of embarrassment. I wanted to do the same, but I couldn't help staring at their dancing feet, their clasping hands, the tight embraces, the beautiful bodies rubbing against each other. How fast they danced and in such harmony! How did they know in advance what to do with their feet and arms?

After the dances, late at night, I would sneak into the gumboot and raincoat room and practice what I thought was jiving. How I longed to jump up from my seat and join those girls the following Saturday! But I never did.

Sometimes we saw classical dances from the South in the movies and we always made fun of them. The music was so painful and hard on the ears, and the basic posture—we called it the 'chamberpot' posture—was utterly ridiculous. 'Looks like she's constipated,' we'd laugh. 'A piece of shit's about to appear any minute!' Everything to do with South India, its language, its culture, was cause for ridicule. As for the North Indian classical style, kathak, which was easy and graceful to the eye, one was certainly very partial to it. But while it was appealing, it didn't attract. The dancers seemed so keen to prove mathematical points that they lost whatever grace they had in trying to execute the steps.

Besides, we were the convent crowd. Anything to do with Indian culture was sneered at. Indian culture was only for the middle classes, the locals, the frogs-in-the-well who were not aware of the world outside. Indian culture was for the Hindiwalas, not for the elite who conversed in English. And I was part of that charmed elite; my Hindi was so atrocious that only Bombay taxi drivers could understand it.

I continued to read a lot in school. I devoured some very 'grown-up' novels: *Tropic of Cancer* and *Tropic of Capricorn*, *Lolita*, *Lady Chatterley's Lover*. Farida Jalal's mother used to bring these novels when she came to visit Farida at our boarding school. I would take the books and lock myself in the toilet, spending hours reading them. I was fascinated by free, wanton women in literature. I remember a passage in one of the books in which the woman walks out onto the moonlit beach, confident that the man will follow her. As they gaze into each other's eyes, there is an electric tension, and she slowly takes his hand and puts it on her breast. I remember sitting on the potty, reading the novel, and when I came upon that passage, I shut the book and imagined the scene over and over again. I was flushed with a great sense of shame and excitement. Shame because a woman had made so blatant a move. And excitement because she wanted something forbidden, and I knew what she wanted.

Would any man ever want me, I wondered. I was sure not. Who would desire a kali-kaluti? I would never live such a scene. Pity. I would wrap my arms around me and hug myself tight, pretending that some handsome Romeo had taken me in his arms. Many were the men and boys I embraced and kissed in my fantasies—my sister's boyfriends, my uncles and cousins, loafers I'd seen on the streets. I imagined myself with all of them, and thus kept myself happy. I prayed fervently to all the gods in heaven to send just one man my way. He need not be good looking, rich, or even a very nice person, so long as he was willing to marry me, give me a home of my own, and ten children at least, so that I could spend all my time in loving my children and bringing them up. I swore that no child of mine would be neglected. I would love them all the time.

But the years passed and I had still not sprouted boobs. The periods hadn't started. My sister was wearing bras at the age of twelve, and here I was, flat even at sixteen. Which man would want a wife without breasts? I had a terrifying notion that women who didn't get their periods became eunuchs, and I visualized myself turning half-male, slowly but surely. If anyone found out, they would give me away to the band of eunuchs who came singing and dancing and making obscene gestures at the men, embarrassing the women and frightening the children. No, I had to protect myself. No one should ever know my awful secret. So every month I spent all my pocket money on a packet of sanitary napkins and on fixed days every month I threw out the pads. Every other girl was embarrassed by her periods, but not me. I made a bold exhibition of the fact that I was menstruating. When the others hunched their shoulders forwards, embarrassed by their new breasts, I would wonder at them. Being flat-chested was my greatest sorrow. Wouldn't God give me at least enough to fill the smallest bra?

Then on New Year's Day, 1965, I took off my pajamas and *there was the great red stain*! It was the happiest day of my life. I skipped and danced and sang and was quite beside myself. Of course, no one could understand my euphoria, and I was certainly not telling anyone about it. Who says that magic doesn't happen? During the next six months there was great activity in the top half of my body. The glands filled up, the breasts grew and grew, and I was so proud that I walked about with my chest thrust right out for everyone to see. This pair was for real. 'Shameless girl!' my mother would say. 'It looks so bad, why don't you wear bras?' And how could I tell my mother that I wouldn't dream of enslaving and restricting that which I had yearned for so desperately. If my boobs shook about and bounced around when I walked, it was very satisfying for me. My mother used to tell me that one went through 1,24,000 births before being gifted by God with the human form. Wow! What was I going to do with this fantastic gift? Let it rot!

I was big-breasted, my waist remained tiny, and my hips filled out. In college (St Xaviers, which I joined in June 1965) the boys were always whistling at me, and it was suddenly too much of an experience. I would go bouncing all round the place, and that was how I got branded as 'chaalu' and 'fast' in college. In a perverse way I was happy being called those names because it meant that everybody knew I had boobs. 'She's a real cheap dame, yaar, she doesn't wear bras,' some boys would say. That I could bear. But when one of the senior boys remarked, 'They're not real, she's wearing falsies,' I burst into tears.

Armed with my impressive boobs (size 37) and evidence of my womanhood—my periods—I confronted life head on. It was a charmed life. I was invited to all the parties in college because I was the sexy chick who danced with all the boys, real close. I enjoyed their discomfort immensely. How their breath would quicken, how hard they would press their thighs against mine, how surreptitiously their hands would try to brush against my breasts. I would do all I could to get them to touch the priceless pair, to feel them, caress them, squash them, kiss them, but college boys in my time were a bunch of nincompoops, scared of girls who were not scared of them. Scared to do anything that they hadn't initiated, where they were not the seducers. I don't think men have changed very much since then.

'That's a very fast one, be careful of her,' the boys said to each other. 'She's just out to have fun.' And what was wrong with that? They didn't have marriage on their minds when they asked a girl out, did they? And what the hell was their kind of marriage anyway? Wasn't my mother married to my father? For as long as I could remember, I had only seen my parents quarrel, which ended sometimes with my mother being knocked around a bit. I had never seen my father even gently caress my mother's hands. I used to wonder whether they cared for each other at all.

I wanted some man to want me madly and marry me, but there was nothing attractive about the marriages I saw around me. The famous music director who was our neighbour used to beat his wife every night. I would often see her sitting out on the stairs, crying. I had seen so many of my mother's friends and our neighbours' wives crying because their husbands ill-treated them. There was always another woman. Why couldn't the husband be nice to his wife, specially since he was having such a good time anyway? Why should he beat her?

And then, why couldn't the wives find someone else for themselves? They always said, 'for the sake of the children', and yet, I remember, as they played cards every afternoon, laughing and gossiping before they found out about the other woman in their husbands' lives, they talked openly about how they would love to screw that man and that, or their favourite film star. But the moment they discovered that their husbands were giving it somewhere else, their world crumbled, they became nervous wrecks, they couldn't fend for themselves in this wicked world. I always wondered at these women. These same women who yelled obscenities at each other, who abused their servants and thrashed their children, who viciously attacked their neighbours, who fought with the vegetable man and bullied him down to half the price, who elbowed their way through crowded markets and temples, couldn't dream of fending for themselves.

There was one couple, though, who seemed happy. But then they were not husband and wife. They were man and mistress. The man was a friend of my father's who came to our house often. He was married, but we only ever saw him with his mistress. They were the most loving couple I had ever seen. He was around forty and she was twenty-five. But the caring they shared, the way they looked at each other, the way he touched her hand or brushed past her, the way he spoke of her, all that made me think that they were the only ones who knew what love was. That was the kind of love I wanted. If it meant being a man's mistress and not his wife, that was okay by me.

O

Being a 'good girl' was never important to me. In fact, I always wanted to be the bad girl. Since nobody cared about me in any case, I would rebel against everybody and everything by being a bad girl. The servants at home called me 'Nirali' because I never did the things that good girls my age were supposed to do. Even in those days I wasn't disturbed by what people thought of me. What the neighbours said or what the world felt never ever concerned me. (Just as today it does not bother me if I am thought of as an immoral woman. I think I am a very good woman. I've always felt very good inside. Naughty yes terribly naughty, but certainly not a bad woman.)

In college I was bunking classes all the time—I saw no purpose in attending; everything was so easy and boring. Besides, I had too many boyfriends, with whom I went out during college hours. My mother used to beat me whenever she found out. If boys called up at home, she would get suspicious. 'Kyon phone kiya?' she would ask, and I had to make up all kinds of stories about library books and notes.

There were two gangs in our neighbourhood, one led by Vinod Khanna and the other by Anil Johar (I.S. Johar's son). Vinod's gang had people like Harshad and Kika and Keku and Kaku and whatever, and Anil had Biddu, Aliah, Noni Kapoor, Pratap Shivdasani and a very handsome chap called Anil Malhotra. Almost all social life in the Bombay of the mid-sixties revolved around these groups. Bistro and Volga, right next to each other in the Fort, were the places to go to. In Churchgate there was Napoli, and Venice at the Astoria, where Biddu used to sing as the lone Trojan, with his crowd gathered all around.

I was sixteen, just out of school, determined to be a bad girl, and I was fascinated by these gangs. I admired them from afar. Girls were told to stay away from them. They often had fights, and people ended up getting hurt. Moreover, they had all these parties where, we were told, the lights would be dimmed, hard liquor served, and—this was the worst bit—girls and boys would dance close and kiss. This of course only increased my curiosity, and soon I was accepted by both groups. I went to their parties and discovered that it was only natural to dim the lights for people to dance close. And there was nothing very wrong with letting a boy kiss you.

Those were crazy days. We would go into town from the suburbs (those of us who lived there) just to dance, to freak out doing the twist or whatever else was fashionable in those days. We lied to our parents if they saw us coming back early in the mornings—we'd gone out for an early morning walk, we'd say. Sometimes we'd tell them we were going out of town for a youth conference. They'd drop us off at Bombay Central station to make sure we went, but we'd hop off at Dadar or Juhu. I was supposed to be a good dancer. When I came on the floor, everyone else would move away and I would have the whole area to myself. I think I was declared 'Twist Queen' once.

It is funny how that scene just dissolved. I think the beginning of the end came when Vinod fell in love with Anil's sister, Neelam (whom I used to idolize), and then both gangs aged. Biddu went to England and later became a star. Neelam acted in a film and then got married and went abroad, to do nothing but be a wife. With time all the glamour was gone.

We were all naïve then. The psychedelic, drugged-out sixties hadn't really hit us. The girls, for instance, had to be discreet. They were not supposed to smoke or drink—perhaps the odd cigarette in the toilet, but no more.

When I left that set and became a model, I became part of the ad circuit and it was a completely different world. No more Venice and Volga. It was now the Chinese restaurants and other places which had cubicles in those days, and a *lot* could go on in there. The advertising crowd got into acid rock, proper psychedelic parties, and all sorts of things.

But I was still naïve, I suppose. Some time later when I opened the city's first real disco, 'Hide Out', just under the Marine Drive flyover, it became a haven for hippies and junkies. I didn't know that charas was illegal. The yanks—draft dodgers, mainly—introduced me to it and I was soon making joints and selling them to the freaks. It wasn't surprising, really, that the police shut the place down.

first loves

In the second year of my college I met Jalal. He had already graduated, but he was in the college canteen every morning and noon, eyeing me. There was something attractively rakish about him, a sort of I-don't-give-a-damn attitude which appealed to me. The college girls kept away from him, saying that he was part of a gang of 'pucca Mussalmans' that got into knife fights. The way they said 'Mussalman', it implied being cheap, dirty, violent, immoral and low-class. I would sit with my girlfriends around our favourite table, and Jalal was always around, smiling and laughing loudly to attract my attention. And he did. We soon started spending a lot of time together.

Jalal was as uninhibited as I. We would go off to nearby hill-resorts, book ourselves into cheap hotels and spend the whole day in bed. I loved him dearly. For me, he was the husband I had always wanted, the one who would give me my ten children and a happy home. That he was Muslim, that his family and mine would never agree, didn't bother me in the least. I loved him, and he loved me. We skipped college every single day for almost a whole year. Jalal was not the first man to have me sexually, but he was first man I had consensual sex with, and it turned out to be not such a great thing after all. I had built it up so much in my mind since childhood, and now I wondered if this was really that great passionate event for which people even killed one another. I'm not saying that I disliked sex, or that I was disinterested in it, just that I was disappointed. Very disappointed. Jalal was not bad in bed, but my body did not experience that fire, that earthquake, that tornado, those rainbows which I had expected.

Jalal was waiting for his rich uncle to die so that he could inherit all the wealth and then do something grand with it. I was absolutely against this attitude and urged him to go to the States for higher education and not waste his time waiting. It took me three months to convince him. We met secretly, as usual, the evening before he was due to leave and wept bitterly for each other and for our love and made so many promises, intending to keep every one of them. We exchanged rings in a very solemn and heart-rending little ceremony on the landing between the third and the fourth floors of a building. I had had to steal my uncle's watch and pawn it for the money to buy the ring which I put on Jalal's finger that evening. He slipped a beautiful ring studded with nine small diamonds on my finger, and there it has stayed ever since.

For three whole days after Jalal left, I stayed at home, suffering and romanticizing my situation. I did all the house work and helped my mother in the kitchen and embroidered and sewed and thought to myself that I would lead this life for two years till my Jalal returned and married me. I did a splendid job playing the ideal lover pining and waiting for the faithful beloved who has gone away, across the seven seas. I played the part for three days and I would certainly have continued to do so for a full two years had life not interfered with my plans. Who can predict what will happen, against all one's good intentions! My little sister had to spend the day with a friend of hers, and she was too young to go on her own, so big sister readily agreed to escort her to the friend's house and spend a boring day watching the children play. I rang the doorbell and a male voice said, 'Come in.' I entered and saw a man sprawled on the couch with a book in one hand and a pen in his mouth. He was tall, slim, and very attractive. 'And I was just writing how the sun rose with great majesty on the horizon—now I know I was wrong,' he said.

'I beg your pardon?' I said, a little flustered.

'I said I was wrong. Because now I know that the sun never rose at all . . . at least not until now.' I blushed. It was such a nice feeling to get compliments from strangers, especially good-looking strangers. 'I'm the big brother, Anil. Come in, make yourself at home. Anita has gone to a movie with all the other girls and left one ticket for your sister. Let's go and drop her there. You can sit with me and have tea, and I will read you all my poems . . . No, I will now begin to *compose* my poems.'

He laughed a lot. You got the feeling that he was sweeping you off your feet all the time. He was such an easy man to be with. I liked him immediately. He was an Air Force pilot and had many girlfriends. He loved all of them. I was soon accompanying him on all his dates. As he leaned over, clasping the girlfriend's hand and telling her how he could not live without her, he would be nudging my foot under the table. I always pretended to be engrossed in his poems, which I read all the time. I couldn't help smiling at that lovely man. He meant no harm to anyone. He just wanted to give joy. In a single day he would meet four or five girlfriends. He never repeated himself. He had something different to say to each one of them. And I went with him, everywhere.

My father, an orthodox, conservative bania at heart, was very strict about what we wore and where we went. We couldn't wear sleeveless blouses to college (my sisters and I fooled him by leaving the house with sleeved blouses worn over the sleeveless ones), and we had to be home by 7.30 in the evening, not a minute later. Going out at night for parties or dinners was out of the question. But everyone seemed to be having fun at nights. I had had enough of day parties in college where the boys would draw all the curtains, then dim the lights and pretend it was night. I had had enough of make-believe, now I wanted the real experience. I dared to ask my father once if I could go out at night for a girlfriend's birthday party and he refused. He was shocked that I should even have asked such a question. 'Girls from good families don't go out at night. Wish her in the morning. If you want money to buy her a present, I'll give it to you.'

I was upset. What did he mean, good families? He belonged to a true bania khandaan, he said his prayers every morning, but didn't he drink every evening? He did not smoke, but did he not gamble in the club? He often came home drunk and beat his wife, didn't he? I had no proof that he cheated in his business, but I was willing to bet that he did (if you're doing business, you cheat—that's simple business law). Was all that okay in good families?

'What is it that I can do at night that I can't do during the day?' I ventured boldly. His response was a slap that I remember even today. His blood pressure shot up and he was panting and red in the face, stuttering incoherently with rage. I stood there, proud and bold. I knew that I was right. The feeling that I am right has always given me a fantastic sort of courage. 'You will do as you're told, understand!' he screamed. I had a great desire to cry, not because I was afraid or hurt by the slap, but because of my inability to say what I wanted. It was the frustration; I knew that if I was given the chance to discuss this topic openly with him, he would lose the argument.

'But daddy, why can't I go out?' I muttered.

'Because I say so, and that's all there is to it. It is an order. If you want to live in this house, you will do as I say. And don't ever defy me again, or talk back to me. I'll break both your legs!'

But I had my way despite him. I would tie a long piece of string to my foot and drop the remainder of the string over the window ledge. We stayed on the second floor. Anil and his friend Rajesh would come late in the night and switch on their headlights. Spotting the white string hanging over the ledge, they would give it a big yank. My foot would jerk up and I would come awake immediately. I would get out of bed quietly and creep down the narrow passage, past my mother's bedroom and down two flights of stairs, with my Pomeranian under my arm, and go off with the boys to wild parties. I would inevitably arrive at the parties when all the 'good, decent' girls who were permitted by their parents to go for a little while were on their way out. So I became the 'fast girl' who couldn't give a damn about how she dressed, as I mostly came in my night clothes or wore a kurta-pajama, as though I was planning to stay the night with whoever was free.

I wondered why women who went out at night had such a bad reputation. I, for one, did not have any sex on those wild night outings. We laughed a lot, went on fast drives, watched the sunrise and talked about life—in short, we were like brothers. Anil and his friends would tell me about their escapades with other women and talk with great sarcasm about those goody-goody girls who put on such an air of morality, but who were, in their opinion, the real 'fast' and sexually frustrated ones. I would be aghast to hear them talk of their steady girls' sexual habits and what-nots. I knew which girl was good in bed, which one liked to be fingered, which one gave a hand job and which one used her mouth. Whenever I talked to those girls at parties and they replied to me in a very prim tone, I would imagine them doing the things that the boys had told me about and I would roar with laughter. I wanted to hug each one of them and say, 'Drop this stiffness, relax,' but never got down to doing it.

My parents never discovered that I had ever gone out. One morning, however, I come in a little too late, and my father was awake and having tea. I rang the doorbell, he opened the door. Seeing me in my pajamas, with the dog at my heels, he asked good-naturedly, 'So early in the morning?' and I smiled happily and said, 'Walking the dog on the beach. You know, early to bed and early to rise makes you healthy, wealthy and wise.' 'Good girl', he said. I wondered about that early to bed, early to rise business. I had come home so many times in the early hours and all around me, on the sidewalks and roads, I had seen only garbage collectors, milkmen, watchmen, drunkards, and the occasional late-night traveller returning home. I never saw a wise, healthy or rich man. They were all asleep in the early mornings.

Anil said that I was his favourite girlfriend and I believed him. Perhaps he said the same thing to others, in other cities, but what did it matter? He meant it when he said it, and I enjoyed being with him tremendously. But my love letters to Jalal continued, irrespective. Of course, there was no question of writing to Jalal about Anil. It never occurred to me to do so; Anil was not meant to be a permanent fixture in my life.

O

I had a girlfriend in college, Rani, who lived with her father, Dinkie, and her step-mother, a beautiful English lady, very elegant and refined. The father was a very suave, well-dressed businessman who owned race horses. He would take Rani and me to the races and give us tips on the horses. I always won. I admired the man, and he was always being special to me.

One day he asked me to come home for lunch with Rani and him, as the wife had gone off for a few days. The next day he took us out to a very lovely restaurant and gave us the best food.

He insisted on dropping me home at night. He chatted gaily in his big beautiful car which was always driven by his chauffeur. As he dropped me, he said, 'I want to invite you out for lunch tomorrow, but this is only for you. I don't want to call Rani, as she's spending the day with her mother. Will you do me the honour of accepting a lunch at Rendezvous, at the Taj?' I was utterly charmed. Lunch at the Rendezvous! I had heard that it was the most expensive restaurant in town, and this suave man was taking me there. How could I refuse?

I was at the Taj with him the next day, still a little dazed. I had taken great pains to look like a lady. I had even worn a sari for the occasion, and put my hair up. I think every young girl is pleased by the attention of a suave older man, specially if he treats her as an equal and does nothing to conceal his admiration for her. He ordered wine. I felt so grown-up, so fashionable. I sipped at the drink daintily, and chatted nervously for two hours. By the end of the meal, I was high and happy. After lunch, he said he would take me to his friend's house 'to meet the friend'. I was a little drunk, but I knew what was on his mind. I hoped that it might not be so, but I was in no state to refuse. Of course I was a little apprehensive, but not terribly afraid.

I woke up in a large bed in 'the friend's house' around six in the evening. I remembered what had happened and the depression started. I burst out crying. I'm sure it was the after-effect of the wine, but at that time I felt cheated. I felt I had been had and I refused to talk to him. He was silent all along as he dropped me home. Before I got off next to our building, he held my hand and looking really crestfallen, said, 'Forgive me, I was high, and I cannot ever forgive myself for having hurt your feelings.' I got out of the car and he drove off. I didn't know what to feel. Of course I believed him.

The next morning, a big basket of flowers arrived, the first in my life. With it there was a note: 'Please forgive me. If you do, then call. I am waiting anxiously by the phone.' I wondered what to do. It pleased me to know that such a worldly, grown-up man was suffering on my account, that he was in turmoil because of me. I called. 'You have given me life. Thank you. Will you give me another chance, just to make up for the lapse? Will you have lunch with me this afternoon?' I agreed. The events of the previous afternoon were repeated, after two bottles of wine this time.

I met Dinkie every afternoon after that at his 'nest'. I don't know why I kept meeting him, since I knew that all I felt for him was physical attraction, and that too because of habit. I still had not felt those tremors, those rocking explosions that one is supposed to feel in sex. It was during this time that the restlessness started. There grew in me a need to be elsewhere, to live another life. I decided to join Air India as an air hostess. I went for two interviews and got through. But my father didn't let me join.

While still at college, I had started doing a bit of modelling on the side. I had kept this a secret from my family. But one day, there I was, sprawled on the front page of the *Times of India* in a brief nightie, modelling for Bombay Dyeing. My father called out to me. 'What's this?' he asked quietly. I looked at the picture and went into a nervous giggle. 'Goodness, looks just like me, doesn't she?' I said. His voice shook with suppressed rage. 'Why did you do this? Did you have to embarrass the family and ruin its good name?' What would people say? How could he show his face to all his friends? Why, why, why? he kept asking. 'For money,' I said finally. 'What do you need money for? Don't you get food at home? Aren't your college fees paid? Don't you get enough clothes and money to spend on transport? Don't I give you enough pocket money?'

'Daddy, I want to work. I want to be independent.'

'What do you mean, independent? What can you do if you are independent? Can you eat more, laugh more, study more? I want none of this nonsense, and if I ever catch you modelling again, you'll be thrown out of the house! Understand?'

I understood. I had to get out of that house. But I would do it on my own terms.

I was made to promise that I would never model again, and I did, but of course I had no intention of keeping that promise. How could I? I had just got a taste of earning my own money and there were quite a few modelling offers coming my way—Signal toothpaste, Nescafé. I hadn't chosen modelling as a career, it had just happened. It was Mrs Swaminathan of J. Walter Thompson (who later died of cancer) who had selected me, and now advertisements were pouring in. My contemporaries were Meher Mistry, Anabella Crawford and Shobha Rajadhyaksha (now Shobha Dé). I started doing fashion shows, earning more money than I had ever handled, and had the time of my life.

meeting kabir

It was September 1968. I had just finished a modelling assignment at Bensons and was sitting with Suresh Mullick (the head of Bensons at the time) in his cabin drinking coffee. My back was towards the door, and I heard it open and this deep, husky voice said, 'May I have the golden key to the executive toilet?'

I turned around, and could hardly believe my eyes! There stood before me the handsomest man I had ever seen—a beautiful hunk of a man, tall, broad, wearing a crumpled white shirt, black trousers, and a devastating smile. He nodded briefly at me and vanished with the keys. With him went my breath. I turned to Suresh, more than a little dazed. 'Who was *that thing*?' I asked. 'And why haven't I been told about *it*?' Suresh looked amazed. 'What! You don't know Kabir? He's been with us four months already.'

Four months! Where had I been wasting all my time? I composed myself, because I knew that the miracle would return with the golden keys any moment. He re-appeared. Suresh introduced us. 'Meet Protima Gupta, she models for us. And this is Kabir, our film and radio chief.' I summoned my most provocative smile. 'I've seen you before,' I said, 'in Delhi. On stage, I think.' He smiled. 'You must have. I've done many plays in Delhi.' A brief, formal two-minute conversation, then he excused himself and was gone.

My spirits were soaring, and at the same time I felt a tremendous dejection. He'd been in Bombay long enough, he must have countless girls throwing themselves at him, he must be going steady already. Perhaps he was already in love . . . Where could I figure in all this? A few weeks later I was called to do the Liberty shirts film. Kabir was heading the unit and the shooting was scheduled for the next day. I was told that I was one of the six girls required to dance sexily around a bonfire. I knew I had to play games to even be noticed. So I rang Kabir up late in the evening and said, 'I'm sorry, I don't think I'll be able to do the film, my parents are objecting to my going out at night. Not possible.' He was quite upset. 'I'll let you off early,' was the best he could say after much deliberation. It was true, what I'd told him about my parents, but of course I went.

At the shoot I found myself in the company of Gazalla Gill, Shobha Rajadhyaksha, and three other girls. We all sat around the fire and talked at length about The Man. The girls were all crazy about him. So was I, but I wasn't about to say so in front of all those models. 'Yes, he's tremendously good looking,' I said, feigning disinterest, 'but . . . he's not vibrant and attractive, there's something vital lacking in him.' They ridiculed me; sour grapes, they said. But I would not budge from my opinion. I discovered that his girl of the moment was a young Bombay model, and that he was already engaged to some girl in Delhi. Nevertheless, I was determined to be associated with this gorgeous man somehow. No one else could matter now.

It started out as a bet with Shobha and Gazalla. I bet them, in a great show of bravado, that I would soon have Kabir Bedi eating out of my hand. I didn't quite believe this myself, but a show of confidence was necessary. All through the shooting, I played silent eye games with Kabir. He probably does this with every other woman, I thought. After the filming all the girls piled into his car, a red Standard Herald, and he volunteered to drop everyone home. I was full of cocky excitement. Sitting right behind him, I regaled everyone with jokes and songs and excessive laughter (which is my style, I know). We approached my house. He slowed down the car, just a little bit, and I said breathlessly, not really meaning it, 'That's my house.' But he simply drove on, saying, 'I'll drop you on the way back, let's drop all these girls first.' I couldn't believe it! He had actually said it. I was stunned; the girls were silent, a little embarrassed. But the air cleared quickly and I became more vivacious, more happy, totally full of myself. Gazalla whispered as she was getting off, 'Phone and let us know what happened.' I promised I would.

Now that Kabir and I were alone in the car, I quietened down, wondering what to expect. I didn't know whether I wanted to go to his place or not. In fact, I didn't. The excitement was already too much. Maybe he thought that too, or maybe he too was playing games with me, sussing me out. He drove me home. It was a quiet drive, full of tension, of expectations, of wondering what he was thinking about, of wanting to be close but not too close, of expecting him to make a move but hoping he wouldn't. And suddenly I found myself below my building. I got out of the car, very awkward, not knowing what to say. I walked across to his side and said goodnight. He made a slight movement with his head and I quickly put my face into the window, thinking he wanted to kiss me goodnight. He pecked me politely on my forehead. 'Goodnight,' he said, 'see you sometime,' and drove off.

I didn't know what to make of it. Perhaps he realized that I wasn't worth it. Maybe after seeing me at close quarters he had decided that I wasn't really worth his while. He was disappointed.

I didn't for a moment think that he might be shy or conservative. A little dejected, and a little happy, I went home, unlocked the door, and slipped in unnoticed.

For the next three weeks I was a crazed creature and drove my friends Nani and Kulbir Ghumman crazy with my desire to see Kabir again. But I wanted to see him 'accidentally'. I hated the idea of letting him know that I'd specially come for him. I did meet him soon, and truly by accident. It was in the gents' toilet of Shanmukhananda Hall. I was standing in front of the mirror, wearing a superb golden bikini, dabbing on shiny silver dust on my body. I had been hired to dance with a rock group. A huge metal cage had been put up for me to dance in. I was the go-go girl. Suddenly the door flew open and in walked Kabir himself.

'Hi!' I said. 'How come you're always looking for a loo?'

'Sorry!' he started, a little embarrassed. 'But I thought this was the gents' loo.'

'It is, that's why I'm here.' I thought I was being quite clever. He came over and stared shyly. 'You're dancing in that? You look super!'

'Thanks! What are you doing here?'

'I'm in charge of lighting.'

Every ounce of charm I could muster was on my face. My eyes caught his and stayed locked. He was uncomfortable. I enjoyed his discomfort. He coughed nervously and excused himself. I was ecstatic. I danced superbly that night.

I invited Kabir to my birthday party a few days later at a friend's place. He came, seemed disgusted by the kind of people who were there, hung around for some time, and then went home. I was quite upset. I wanted to go with him, but couldn't because Dinkie was there. Dinkie was really quite a sweet, precious old man. I wasn't seeing him as often as I used to, but I still adored him, despite the manner in which he had seduced me. He was such a gentleman, so fatherly and so generous that it was impossible not to like him. For a while he was all that I needed. But after I had met Kabir he couldn't possibly matter as much to me as he used to. Dinkie sensed this and was beginning to get a little jealous.

After the disastrous party I redoubled my efforts to get Kabir into my life. I would sneak into his office at Bensons and go through his diary. He always wrote down his appointments and dates meticulously. I would note down all his appointments and make sure I landed there on some pretext before he did, so that he would never imagine that I was following him. His favourite restaurant was Bombelli's, where he often went after office hours for tea, alone or with his dates. I would be there too, always with a new boyfriend, always laughing, full of fun and cheer and having such a good time. My theory then was that I had to get this man. The only way to get him was to get him to notice me. The only way he would notice me was by my absence, since my presence was so full of vitality, energy and laughter. I wanted him to get used to seeing me every day, accidentally. Then, after he'd seen me continuously for two or three weeks, I would suddenly vanish for a whole week, so that my absence would be noticed. Once that happened, the rest would be easy.

That was exactly what I did. When he met me after my week's absence, he invited me to adman Gerson da Cunha's party. I went with him to his house where he wanted to bathe and change. This is it, I thought. He's now going to make his move—you don't invite a girl for no reason to your pad. But he was a master game-player himself. He did nothing. He bathed, changed and led me to the party. I was bored stiff with the advertising crowd and wanted only to concentrate on Kabir. He smiled a lot. His eyes, I noticed, were an odd colour. Sometimes they were blue, sometimes green, but mostly gold, with warm brown flecks in them. He was dressed very badly—his shirt was two inches too small for him, the collars were frayed, his trousers were ill-fitting and the shoes worn out. But he didn't seem to notice and I loved him dearly for that. (I have always loved men when they are not fussy about how they look. In fact, I remember how my heart had gone out to a friend's husband who had arrived at a party with two different coloured socks and wearing chappals. When someone pointed this out to him, he wasn't embarrassed at all. He just laughed. I would have slept with him there and then, for these things always melt my heart, and when my heart melts, there are no barriers.)

Kabir was busy chatting with everyone at the party. I was being ignored. On our way back there was a definite tension in the car. We passed his house, and my heart sank a bit. He wasn't even asking me whether I wanted to come to his place or not. Halfway home, he slowed the car, muttering something about a flat tyre. I smiled, thinking what an old line that was, and waited in suspense for the move. I was very interested to see how he would manoeuvre it, what he would say, how he would look at me. I have always found initial moves extremely awkward and embarrassing. I wanted to see whether this one would be any different. He stopped the car, got out, walked all round the car and got back in. 'False alarm,' he smiled and drove me home. At the porch he merely held my hand, said 'Goodnight' and drove off. No mention for another date, nothing. How could a man be so goddamned difficult!

Soon afterwards, Nani and Kulbir Ghumman arranged a dinner for four at their place. I thought Kabir wouldn't turn up, but he did. It was a full moon night and we decided to have dinner on the terrace. We all sat and smoked pot. I was so aware of Kabir's presence next to me, and aware that he was aware of mine too, that it was electric. At some point Nani and Kulbir went downstairs to bring the food up, and suddenly—I'll never know how it happened and who made the first move—we were in a tight embrace and he was kissing me tenderly, then passionately. It seemed to go on for ages. I remember seeing, from the corner of my eye, Nani and Kulbir appear with the food in the doorway and then quickly disappear. It lasted only a few minutes, and Kabir became very self-conscious after that. We all ate dinner quietly.

Kabir and I left together. He stopped his red Standard Herald outside my apartment building and asked, 'Do you have to go home tonight?'

'Yes, my father will kill me.'

'Tell him you spent the night at Nani's.'

Even though I knew I would never be believed, I threw caution to the winds and said, 'Let's go.' At that moment I did not care if I never went back home. I was with this gorgeous man and I wasn't about to miss out on anything that would happen. I was certain that this was the night when he would fall truly and madly in love with me. He would become mine; my life would never be the same again.

We went to his pad. I changed into his kurta and snuggled under the covers of his bed. It was a small bed, not one on which two strangers could sleep at a polite distance, and I waited a little shyly for him. I was now full of apprehension. I was unsure of myself, my surroundings. I didn't really want to go to bed with him. Suddenly my conditioning all came back to me. I knew I shouldn't make it so easy for him. I had to have some respect, if he was going to be in love with me. I was not a virgin. I'd had a couple of boyfriends before and I was already engaged to Jalal, but I was not confident in bed at all. By the time Kabir emerged from the bathroom, I had made up my mind that there would be no love-making tonight. I would tell him that, and I would make quite a point of it. My honour would remain intact and I would gain some kind of respect and admiration from him.

He got into bed, switched off the light, turned towards me and gently took me in his arms. He hugged me tight and whispered, 'Let's not make love tonight. I just want to hold you close and go to sleep. Okay?'

I could have hit him! The cheek of the man! I was furious. Did he think I wanted to sleep with him? How dare he say it first! How dare he insult me! But I kept quiet, and though I was seething with rage, I simply nodded my assent and cuddled up to him. Ten minutes later he was snoring softly and I lay awake thinking of the hell I would face the next morning from my father and mother. I wanted to laugh at the absurdity of the situation.

In the morning I shared his breakfast of two fried eggs, two toasts and one cup of tea. We went to the film laboratory for his work because I was petrified of going back home. I finally went home late in the afternoon and lied, hoping for the best. Nani would be my alibi. I got away that time.

I thought of Kabir all night. He had to be part of my life. What was his story? What was he all about? I knew that he used to present TV shows in Delhi. He had given up his ambition of joining the IAS because he had realized that the film medium was his thing. As far as he was concerned, he'd reached the top of whatever he wanted to do in Delhi, so he had come to Bombay with Rs 500, looking for his fortune. He had joined Lintas advertising, was with them for a year, and then joined Bensons as chief of film and radio. He made all the ad films there and had won a few awards and merit certificates. I had heard that he was engaged to an artist in Delhi, but had broken off his engagement after coming to Bombay. He was staying as a paying guest with Mrs Delph, who had this beautiful large house with four rooms, an empty swimming pool and a beautiful garden with the sea just below. She liked having young bachelors as paying guests. The room he had was much too small for a man of his size, but he had done it up beautifully. I loved his taste immediately. It was the same as mine. The bedsheets, the hangings, the paintings, were all terribly Indian and very, very colourful. He seemed perfect to me.

He rang me the next day and asked whether there had been any trouble with my parents. I concocted a great story about how I had been tortured, how I felt utterly humiliated, how I was dying to be independent and free from all oppression, and how I had been thinking about leaving home for months now. He promised to meet me that evening. When we met, we talked about me and my problems. 'Why don't you simply leave and be independent if that's what you want?' Kabir asked matter-of-factly. Why don't I, I wondered. It seemed the most natural thing for me to do.

I knew I had money in the bank from my modelling assignments, enough to see me through six months. I was at that moment involved with a fashion show for the Navy, my first fashion show as producer and designer. That would pay me well too. I knew that if I continued to stay in that household, I would have to get married. They had already started talking about some Modi and saying things like 'Ladki badi ho gayee hai; better get her married before she gets into some trouble.' Murli Deora had only recently asked my father for my hand in marriage and I was petrified. I saw myself becoming one of those marwari-bania wives and the thought was horrifying. I had made up my mind that my life was going to be different. At the most it would be a failure and I would die thirty years before my time, of disease or suicide or whatever. I didn't mind even if I became a prostitute—anything would be better than the mundane life of eating, sleeping, raising kids and entertaining my husband's friends!

I went home and thought about it all night. By morning I had made up my mind. I called Dinkie and sobbed on the phone. I told him how badly my father had treated me, how utterly miserable I was and how I was going to run away from home. He was very upset and tried hard to dissuade me, but I was adamant. I knew I had to play this very smartly. I wasn't at all sure of Kabir, though I wanted to be. I was sure Dinkie would help me, and I had to use him to get Kabir. Once I had a pad of my own, my relationship with Kabir would only improve. I met Dinkie the next day and sobbed uncontrollably. The great advantage I had in those days was that I invariably always believed my own lies very quickly, so that it was easy for me to put up a tremendously natural performance. Dinkie promised to look for a flat for me.

I made it quite clear to Dinkie that I wouldn't live in any seedy place. I needed a small room, but in a posh area. At that time, only cheap girls from bad families stayed alone. And then too it was because they were probably being kept by some old man. I could have none of that. I couldn't have people thinking I was a high-class prostitute. Dinkie understood, and he found just the right place, a lovely room with a balcony and attached bath. It was expensive, and I had money enough to survive only for six months, possibly less. But youth was on my side, and when you are young six months is a long, long time. We would see about tomorrow when it came. Right now I had to plan this perfectly.

Dinkie was respectably married, and had a reputation for being protective of young girls, so all this was done secretly. It was all to my advantage anyway. He merely gave me the address of the place and asked me to go have a look and let him know whether I liked it. He would take care of all the necessary formalities later. I took Kabir to see the pad and he loved it. There were three South African students staying there at that time and they were leaving at the end of December. I could move in any time after the first of January 1969. Dinkie was informed and he paid four months' rent in advance.

Now I had to start a quarrel at home so I could stomp out of the house. It took me days to work myself into a mood, for I was truly petrified of my father. It was Christmas Eve. Kabir rang up and asked me out. I was thrilled. He hadn't called me for a whole week till then and I was getting a little worried about my relationship with him.

I walked up to my father.

'Daddy, I want to go out for a party. It's Christmas Eve.'

'So? What have we to do with Christmas? It is not our festival. No, you cannot go.'

He went off, grumbling. I was to meet Kabir at 9.30. If I went now, after having told Daddy about it, he would know for sure and there would be hell to pay when I got back. I was not ready to face his anger. I called Kabir. 'I'm afraid,' I said. 'If I go out with you tonight I shall not be able to return home after that.'

'Then don't return, where's the problem? You're getting your house next month anyway, right? So move out tonight.'

'Where will I stay?'

'You're most welcome to stay with me, if you like. I know it will be uncomfortable for you. There's only one bed, and I am a paying guest myself, but those are small problems. You have to make up your mind.'

That decided it for me. 'Okay. I'll see you at nine-thirty.'

I took a few clothes and put them in a plastic bag and made quiet preparations for my first break in life. I sneaked out of the house. When I got into Kabir's car, a great relief swept over me. I could have sworn that it was the happiest moment in my life—next to New Year's day 1965, of course. There is something cleansing, something purifying when you move from one state to another. It is as if you had been stagnating in one place, in one dead emotional state for too long, and if you hadn't moved on you would have rotted, deteriorated, died. There must always be change. I have felt that same overwhelming relief, that tremendous sense of freedom and mad joy fill me up every time there has been a great shift in my life, and there have been many.

They found out at home soon enough. The police were informed, the neighbours were alerted; the family mourned the escapade. I phoned two days later, just to say that I was well and had no intentions of coming back, and that they were not to worry. It was my mother whom I spoke to, and before she could say anything, I had hung up.

A few days later, as I was walking down Marine Drive, my

father's car drew alongside and stopped. 'Get in,' he said. Stunned, I got into the car quietly. He's going to beat me, I thought. I didn't care if he did, I would show him that I was free of him. But he did nothing of the sort. He drove me straight home and said, 'I don't want to know where you have been. I don't want to know anything. I'm just glad that you are back. I couldn't bear the strain of this happening.' And having said this, he lay in bed and slept. He stayed home for two days and I wondered how I was going to get out again. On the third morning I approached him, cautiously. He was looking well-rested and happy. 'Daddy, how are you feeling today?' I asked nervously.

'I feel fine,' he said. 'For the past eight days I have been in a daze, and I'm now fit enough to go to the office.'

'I'm really glad that you are well, Daddy. I could not leave while you were in bed. Now I can go.'

'Go? Go where? What is all this go, go, hanh? What has got into you?!' His temper was rising, his blood pressure was shooting up. The doctors had told him that he had to be careful, but he never listened. I looked down, unhappily. Why was he making it so difficult for me? I was not going away to hurt him. I had no intention of causing him pain. I just wanted to live my own life. Was that really so terrible? I couldn't let him marry me off to some man of his choice, I couldn't accept a mediocre existence like my mother's, like his own, like that of so many other people I knew. The world was full of women who had families, husbands and homes. There was no need for one more. The world would not miss one dropout. I didn't know where my life was taking me, but I did know that nothing could stop me from doing what I felt was right. And at that moment my leaving home was imperative. It was willed by the gods themselves.

I told my father simply that I had to leave and that he should understand. He flew into a rage. 'All right, get out! Get out of this house and don't ever show me your face again. From today, you no longer have a father and as far as I am concerned you are dead. Don't even dare to step in this area or I'll have your legs broken. Get out!' He was trembling. I longed to bend down and touch his feet, something I had never done in my life. But his anger prevented me from doing so. I wanted to tell him not to be angry with me, to forgive me, to understand that I was only doing what I felt I needed to do with my life, but I couldn't speak. Choking with emotion, I ran out of the house and made it somehow to Kabir's house, where I sobbed till evening.

Kabir and I started living together. I never took up the place Dinkie had arranged for me. About a month after I had moved in with Kabir, we went to Goa for a weekend by the sea. On our return I found my brother outside our door. He looked sad.

'What are you doing here?' I asked. He didn't reply. He took Kabir aside and said something to him.

Kabir came towards me, looking very concerned. 'Now, darling, you have to be brave, and you have to be calm . . .'

'What is it?' I asked, suddenly scared. I knew it was something terrible, and my heart was thumping with apprehension.

'Your father . . . he's dead . . . in a car crash, two days ago.'

I nodded stupidly, stunned.

'Come, I'll take you home.' Silently we went home.

He left me downstairs, saying he'd fetch me in a day or two. What could I say? I hugged my mother.

O

Kabir and I moved into a new place which we hired for Rs 700—he paid the rent and I bought the food. Living with Kabir 'in sin' was a wonderful experience. Just the idea of 'sin' made it so adventurous, so colourful, so utterly wicked. Of course it was mostly play-acting at being married—cooking for your man, mending his clothes, looking after the house and generally doing all the exciting work which married women find such a drag and a bore. I can't say we were always at our best, but mostly we were, because we both knew that besides the love we had for each other, nothing else bound us, and we were free to go our different ways if the relationship did not suit us. This really strengthened our future relationship—what we share now—because it all came out of love and shared feelings and not from any economic or social dependency.

Getting to know each other's habits and eccentricities was full of surprises and laughter. I could easily have walked out of his life for any of a number of petty reasons—he snored too loudly, he hogged the entire bed, his armpits smelt, he greased his hair with smelly oil—and he could have done the same. But because we were not married, we didn't take each other for granted. I learnt to love him not only for his good looks and gentle voice, but also for his varying moods, his entire being. I loved him for his fantastic mind; I was in awe of him and his very intelligent-sounding friends. All in all it was a period of gradual ensnarement—a period of joy, laughter, sensitivity, creativity and love.

Of course it could have gone wrong. But we were both economically independent, and as for the social stigma, we never had any fear of it. The main negative factor—parents and relatives—remained. They were quite orthodox, the sort who would say: 'What will people think? How can we face anyone?' They suffered socially, though not much, and managed to make us feel guilty. There was briefly, in the beginning, a struggle between my heart and my conscience. My heart won. I reconciled myself completely to the guilt. I said to myself, 'You're dying to do it, might as well accept yourself as you are.' That done, it was easier for others to accept me as I was.

Another negative factor was the thought that Kabir might leave me and that I would have become too emotionally involved by then to take it without some sort of breakdown. But even if that happened, wasn't it better to quit without nasty court procedures, haggling over alimony, social scandal and all the rest of the mess that goes with divorce? Yes, the risk was worth it. And after all, what would I have lost by taking the risk? Nothing that really mattered to me. And funnily enough, society, I knew, was not going to reject me for it.

Kabir introduced me to Buddhism and mysticism (his mother, Ooggee, was a Buddhist nun), and the joy of living became a reality. We went through the most incredible experiences together, and because of him I discovered true freedom. I can frankly say that had he not been beside me, protective and strong and believing in all that I dreamed of and did, I would not have done or said half the so-called scandalous things I did.

Kabir was fairly anonymous in Bombay before he paired off with me. I was already known as a model, a scandalous girl—I had a reputation of my own. People like Vinod Mehra and Randhir Kapoor were my college friends. Nobody had heard of Kabir until then. Sometime after we started living together, he got an opportunity to do the advertisement for Wills cigarettes, and then he became known as the Wills man. And we became known as a couple who were heralding in the era of permissiveness, primarily because of my friend Anees Jung who wrote about us in *Eve's Weekly*, *Junior Statesman* and *Youth Times*.

It was not that we did things which we did not believe in. If we smoked hashish, if we had LSD, if we arranged wild parties, we enjoyed them. And many of the other things that I did were for me just ways of expressing myself. These things shocked people, those dead armies walking around, and it was they who made me a mini-celebrity. (Though I will not deny that I was an exhibitionist. At that time I had to fight to be in the limelight, especially with someone like Kabir after he started modelling and then joined films. When Kabir first came to Bombay, I was the one who introduced him around. Then, suddenly, the roles were reversed. I remember walking in with Kabir for the premiere of a movie and a photographer pushed me aside to take his pictures. I was quite angry.)

I wanted a relationship with Kabir, I did not want a marriage. I saw no reason for it. In the beginning Kabir didn't want marriage either. But when I became pregnant with Pooja, he said that we should get married. I accepted that, just as I had accepted the number three status in his life—he had made it quite clear to me before we started living together that his work and his friends would always come before me. So, we had children, which I wanted, and we had a marriage, which I did not want.

marriage

We married, Kabir and I, on 14 October 1969. The card we had was a very beautiful one—deep ochre handmade paper. Each card was personally signed by the two of us. It was different, pure class. Everyone would talk about it. Of course, it was mostly Kabir's idea. He was the more creative, the more intelligent of the two of us. The wedding itself was different. Sensitive and beautiful. We had decided to marry in a Buddhist temple and had spent three days looking for the right one. They were three miserable days for me, for I was already two months pregnant and was going through a wretched, nauseous phase, throwing up every ten minutes or so.

Kabir's mother had arrived in time and was looking after all the arrangements. My family was quite agitated, getting together expensive clothes and gold jewellery to present to me as some sort of dowry. It was quite unnecessary, and I told my mother so. After all, I had run away from home almost a year ago and had been living with Kabir 'in sin'. My mother in fact had not spoken to me since my father died because she blamed me for his death. But now that I was marrying, she made up with me—she had been so sure that no one would marry me, that now she was relieved. She brought me clothes and jewellery, which I found horrid. I wasn't being married from that house, so why should I be given anything? She said, 'Dete hain sab. Security ke liye.' So I retorted, 'You didn't give me any security when I needed it most. At that time it was "Log kya kahenge!" ' But mothers are mothers and mine was particularly so. She always took her role rather seriously and suddenly, despite the manner in which I had left the house and Kabir and I had come together, tradition became terribly important for all concerned.

The ceremony, finally, was a very simple one, done according to Buddhist rites. Only the two families were present.

Pooja was born seven months after our marriage. Both the families were there, and Kabir was by my side throughout, holding my hand. There was music playing for my benefit and my favourite painting had been put up on the wall before me. And to keep my mind off the pain, I kept singing, 'I'm a tiger, I'm a tiger.' It was a normal delivery. I had a baby, something I'd always wanted. It was a miracle.

o

Less than a year after we married, Kabir joined films and we moved into a flat in Juhu. I didn't really want him to join films. I have always had a thing against the film industry—I knew the film crowd, not just through my friends in college, but also through my mother's friends, who included Nargis Dutt, Kamini Kaushal and Smita Biswas. Had I wanted to make it in films, I could have; at different times in my life I have had offers from people like Raj Khosla, Mahesh Bhatt, Johnny Bakshi, and even Girish Karnad. But I was never interested. I wanted a free life and films tie you down completely—you eat films, you drink films, you sleep films and you dream films (which was exactly what Kabir started doing). Films are like that jealous and embittered woman who catches hold of you and locks you up, and you can never get out.

The first film Kabir signed up for was O.P. Ralhan's *Hulchul*. We started moving around in the 'filmi' circles and we were a hit pair. I would sit with some of the women at the filmi gatherings and watch Kabir circulate, talking to producers and smiling at the actresses. I would notice the starlets look at him, some with longing and admiration, others with badly disguised lust. All of them in awe of him. It amused me and I wondered how he took all this. I knew how shy he was. I was glad the women were making their attraction for him so obvious, it was good for his ego. I felt very happy, enjoying all the adulation and applause by proxy.

At a big film party hosted by O.P. Ralhan, Mrs Ralhan nudged me and said, 'Keep a tight grip on your husband. You don't know how bad the film industry is. Before you can even blink, someone will have grabbed him.'

I laughed. 'Don't worry,' I said, 'Kabir is not like that. He has a very different sort of mind.'

'Every wife says that in the beginning,' she said sadly. 'But I have seen many women suffer. Don't say I didn't warn you. You will remember my words one day.'

I went up to Kabir. He was smiling and chatting with a friend, Sonia Sahni. When she saw me, she linked her arm with Kabir's and said, 'Don't be so selfish with your husband, yaar! After all, you'll have him all your life, so let us share him now.' I liked Sonia. I laughed back, saying, 'I'm not his mother, yaar! He'll never need my permission. In any case, when he's getting a good thing for free, he'd be a fool not to take it!'

Kabir smiled uncomfortably and retreated. I found myself a seat and went back to watching everyone. I felt entirely confident about Kabir. How naïve and stupid of Mrs Ralhan to warn me about losing my man to another woman. This sort of thing happened to other people, like rape and murder. Marriages failed in other people's lives. Love vanished from other people's lives. I was different, my husband was different. Ours was not an ordinary marriage, there was a lot of understanding and love.

Another day, another party, and someone whispered to me that Kabir and Zeenat were having an affair. I knew Zeenat from my school days and had been meeting her quite often. I liked Zeenat. She was intelligent, attractive and hip. My type of person.

'So what?' I laughed. 'It shows he's got good taste, no?'

I tried to visualize them together but the image wouldn't stay. I shrugged and smiled to myself. At home I told Kabir what I'd heard at the party. He laughed.

'I don't have a single scene in the whole film with her! She's a nice girl, I enjoy talking to her.'

I didn't let it go at that. I wasn't really jealous, but I was trying to provoke him into saying how much he cared for me.

'Sonia Sahni said she's very attracted to you. How do you feel about her?'

I saw Kabir stiffen. 'Listen, darling,' he said gravely, 'you're going to hear all sorts of things about me. And in this film line one learns to play along. It's important to my career that the actresses are attracted to me.'

That made me angry and I said sarcastically, 'Really? How?'

'Well, if an actress wants you she chases you, and when she can't get you she tries to find ways of being together with you. So she suggests your name to her producers. One has to just play the game . . . Look, if you're going to be in this mood, I don't want to discuss anything more with you.'

That hurt me. I didn't understand his logic. If his work demanded such a hypocritical behaviour from him, it was better that he gave it up. He seemed so false and cooked up to me. His explanations sounded hollow. I was furious that his mind should reason in this manner. I burst out crying and hugged him.

'Just hold me close, please! I'm feeling insecure, that's all. Everyone in the industry warns me. At first I laughed at them, but now it hurts.' Kabir held me tight and comforted me, saying that I should not listen to the idle gossip of frustrated women. The important thing to remember was that he loved me the most in the world. I slept, comforted, but only for one night. The insecurity returned, and finally Kabir became impatient.

Late one night, a very well-known and flamboyant film star landed up with a girl. 'Hi,' he said, 'just thought we'd drop in. I didn't know Mr Star was such a good pal of Kabir's. I was confused. I sat in the living room. Kabir beckoned to me to come to the bedroom.

'Let's leave them alone. After all, it's not easy for an actor to take a woman anywhere. People talk in hotels and places. Make the bed for them outside and let's got to sleep.'

My first reaction was shock. I was horrified. This was my *house,* damn it, not a brothel. And why *our* house? Surely he had other friends. We were not even his friends, he'd never come home before. It must have been decided between Kabir and him on the sets only a few days ago, I was sure. Why was Kabir doing this? Were these the kind of things he would have to do to rise in the film world?

In the morning my anger had died down and I realized how insidious this sort of thing could be. Watching Mr Star in our balcony, I felt faintly proud that he had trusted *us* to be discreet.

As far as I am concerned, my marriage died when Kabir joined films. I lost him to the film industry. After that it was just a continuous process of moving apart. It happened in slow motion. It was a slow build up, so slow that we didn't see it coming. Like sitting in a revolving restaurant—only when the purse you left on the window sill next to your seat is no longer there do you realize that you have moved, and moved plenty.

But I was still madly in love with Kabir. Ever since we had

met, and especially after we started living together, I was struck by that man. I hero-worshipped him. He had intellectual friends, most of them rich and many of them artists. They could all hold their own in any conversation. I wanted so much to be like them. I would watch, listen and learn. There was a film we had seen about a man who had a mistress and whose wife killed herself because of this. For me that man was a villain. But Pearl Padamsee said that it was the poor man who was the unfortunate one, that he was the one who had suffered the most. I was amazed at this insight—that there could be so many perspectives; it was not all at face value. Only dolts like me would see things as they were presented to us.

I was convinced that I couldn't think for myself. I was just a bimbo. The only assets I had were my youth and sex appeal, and I used them to their fullest extent. I dressed outrageously—see-through fabric, plunging necklines, halters, skirts with slits all the way to the top—to compensate for my lack of artistic and intellectual faculties.

In time, particularly after I saw the hypocrisy in Kabir once he had joined films, I picked up confidence and soon saw his clever, chattering friends for the frauds they were. I felt a sort of contempt for their rambling insights, their intense philosophy and their artistic pretensions. I read and listened to J. Krishnamurti, I went to meditation camps, and I cultivated an acid tone of my own. I became the bold girl I was in school and college and pitched into every discussion, always coming out the winner. No one could argue with me, and I wondered whether my father had indeed been right in seeing a lawyer's vocation for me!

My star-struck attitude having vanished, I was left with Kabir as less of a hero and more of a man. I was just not attracted to him sexually after that, perhaps also because he was hardly ever around. He was firmly in the film groove and was busy all the time. The film world was his only world now, but it was not my world, and for all my glamour and 'hipness', it could never be. Kabir only talked films and about film folk. He had even started defending the whole set-up. In the beginning there were great vows of not being swallowed up in the filmi duniya, but now he was so much part and parcel of it that he found it difficult to maintain his interest for long when talking to a non-film person. He was not as interested in people as he was before—plain people who would flock to him for advice or simple comfort. The new Kabir was not really reaching out, he was dedicating all his time to himself. He was happiest when holding forth in a group of young stars or directors. He was still sensitive, and a little naïve, but I was losing him.

I used to tell Kabir that I had made many men unhappy and miserable and I was sure that I would be hurt in turn sometime. I dreaded the moment and knew instinctively that the only person who could ever hurt me was Kabir himself. I was never very sure of him. The day I married him, I knew it was not to last: I knew it because I wasn't at all confident about myself. I was sure that some other woman would steal him from me. And she would be right too, for what was I worth anyway? I was so prepared for this to happen that when I saw signs of it, I was relieved—and yet utterly miserable. My insecurity was guaranteed.

In those early years of our marriage he had seemed much too intelligent, too good looking, too kind, too wonderful a man to be mine for long. I lived in constant fear. Every time he looked at or spoke to a girl, I knew the end was near, and so I always cooked up illnesses or affected traumas to keep him and his affections. When he joined the film industry, there were women around him all the time and I became paranoid. Sonia Sahni and others would say that it was unfair to keep Kabir all to myself, and I would say confidently, 'Why don't you try?' But that was plain bravado.

It was clear that I couldn't stop affairs happening, so I took the attitude of 'I don't care, because I understand.' When the starlets asked me how come I didn't mind my husband flirting or having affairs, I would laugh and say, 'Well! He'd be stupid to refuse something that came so easily and cheaply,' hoping that would put the women off. But I only hurt myself every time, imagining what was happening and burning within. I suffered, and there were times when I thought that if Kabir knew of even a fourth of my pain, he would go down on his knees and ask for my forgiveness. But of course he never knew.

He made me believe that he had to behave in a certain way if he wanted to stay in the industry. He would have to flirt more than the others since for an actor marriage was a very major handicap. Like an idiot I believed almost every word of what he told me. Perhaps he was stupid enough himself to actually see things that way. It became clear to me soon enough that he was so ambitious that he would push aside everything that came in his way. Before marrying me, he had said, 'My work comes first, my friends second. You will come third.' And it had stayed that way. This had not offended me in the beginning—he was doing me a favour by giving me any place at all in his life—but later I began to resent it.

We were both looking for sex and companionship outside marriage. He became like a big brother for me. Perhaps he too felt the lack of being needed as a 'man', or perhaps he did not and in fact felt guilty for not having any sexual feelings for me himself. Anyway, for whatever reasons, we had stopped having sex.

O

Early in 1971 I had a miscarriage. I was shattered. The depression was overpowering. I had barely returned from the hospital when Kabir told me that he had to leave for Manali to film *Seema*, his second film. I was extremely sensitive after the miscarriage, and the thought of being alone terrified me. It seemed to me that I wouldn't survive. 'Don't leave me alone, please!' I cried to him. He explained gently that it was beyond his control. He would have taken me along, but my health did not permit it. He couldn't cancel his shooting schedule, for it would mean a great financial loss to the producer. Poor Kabir. I could see how difficult it was for him, but there was no other way. He went.

I cried myself to sleep that night. Early the next morning, as I looked out at the sea, I saw our neighbour, a young German, returning from his morning run on the beach. I had noticed him in the compound of our building a couple of times before and knew that he stayed next door, with three other Germans, also engineers but much older. Watching him that morning, I was struck by how handsome he was, and how naturally masculine with his athletic physique, bronzed skin and brown hair.

Two days after that was Holi. A big group of friends were at my front door, yelling for me to come out. I had decided not to play Holi that year, as a mark of respect to the child I had lost. But the screaming and pounding got louder and I opened the door. I was pulled out and plastered with red, blue and green colour. I grabbed some red gulal from someone's hand in order to retaliate, and at that moment I saw my neighbours' front door open and the young German emerged with his camera to take pictures of the whole tamasha. I rushed up to him and smeared the gulal on his face. One of his elderly friends grabbed my arm and tried to stop me. I threw the remaining colour on him. He let out a loud yell and doubled up. The powder had got in his eyes. I tried to help, apologized profusely, and in all this commotion we got talking about the festival. I explained what Holi was all about and they invited me to have tea with them. They had been in Bombay for barely a month and knew nobody except their company people. I promised to show them around as soon as I was better. The following evening they invited me to dine with them. They were curious about everything Indian and I was charmed by their warmth and friendliness.

Two days later I was invited to a party at Nana Chudasama's house. I needed an escort. I wanted to go with Fred, the handsome one, and decided to take a chance. I rang their bell with great apprehension. The door opened and Fred stood there, smiling.

'Hello! Come in.'

'No, I just wondered if you'd like to accompany me to a party. I'm afraid I can't invite all your colleagues but I'd said to myself that I would invite whoever opened the door. Will you come?'

Fred was delighted to be my escort. The party was a nice, quiet affair, and I sat talking to various people all evening. I felt a little guilty that perhaps Fred had not enjoyed himself and so suggested we go and dance at the 'Hell' discotheque. He loved the place. We danced and laughed and got pretty high. By 2.30 a.m. the slow numbers had started. Fred took me in his arms and our eyes met. A shudder of energy went up my spine and I looked away hastily. We danced quietly for about fifteen minutes. It was as if there was no one else around.

The tension became unbearable. 'Let's go home,' I said in a low voice. Silently, we drove home. My mind was in a whirl. How would the situation develop? Did he expect to share my bed tonight? Did I want it so? I had no idea what I wanted. I was terribly attracted to him but I was frightened of having sex. My husband was not home, but I did not want to violate the harmony of our existence. I wanted to be cuddled and hugged and given warmth but I was unsure about sex. Then we were home. Very tensely, I reached into my handbag for the house-key. I opened the front door, turned around and smiled at Fred. 'Thank you, Fred, you've been very precious.' Silently, he leaned forward, kissed me on the forehead, then turned abruptly and walked down the passage to his house. I stood at the door, hoping he would turn around, see me, come back. But he didn't. I sighed with a mixture of relief and dissatisfaction.

The next morning Fred brought me a bunch of flowers which he had picked from the trees by the seashore. His blue eyes twinkled merrily. 'Coming for a swim? Bring your daughter too.' We had a wonderful time, the three of us. He had tremendous energy and warmth. It surprised me to see how gentle he was with Pooja. She was eight months old, barely toddling, but she chased after him, falling over herself, laughing hysterically. He horsed around with her all morning and watching them I began crying. It had been ages since Kabir had spent such a day with us, ages since I'd seen him laugh freely and felt my heart soar. He was caught up completely in his world of films and film-making, which was not my world. I had been reduced to playing the patient wife waiting dutifully at home. How insensitive Kabir had become to my needs. I suddenly felt a great pity for myself.

A week went by in the same fashion. Fred would pop into the house briefly, just to yell a 'good morning' to me, then rush down to the compound to play with Pooja for ten or fifteen minutes before going off to work. He would return late in the afternoon and take us to the beach, or to Sun-n-Sand Hotel for huge ice-creams. He would insist on camel rides for all and pretend he was a sheikh who was kidnapping the beautiful Oriental princess, taking her to the land of milk and honey. After dinner, I would put Pooja to bed and sit out on his veranda, sharing his cigarettes and drinking rum with him and his colleagues. In that week I fell head over heels in love with Fred—Seigfred Kinzel. He was understanding and patient, a warm and happy person. He was everything that I needed at that moment in my life.

I knew that Fred cared for me. Perhaps he loved me too. I would sometimes see the pain and the desire in his eyes, but he always controlled himself. One evening as he was kissing Pooja goodnight, I turned up my face, my eyes closed, and whispered, 'What about me?' I waited an eternity and nothing happened.

Confused and embarrassed, I quickly opened my eyes. He was standing close to me, staring at me, a pained expression on his face. 'I'm sorry,' I said quickly, 'I was only joking.' His expression did not change. 'What's the matter, Fred?' I asked. 'Did I do something wrong?' He kept looking at me, then turning around slowly, he went into his house.

I didn't see him the whole of the next day. I couldn't get him out of my mind and I was very agitated. I couldn't understand what was wrong with him, what had upset him so. I wanted to go to him, to sit and chatter with him, but something held me back. I sat at home, alone and wretched, and didn't sleep all night. The following morning I heard Pooja's gurgly laughter and her shrieks of delight, and Fred's deep laugh. I rushed out into the corridor and found her sitting astride his shoulders. He was pretending he was a mad bull and rushing wildly at the walls, almost crashing into them, but turning away just in the nick of time. I was overjoyed to see him in his happy mood again. I began to laugh hysterically. 'Come and have breakfast with me. I've declared today a holiday,' he said. We trooped into his house, sat on top of the dining table and ate like savages. Pooja toddled off to play with Uncle, a wonderful man employed by the company to look after the Germans. Fred piled a lot of butter and marmalade over a toast and offered it to me. I put my hand out to take it, and Fred held my hand. I looked at him. He was staring at me. My heart started hammering violently against my ribs and I couldn't look away.

'If you want me even half as much as I want you, then remain here,' Fred said. 'If not, go now, and don't see me again. It would be best for us both.'

'I love you,' I said, choking on my words, and burst into tears. He embraced me gently and licked the marmalade off my fingers, kissed away the tears and the running mascara, and carried me off to his bedroom.

I was amazed at my hunger. I would go to Fred early every

morning, in the afternoon, when he returned from work, then at night, and it wasn't enough. For almost a month, the two of us lived as if the world did not exist for us. I was not a married woman, he was not a foreigner who had only a few months left of his stay in India. Fred, Pooja and I were like a happy family. He wanted to take me away to Germany along with Pooja, marry me, and set up a beautiful home where we would live happily ever after. And then one morning Kabir returned. I was surprised to find him back. I felt strange towards him. Something vital had changed in our relationship and I felt odd being with him, even just talking to him. We made small talk and I busied myself with unpacking his clothes. I thought of Fred, and a warm glow of happiness suffused my being. I wanted to be with Fred. But how could I tell Kabir? Would he be terribly angry and hurt? I didn't dare tell him immediately. Perhaps when he had settled down a bit, I would confess all. I was sure he would understand. After all, I hadn't meant to cheat on him.

As the evening approached I started getting excited. I heard the horn of the car and I knew Fred had arrived. I rushed to the balcony and saw him get out of the car. He looked up at me, winked, waved and disappeared into the elevator. My heart beat faster. Kabir was lounging in the living room, and the doorbell rang merrily. I opened the door, and before I could warn him, Fred charged into the living room, yelling for Pooja. He saw Kabir and froze. That split second seemed like an eternity. Then Fred smiled, a little unsurely, and said, 'Hello! I'm Siegfred Kinzel, I stay next door. I bought some sweets for your daughter. She's a beautiful little girl and I love her.' They shook hands. Kabir looked at him a little nonplussed. Pooja waddled in and with a tiny shriek of joy, rushed to Fred, clung to his neck and said, 'Chalo ghoda.' Fred got up with Pooja still clinging to him. 'Chalo memsahib,' he said and then to Kabir, 'Bye, Kabir, nice meeting you!' I rushed after them, saying loudly, 'Fred, don't take her to the beach today. And stay a little longer next time.'

I went and sat beside Kabir, waiting for him to ask me about Fred. He didn't say a word. I started making small talk again. He got up and went to his study, pretending that he was engrossed in some book he had started reading. I was sure he had guessed.

I knew I had to tell Kabir about Fred—to me the marriage we had was of little value compared to the joy Fred had brought into my life. A week before Fred was to leave his company and go back to Germany, I told Kabir about him. I was unhappy with our marriage, I said, and in love with Fred. I was going away. My decision was final. Kabir broke down, wept, said that he was still in love with me and begged me to stay and give our marriage another chance. Of course he had some of his old hold on me—I gave in, but told myself that I would only stay with him long enough to help him get over the hurt and the initial shock. I promised Fred that I would join him in Germany in a few months. Fred knew I wouldn't and told me so. I believed I would. I couldn't see at the time what must have been obvious to Fred—if I was staying back to save the marriage, clearly I wasn't prepared to opt out of it. As it happened, Kabir made the effort and I decided to stay with him.

I went to Sikkim around this time, to be with Ooggee Dadi, Kabir's mother, at the monastery in Rumtek. Ooggee had renounced the world and chosen for herself the life of a Buddhist nun, in the Kagyupa Tibetan Buddhist tradition, while Kabir was still very young. I spent three months in Rumtek and it was there that I realized I was carrying a child. On my return to Bombay, Kabir asked me whether it was his baby or Fred's. It was a very difficult time for me but I am glad I had the guts to say 'I don't know'. I wished to God the child was Kabir's. Meanwhile I had written to Fred in Germany, telling him that I was pregnant. Fred was convinced that the baby was his. Siddharth was born, but how could I be certain, till he was a little older, who his father was? I lived in agony. I could understand how Kabir felt looking at Siddharth and wondering whether he was his child or Fred's, and that made me feel worse. Fred kept sending presents for Siddharth and asking for his photographs. He had no doubt that Siddharth was his child and wanted me to come to Germany and live with him. But it was much too late for me by then. I had made my decision to stay with Kabir.

Siddharth's birth was in complete contrast to Pooja's. It was a difficult pregnancy. I had to have injections to keep the foetus inside. There was a constant danger of miscarriage. It was almost as if the baby did not wish to be born. I was advised complete bed rest and eventually had a Caesarean delivery. Siddharth was born a blue baby. Kabir was not with me this time, he was away on an outdoor shoot.

As far as I was concerned, Siddharth was my child, and that was all that mattered. I stopped corresponding with Fred completely and lost touch with him. He moved out of Germany and went to USA at some point and that was the last I heard about him. It was only when Siddharth reached puberty that we could be one hundred per cent certain he was Kabir's son. Kabir never let this affect his relationship with Siddharth, though years later, when I told Siddharth about the exact circumstances of his birth, it did cause some misunderstandings and tensions between mother and son. [*Though by then Siddharth was already behaving erratically, suffering from depression and mood swings, which was diagnosed as schizophrenia much later.*]

o

After I had my kids, I began to get a little more responsible. I could not suffer the film set at all now. I found film people tedious and tiresome. None had any sense of humour and very few of them were worth associating with. I had no great desire to hear some producer go on for hours about how great some shot in his last film was. My time was only for my children.

I am a born mother'. As a child I mothered my toys, the little statues of Ram, Lakshman and Sita. I bathed, changed, perfumed and decorated the idols; I crooned lullabies to put them to sleep; I sang and danced to entertain them. The best five years of my life have been those that I spent doing all this for Pooja and Siddharth when they were babies. We were inseparable. I made them bunk school often. We went camping, swimming, walking, built castles on the beach and many castles in the air; we cooked, laughed, dreamt dreams together. I was nominated the 'perfect' mother by all my friends and acquaintances and by my children.

With my babies around, there were times when I did not even miss Kabir. I sometimes suspected that I had married primarily to have my own children—little people whom I could dress, feed, put to bed, sing and dance to, and who could, unlike the idols of the gods of my childhood, respond to my caring.

Kabir had little time for the family. By mid-1972 there were signs that his film career would take off. He hadn't delivered a hit yet, but there were some people in the industry willing to take a chance with him. And Kabir was more determined than ever to be a star, though on his own terms. We were not exactly rich, but we had more money now than we ever had before. At a party in 1971, when Kabir had just joined films, Barota Malhotra (industrialist Jayant Malhotra's wife) had said, 'Kabir, when you become a big star, the first thing you'll do will be to buy a big, flashy filmi car.' We had laughed at the sheer idea of it. Barely a year later we had acquired a Pontiac, a big hulk of a beauty. I have never felt more alienated from ordinary people than when we travelled in that beauty. Once it broke down at Bandra and nobody came forward to help. They stared at us, full of hostility, resentment and bafflement, and we realized what we were doing to ourselves. It was an eye-opener and I think Kabir decided right then to get rid of that monstrosity and settle for a smaller Indian car. The tide then was definitely anti-affluent people—the capitalists, the black-money hoarders. One believed at the time in Indian-made things. Kabir also started his own style in clothes—

Indian silk kurta-churidars. It became him.

Later that year Kabir went to America and returned with a whole new attitude. He was full of everything American. Everything Indian was wrong—its management, its government, people's mentality, and what have you. 'We're leaving this fucking country,' he would say. 'We'll go to America and do things.' We were going nowhere, I told him. This was our country. This was us. But he was completely disillusioned with it; there was incredible poverty here, too many potholes, too much filth. 'This is a black-and-white country,' he said, 'America's a pop-coloured country. He bought himself very mod clothes and gave himself a mod hairstyle. Gone was the Indian image, the silk churidars. He was now the swinger of the seventies. He wanted to do films for the American market.

The elusive hit was taking too long to happen. There were no queues of producers and directors outside our door waiting to sign him up. He would brood at home when his shootings were cancelled. He was terribly restless, perhaps also insecure. Doing nothing didn't agree with him, and the financial squeeze worried him, though he wouldn't let on. 'It'll come, never worry about money,' he would say. But to me it seemed that he was worrying himself unnecessarily. He didn't realize how terrific he was on screen. Didn't he realize what a large fan following he had? But he continued to wallow in insecurity and nervous tension. It was a terrible phase.

By the end of 1972 work on two new films had started. He was shooting daily, and suddenly he was a different man. All the recent insecurity was gone. I remember when we drove around in our 'flash filmi' car in the early days, people would see the car and assume it was a big star zipping past and they'd shout, 'Rajesh Khanna! Rajesh Khanna hai woh!' or 'Dekho, dekho, Dharmendra!' Very few people recognized Kabir and I could see he was waiting for his day. Things had changed now. Not completely, but enough. On our way into town once, we heard people yell his name. I saw a smile of satisfaction on his face. I saw pride, a nice kind of pride, and I was happy for him. He would get all the fame and money that he needed.

After the success of *Sazaa*, people thought Kabir would sign any film. But he was still choosy, still finicky about roles. The dancing-singing image was out. He was just going to be The Man. The beard was now permanent. It suited him, gave body to his face and fullness to his chin. His career was still not rock steady, though. He needed a hit. People in the industry were still suspicious of his stock market value. They would wait until the 'hit', and then his price would rise. Meanwhile we were in debt: payment for two cars, land in Delhi, the money we owed the Prince of Sikkim. Kabir's 'friends' in the industry advised him to accept any major roles in films and not insist on lead roles, as they thought he would never make it. After all, he was not going to sing or dance; character roles were the only sensible option. But Kabir was convinced, and so was I, that he could play the lead and still not prance around trees.

Despite three flops—*Hulchul, Seema, Rakhi aur Hathkadi* (which was not so bad)—Kabir remained hopeful. He was banking everything on *Manzilein Aur Bhi Hain* and *Kucche Dhage*. If these two films flopped, then he might as well give up totally. They were his best. He couldn't do better. There was a lot of publicity. All his interviews and write-ups on him appeared at the same time. For one whole month the magazine-reading public were not allowed to forget him. He was everywhere—in *Eve's Weekly, Femina, Stardust, Sensation, JS*. Almost overnight things were improving tremendously. He was so utterly busy with work, outdoors, indoors, at home—everywhere. There was no time to relax and enjoy himself with others, but he was surer of himself and happier now than ever before in his film career. Producers and directors were coming home at all bloody hours of day and night but Kabir would be up and smiling and welcoming and ordering for tea. I hated it, and loved it. People were recognizing him as an intellectual actor. I wasn't sure if that was good for his image. One had the example of Parikshit Sahni, which was hardly encouraging. But there was no room for doubt. I hoped *Anokha Daan* would be a super hit, although I hadn't much cared for Kabir's performance in it. I was curious about how it would change him if the film made it big. He would change, of that I was sure.

Then Mahesh Bhatt's *Manzilein Aur Bhi Hain* happened. Raj Khosla with Danny Dengzongpa, Johnny Bakshi, Mahesh and three others dropped in at 11.30 p.m. after seeing the rushes. Raj was excited and it meant such a lot to all of us that he had dropped by, because it proved that there was something fantastic about the film. They drank till four in the morning and smothered Kabir with compliments and kisses. They were overdoing it and Kabir was a bit embarrassed. He sat quietly, listening and taking in all the wonderful things being said about him. I saw the film a few days later and came away wanting to get drunk just as foolishly as Mahesh was that night and kiss everyone. It was the most beautiful film I had ever seen. I went straight to the mahurat of Rajesh Khanna's *Prem Kahani* after that. It somehow turned out to be Kabir Bedi's party. They were all around us and what a good feeling it was. Kabir was jubilant, but hesitant. He wasn't sure how *Manzilein* would 'go down' with the people. It was not a typical or 'safe' film at all. The central characters were a prostitute and two criminals on the run. The prostitute was pregnant but didn't know which one of her two companions was the father of the child. It was a risk. But you could see that Kabir was full of beans.

I was certain Kabir was going to be the biggest thing after its release. He was superb, he didn't even need good luck. He'd be hounded by producers, directors, and the press. What would he talk about? He would talk to anyone. He could hold forth on anything under the sun. And he did. He was not even a big film name yet, not even a medium name, but he was getting all the attention of the big-timers. People used to say that he was very handsome but still stiff in his acting, and I had agreed. But I was convinced that *Manzilein* would have them all singing a different tune.

Yet, Kabir was being funny, mad enough to be in two minds about accepting B.R. Ishara's new film! He should have been jumping at the chance but not so, he was weighing it, thinking about it. Everyone urged him to sign up. B.R. Ishara was a big name, and the film in its totality would have been good for Kabir, and I told him so. But he thought it right to be seen as choosy, a thoughtful actor with a mind of his own. He had to be different, an utterly futuristic person, so controversial already. Reporters were fooled and so was the press. They thought he was a tremendously confident actor, a very sexually liberated man with weird ideas on everything. They were half wrong. He was just being a sensationalist.

Kucche Dhage, a dacoit-film, was released in June 1973 and it was a big hit. There were press reporters day in and day out at our Ashoka Hotel suite. Kabir talked long and well and charmed them all. He became quite the darling of the press. I remember thinking, 'How he can talk, and enjoy it!' After that he was flooded with film offers. He was suddenly so much more confident about his acting. He was also speaking Hindi beautifully, working hard on the scripts. He was more relaxed, he would come home early in the evenings and spend time with the children, playing with building blocks. It was a very beautiful, peaceful phase. After his acid trip earlier that year—a good experience for him, I think— Kabir had also become more mobile and graceful.

He was still determined to be different, of course. He would voice very unorthodox views on love and marriage. Then he acquired a new clothes fad. No shirts with collars. 'Design me anything that swings,' he said to me, his designer, 'something that's colourful and different. Great chefs don't follow wonderful recipes, they make them. And at the start of his fantastic career he was already talking of retiring in five years to a life of creative writing and painting and being that 'futuristic' man. I found it all exasperating sometimes. Money meant nothing to him, he said—of course it didn't; he only wanted a simple, peaceful existence, with a comfortable house, servants, a nice car, and all the other amenities. I didn't believe he could give it all up once he had it, but if he did do it, my intuition was that he would then take to lecturing people.

In August 1973 *Manzilein Aur Bhi Hain* was banned. It was an exhausting period. Everyone was very upset. There were furious discussions day and night, and Kabir's amazing organizational capacities came through. I had never imagined he could be such an incredible organizer. There were letters to the press, conferences and speeches, and everyone was floored. The whole unit looked upon him as the leader, which he was. They adored him. I could see him being affected by all the attention and adulation he was getting: the self-conscious smile, the edginess when getting into cars with people calling out to him. He could sense the power. He was beginning to lose his charming shyness and his openness and accessibility, which was sad.

Meanwhile the problems in our marriage kept getting worse. My affair with Fred had created tensions, and then there were Kabir's affairs. I remember vividly the time I caught him and someone very close to me, whom for the purpose of this book I shall call Gita, locked in a tight embrace behind the cupboard in our living room, kissing each other hungrily. It was when I was pregnant with Siddharth and Gita had come to stay with us for a month. Another night I woke up and found them together in her bedroom, and he said he was only giving her water to drink. He swore on Pooja's head that he was innocent. He had the advantage: I was the one who had been unfaithful, had fallen in love with a man when my husband was away and had even wanted to end the marriage. It did not lie in my mouth to accuse

Kabir of infidelity. It was only some years later, after Kabir and I had separated, that Gita told me that they had been having an affair since the time I was pregnant with Pooja. Gita had become pregnant and Kabir had asked her to abort the child. That had stunned me. When I hadn't had a single affair, when I was still the faithful wife, he'd been cheating on me. And he had always drummed into me that if I had not looked at another man he would never have looked at another woman. He had started it all—creeping out of the bedroom while I was fast asleep to screw Gita in the living room. She was only sixteen then and a virgin. But he always projected himself as the wronged one, and I suffered terrible guilt. Kabir, unlike me, was rarely stupid or brave enough to come clean about all the fooling around he did.

One occasion when he did tell me the truth was shortly after his birthday in 1973. I had arranged a surprise party for him. We were all having a good time. My friends Gayatri and Kamla walked in around 12.30 with champagne, and after that it was sheer flirtation. I was polite, I was the hostess, after all. I couldn't bear to see Kabir flirt like that. I still wanted to believe that he was not the type, but everyone could see that he was enjoying himself immensely. It was as if I did not exist, or did not matter. The humiliation and pain was unbearable. I went to the other room and stayed there, crying. My old friend Anil Johar came in, shook me roughly by the shoulders and said, 'Get up, you bitch, go out there and fight for your man!' I asked him to leave me alone. He sat there and put his arms around me. 'Sweetheart, crying won't help. Go and fight or stop feeling miserable.'

I cried and fell asleep. When I awoke in the morning Kabir wasn't home. He came in at 9.30 a.m. I asked him where he'd gone. 'You'd never believe me if I told you. I dropped Kamla and Gayatri home, and on the way back I hit two road dividers. I realized I was very drunk and would definitely crash, so I pulled up by the side of the road and fell asleep. When I woke up, people were staring at me and I drove back home.

I wanted to believe him, I half-believed him, but the next day when I accused him again, he admitted that he had spent the night with Gayatri.

My reactions to his escapades were spontaneous and violent, but brief. They were never as harshly critical and devastating as his reactions to my 'misdemeanours'. On my birthday in 1973, Kabir came home tired from shooting and fell asleep almost immediately. It was not yet eight o'clock. The way our marriage was placed, this seemed to me like callousness and upset me more than it should have. I fretted, watching him sleep. I was full of anger, resentment and unhappiness. I wasn't about to be large-hearted about this. There was someone else who loved me. I called Jean Jacques Lebel, my French boyfriend who was in town. He took me out for dinner and I spent much of the night with him. When he was driving me home late at night, I made him stop near the beach, got out of the car and put some sand on my arms and legs. Back home, I opened the door quietly. As soon as the lock clicked, Kabir was up and standing in the doorway.

'Where have you been?' he asked quietly.

'To the beach.' He noticed the sand on my arms and my feet, but he wasn't entirely convinced.

'Who with? Who dropped you?'

'Dropped me? Nobody. I was alone.'

I walked into the bedroom and got into bed. Then he noticed sand in my hair and immediately the suspicion flared up again. 'How come you've got sand in your hair?'

'Because I was lying on the beach, watching the stars. There are always millions of people on the beach. I wanted to be by myself. You should have come, it was lovely.'

He did not believe me, but he couldn't prove me wrong and that made him angry. He muttered under his breath and turned over and went to sleep. I waited, hoping he'd say something nice. I was crying, but he did not turn to me. I wanted to touch him, to be close to him. I hated his cold indifference, the distrust and lack of love. How could I make him love me?

Why did I have to tell him about any of my diversions? But why shouldn't I? Wasn't he my best friend, with whom I could share everything? So what if he happened to be my husband? Wasn't our marriage different? I never meant to hurt Kabir. But the guilt was always there, guilt for causing hurt, and I was never allowed to forget that there had been a hurt. Only *my* deeds were remembered and dissected. I hated and resented that. Why should only I take the blame? And yet I would try to make up in so many ways. I would take the blame and plead forgiveness like some seriously errant child begging for one more chance to prove that she's not a bad girl.

'Please help me, Kabir,' I told him one day. 'I'm so fickle. I don't scheme or plan affairs. I don't even want them, but I can't resist. It's like there's some awful magnet somewhere within me. I know that I can stop it, I should stop it, but everything always gets the better of me and I don't see anything wrong, intrinsically wrong, with whatever I'm doing. The important thing I want you to know is that it is never meant to hurt. . . But you always make me feel guilty and I hate that. I don't want to have affairs. Won't you take charge and help me stop? I'm so miserable, Kabir, so unhappy, and I don't want to be so.'

Kabir looked away, sighed and said, 'I know that you mean every single word of what you say, I also know that you genuinely suffer, but you do so only now. You have promised on so many occasions that you won't give in to another affair and I have believed you, but you can't help yourself. I know that you feel genuinely sorry, but tomorrow you will see or meet another man and you will forget all this drama.'

'Yes!' I sighed unhappily. I wanted to say, no, no, I'm truly reformed and you'll see it won't ever happen again. But the honesty inside just decided to do its own thing. 'You're right. I wish it wasn't so. Isn't there some way I can stop it?'

'You're the only one who can do something about it. Channelize your energies. Do something constructive. Your problem is that you have nothing to do and your affairs become the single most important pastime.'

He had started off lightly, as a friend, but as he warmed up to his speech he became aggressive and sounded condescending, even disgusted. The moment disgust crept into his voice, eyes and face, my hackles rose. He always put me on the defensive. I hated a fight, hated to feel small. I felt the anger rise within me. Why was he talking down to me? Who the hell did he think he was? Holier than thou all the time. As if he had the courage to tell me about all *his* affairs! As if he even cared enough to share things with me! He had nothing to offer. He was a pauper, an emotional pauper. He didn't own me. Why couldn't we be friends? What the hell was so bloody wrong with sex? The whole world was doing it. Did it really matter who was doing it with whom? Didn't solid emotions mean more than fucking? Why should one mean giving up the other? I wanted to be Kabir's friend more than anything else in the world. I wanted to be free and I wanted him to be free too.

Some months later I went to join Kabir in Nepal where he was shooting for a film. There were twenty females in the unit, all lovely, and there was the then famous beauty queen desperate to make it big in films. Kabir fell madly in love with her. It was too obvious for him to deny it. But he wouldn't say it was an 'affair'. He was always couching his own doings in high-sounding sensitive explanations and vague philosophical statements. Everybody else had affairs, but he had 'beautiful relationships'. The woman didn't even love him but he was blind. It was useless telling him, it would only have caused resentment. She wanted to join the movies; she was using him, just as Naseem had used him, just as so many other women would in the future. She wanted publicity and she wanted fun and she was getting it. I felt sorry for Kabir, he would be disillusioned again. However mature and sensitive he might have been, he was very immature in love. Even with me. He had told me just before the Nepal trip that his feelings towards me had changed and that he no longer cared what I did. I knew, of course, that he was only denying the guilt he felt about Naseem. Then I went to a meditation camp and he was in love with me all over again, because I had changed and had become peaceful. More likely, he wasn't involved with another woman at the time.

He wanted to transcend sex, so he wouldn't sleep with me. But his entire attraction to that beauty queen was based on sex. She was not sensitive or deep enough to hold his attention outside bed; he was having sex with her almost every time he met her. Why the delusion? Why sugar-coat the basic desire for an extra-marital fling? To me that whole business of sublimating the sex drive only proved his great preoccupation with sex. He said at the time that there could never be another woman for him after Sarah, but I knew there would be, and there'd also be a new cooked-up idea in his head about the relationship.

Nothing seemed right with our marriage at this stage. We were going in different directions. Kabir had loved my image, I felt, some image he had of what I should have been. For when I was unfaithful—or when he thought I was unfaithful—and when he thought I was loud and vulgar, he clearly did not love me. I had always loved him for what he was, even when he was unfaithful and less than perfect.

It saddened me to see him change from a beautiful being to a common, insensitive, indelicate being. I was convinced it was films and the women in his life that were doing this to him. He had started lying, not only to me, but also to himself. He would get drunk and have one-night stands. He was sarcastic when he spoke to me, and was often mean. I thought he did this to feel less guilty about what he was doing. The film industry was wrecking him. Why didn't he quit films? We didn't need all that money, fame and glamour. We needed love, and it seemed to me that he didn't know the meaning of love anymore.

europe

In May 1974, I went to Europe for the first time. Papa (my father-in-law, Baba Bedi) had shifted quite some years ago to Italy, where he was a highly respected psychic healer. He had set up his own centre for psychic healing in Rome, and it was there that I began my whirlwind tour of Europe. I was staggered by the charm and beauty of Rome. The city seemed to have more loafers than Bombay, and my sari ensured that I was always noticed. I fell in love with the place.

Sensitive, elegant people surrounded me, mostly psychoanalysts, Papa's peers and disciples. Papa was working very hard, but he had made fantastic arrangements for me and I felt pampered. The sky was always clear and the sun shone brilliantly. It was fashionable in Italy to be brown, so I was in fashion. I bought myself a fantastic golden yellow bikini and enjoyed the looks I got. For some reason the people I met there already believed that all Indian girls were beautiful, too beautiful to be allowed to live.

One evening, the Alitalia captain I had met on a flight phoned to say that he was taking me out for dinner with some other people. Captain Alitalia was a good-looking man, but I didn't like his obscene hunger for me. I had told him this repeatedly. Yet I accepted his dinner invitation. He picked me up at 7.30. I was relieved to see that he already had a girl with him.

'We're taking you to a fabulous place run by homosexuals,' he said. 'It's a very chic place where they sing songs about politics and class with a lot of dirty words thrown in. We're to meet the fourth person there, a rich banker. He's the one paying for the dinner.' I hoped the banker would be good looking—and interesting. The scene at the restaurant was jolly. I liked it immediately. As people walked in, the singers started commenting on their anatomy, using four-letter words liberally, making lewd gestures and saying the most obscene things in Italian (Captain Alitalia kept translating the remarks for my benefit, and of course he was enjoying that). The banker walked in, not at all the creature I had hoped for—he was short, round, bald and greasy. His well-manicured hands were the only redeeming feature. He only spoke Italian, but in his mouth the language lost all its sensuality.

After we had finished dinner, the maître de hôtel announced that they would present a bottle of champagne to the lady of the evening. The master would walk around and pick the lucky lady. At this everyone started giggling and laughing and I wondered what it was that they found so funny in this perfectly normal announcement. The master walked slowly to and past each table, commenting on the ladies sitting at the tables. As he passed and said whatever it was that he was saying, the diners roared with laughter. Alitalia explained the master's remarks: 'This one's got too much flesh on the bottom—quite a problem a tiny thing would have making its way through the folds of flesh'; 'Oh, this one looks like a virgin—too tight, too uncomfortable'; and so on and on. The master approached our table. I was excited but very nervous. Surely he wouldn't make those embarrassing remarks about an Indian lady? Weren't Indian ladies known to be graceful and dignified? And I looked like not just another graceful Indian lady, I looked like an Indian princess, draped as I was in a silk sari, wearing a big red tikka and gorgeous gold jewellery.

'Ah!' the master said as he reached our table. 'This very beautiful Indian lady, so beautiful, so charming, is decidedly most deserving of the champagne.' He held out his hand in an exaggerated gesture and I stood up. There was a burst of applause and a roar of laughter. People started clapping in rhythm and singing some song.

With a mixture of embarrassment, pride and anxiety, for I didn't know what I was expected to do, I followed the master to the centre of the restaurant. 'Ah! You just stand here, madam,' he said in English, 'in front of all these people. Let them admire true grace.' I blushed. He put a chair on top of a small table and then a bottle of champagne was brought and put on the chair.

'C'mon, take it,' said the master. I hesitated. It was clear to me by now that something wasn't quite right. I merely smiled shyly and did nothing. 'C'mon, the bottle waits for you.' I stretched, reached out and gripped the bottle by its neck, and before I could pick it, the master's hand was around mine. I tried to pull my hand away, but he was holding it tight. Suddenly a guitar struck a chord and there was a hush. And the master spoke.

'No, no, you must never hurry with the most wonderful things of life.' Everyone laughed. 'You have to appreciate this wine, this bottle. You have to show it how much you want it.' And as he said this he was moving my hand up and down the neck of the champagne bottle, simulating masturbation. I turned my face away, blushing furiously, as the man kept forcing my hand up and down the cork and the neck of the bottle. The tempo of the music increased as the master made my hand move faster and faster. The music was reaching its peak, it was coming to a climax. And suddenly there was a loud explosion as the cork shot out of the bottle and flew up in the air with the heat generated by my hand. White froth gushed out of the bottle and over my hand and spilled on the chair. 'Great show,' hollered the master, and there was thunderous applause and great laughter as I carried the half-empty bottle off the chair and to my table.

I was burning with embarrassment, and at the same time marvelling at the ingenuity of the entire act. I tried to act nonchalant, as if what had happened was the most normal thing in the world. No sooner had I sat down, than the greasy banker put his pudgy paw on my thigh and squeezed it. 'Marvellous,' he said to me. I smiled politely and looked pointedly at his hand. He relaxed his grip, but kept his hand where it was. I was furious. How dare he think that he could do as he pleased just because he had paid for my dinner. I picked up my fork to put the last piece of cheese into my mouth and in doing so, dropped the fork to the ground. I bent under the table to retrieve the fork and on my way up, dug it hard into that fat paw. The oily banker screamed in pain, his hand shooting up above the table. He looked at me sadly.

'Sorry,' I said, 'my fault.'

He paid, and we drove to the best disco in Rome. The guards outside stopped us, the disco was booked for a private party. Pity. As we turned to go, a big black saloon car drew up and out stepped the most amazing people I had ever seen. I had seen photographs of exotic-looking people in weird costumes in fashion magazines from Europe and America, but had never believed such people actually existed. But here they were, the most gorgeous men dressed as women, in long, sequined gowns with plunging necklines and purple, red and yellow wigs with shiny spangles in them. They wore thick black mascara, flaming red lipstick and shockingly high heels. I gaped as they walked into the disco with tremendous sophistication.

I ran to the porch and asked the doorman whose party it was. It was the birthday party of the film actor Helmut Berger. I was determined to get in. I begged the doorman to let me use the toilet. He wouldn't hear of it at first, so I asked Alitalia to make the man see sense—I didn't want to go to the party, only use the toilet. He finally relented. I rushed towards the toilet, then veered to the bar. I asked where Helmut Berger was. The barman pointed to a man dressed in shorts, standing in the centre of a large group. I walked up to him and smiled.

'Hello, I'm from India,' I said, 'I came to wish you a happy birthday. It's such a beautiful party.'

'Why don't you stay? Come, have a drink.' He picked up a bottle of champagne and steered me to a corner table and sat me down. 'Enjoy yourself, honey, I'll just attend to the other guests.'

I smiled triumphantly. What a fabulous creature, this Helmut. So delicate and white, with a blonde wig, and those hot pants—half of his beautiful bum was on display. No model I had seen in the flesh or in photographs had more beautiful legs than his. I was joined by some men in women's clothing who oohed and aahed over my jewellery and the tikka and asked many questions about India. In the centre of the floor a most magical-looking man in drag was singing a sad, sad song. As he sang, he made gestures, as though he was taking off bangles, earrings, clothes. The song was obviously about a woman waiting for her lover. I was told that he was the best imitator-actor-singer around and performed at some exotic nightclub every evening. I sat mesmerized. I had had quite a bit to drink, and I swayed over to him and held his hand.

'You know, I've never seen anything so moving, and I don't even understand Italian,' I slurred.

He held my hands gently and gazed into my eyes. 'Thank you, my precious, but you are so beautiful, tell me all about yourself and don't leave my hand, for I will not let you go so easily.'

It was now nearly four in the morning and I wondered how I could go home. I had abandoned my hosts for the evening and I could not disturb my father-in-law at this time. On an impulse I said to the man, 'Can I sleep the night or what's left of it at your place? I have nowhere to go.' Of course I could, he said, but I would have to sleep in the living room; he had only one bedroom. That was a relief. He looked at me, and then slowly peeled his false eyelashes off and put them in my hands. 'For you, my dear, because you are my friend.' I looked at the lashes, and didn't know what to say. Why eyelashes? Much later I was told that it is one of the biggest compliments a queer can give you, if he likes you.

His living room was not small at all. There was a magnificent couch in which I lay and he covered me with a blanket and put a pillow under my head. He stroked my head gently. 'Goodnight, angel of paradise,' he said, and turned off the lights. I lay there quietly, in suspense. Would he change and then come over to sleep with me? He didn't seem interested, yet you never knew. Well, it was not such a bad thing to happen, he seemed so gentle and friendly. Also, I had never been to bed with a man who dressed as a woman. I waited in the dark, but nothing happened. I sighed with relief and went to sleep.

When I awoke, there was frenzied activity going on in the kitchen. Dishes were being washed and the coffee percolator was working. I propped myself up on my elbows to look around the living room. Suddenly a very thin voice screamed at me.

'Oh, you are awake, how charming. Let me see what Antonio has brought home.' And a thin man in his mid-thirties wiggled his way towards me and sat next to my pillow, examining me. 'Such big beautiful eyes! Do all women in India have such big eyes?' I nodded. 'And those hands, ooh, let me look at them. So slender and so graceful. Antonio,' he screeched, 'come and see these hands.' Antonio emerged. Without his make-up and wig and long dress, he looked like any normal man with a highly sensitive face. He bent down and kissed me on the cheek.

They gave me a fabulous breakfast. The thin one with the screech had a nasty cold and kept complaining to Antonio how miserable he was and how unhappy because his face was swollen and his nose red; he looked so ugly, how could he face the public looking like that? And then in the middle of all this Antonio had gone off and left him alone all night. They were squabbling like a long-married couple. I smiled fondly at them. They seemed like children playing a game. The 'wife' took me to his wardrobe and showed me all the fabulous gowns he had collected, the wigs, the shoes. Then he led me to the living room and sat me down on a chair, firmly.

'Antonio,' he yelled, 'bring me the soap and a jug of water.' Holding my face in his hands, he scrubbed my face clean of all the make-up. 'You have such an oriental face,' he screeched, 'beautiful big eyes. Show it to your advantage, your make-up is all wrong.'

A big box of make-up was brought out, full of crayons and colour pencils. Within half an hour they were finished with my face. I went to the mirror and almost collapsed. I couldn't possibly go out into the streets looking like that. There were six different shades on my eyelids—purple, white, mauve, brown, blue and green. My eyebrows were thin and extravagantly arched. My lips were a flaming maroon. The tikka they had put on my forehead was the third eye of Lord Shiva.

'Now, doesn't that look zappy? You'll cause an earthquake with that face. Traffic will stop and everybody will fall at your feet. Just you see,' said the screeching voice.

I smiled, hesitantly. 'Yes, it's fabulous, but in the morning . . .'

There was horror on his face—'Who says that this is for morning and that for night?! You must conform only if there is something worth conforming to. You are embarrassed by your beauty?!'

What could I say? Could I walk into my father-in-law's place like that? They bundled me off quickly, having extracted a promise that I should come and spend some time in the evening with them. I found myself on the pavement. There was no taxi in sight. I put on my most confident look and walked brazenly down the road. People stared, some passed comments, some stepped back hastily, and soon I got used to all kinds of gestures from the passers-by. Well, what could they do? They could only jeer, or look shocked or laugh. It was just a question of the moment when I passed them. In any case, I did not understand their language. Soon I even started enjoying the attention I was getting. I laughed, I smiled at everyone. They did not know me, so what was the difference anyway? I could easily have done a little jig on that busy Monday morning. I had seen the stupidity of being embarrassed. I doubt if I've ever been embarrassed by anything after that.

But not every Italian I met was as beautiful and sensitive. I remember the wretched man I met in Venice who seemed nice enough till he took me home and tried to rape me. I escaped, but in the morning I found myself without my passport and wallet. The hotel bills had to be paid. The hotel woman was very kind, she understood my predicament and let me stay on and make a call to Rome. I was rescued by Baba's friend who had a crush on me. He came over and we drove to the molester's house. I went in and took my wallet and passport from the people in the house. The man didn't meet me. On my way out, I picked up a large stone and smashed the windshield of his car parked outside.

On the afternoon of my last day in Rome, I was given an acid trip by a man in a hotel. When I revived, hours later, the man had disappeared. I went out and walked about in the Piazza Navona till everything shut down. Then the ruffians came out and stared. Two of them approached slowly, one by one. 'Cigarette?' they asked. 'Light?' The usual ploys. What could they rob me of? I smiled and invited them to chat with me. They walked about with me in the gardens all night, speaking in their charming broken English. There were police cars everywhere on the roads. One of the ruffians lay down on a bench for the night, the other walked me to the house where I was staying. It was early morning when I said goodbye, and there were tears in my eyes. They were the nicest men I had met, the ruffianatos, the scruff.

While in Rome, I became part of what was billed as the biggest musical concert of the year, a festival of pop music that would last five days and nights, with over 25,000 people watching the bands. I had attached myself to a group called ARIA. They specialized in a sort of industrial music—very dynamic, sensitive and creative music. I had been asked to dance on stage while they appeared with their drums and guitars. It was great fun being part of the fantastic world of pop music. I peeled potatoes, carrots and oranges in a big tent, helping out my new friends, preparing for the big event. I was all ready and set for it, but it never happened. All of us freaked on acid and that was that. But there was no disappointment. It was a great experience to be with those gentlest of flower children. I belonged with them. We all drove to Milan, through the beautiful countryside. Rows of neatly planted trees flashed by, then fields of red poppies interspersed with patches of white flowers. The sun peeped out from behind great big white clouds, sleek cars kept passing by and every now and then some happy soul would start strumming his guitar and everyone would join in, singing happy songs. Why couldn't everybody in the world have such a beautiful time, I thought. I loved the whole world and was quite prepared to believe that the whole world loved me.

I wanted to extend my time in Europe, and Kabir was being indulgent—people asked him when his gallivanting wife would be back, and he'd laugh, 'She'll be back when the money runs out.' We wrote to each other regularly, and I accepted, away from the tensions of Bombay and the house we shared, that I could never stop loving him. One of his friends in Italy said one day that I reminded her so much of him with my mannerisms and expressions, and I thought that it was the biggest compliment anyone could have given me.

o

From Italy I flew to Paris to be with Jean Jacques, my French boyfriend. His parents were awed by the black witch from India. The father would rush off on some pretext or the other whenever he found himself alone with me. Finally, I think, the tension got too much for them, and they gave their son money to take me away and travel through France. I preferred that. After Rome, Paris was an anti-climax. The city did not have enough vibes, and French men were truly disappointing.

France was really not my scene. The men there had a strange, sadistic streak in them, it was there to be seen on the face of every Frenchman. You only had to look a little carefully and there it was, the sadistic look, behind the strict, stern lines along the cheeks and around the mouth. I went out for dinner with one Frenchman, and as though he was asking me what sort of dessert I'd like to have, he asked me casually, 'What brand of whip do you prefer?' I almost choked on my food. It was the same everywhere—a total obsession with orgasms. Not sex, but orgasms. They would try every method, every conceivable object and idea to achieve the perfect orgasm. It was a must almost every night. Dinner, then to the bars for drinks, then the discotheques for dance and then the Orgasm. It was a little frightening to see a total lack of feeling, sensitivity and emotion where sex was concerned. To each his own, I told myself. After all, they had Marquis de Sade as their ancestor!

While Paris was a disappointment, London surprised me. I was convinced that the city would bore me and hadn't been too keen to go there. But I had a wonderful time. The highlight was the frequent tripping—I had the most intense and liberating visions. And through each trip I ached for Kabir, longing to reach out across continents and oceans and touch him. He was my man, there was no doubt about us anymore in my mind. I had heard that he was planning to leave for Malaysia soon for the shooting of *Sandokan*, the Italian television serial in which he was playing the lead. I dropped all plans to travel through Switzerland and flew back home—I needed to be with the man I loved. At that time our marriage seemed to me a beautiful relationship full of love. The people I had seen over the past months in Europe appeared a sad lot, never really connecting unless they were having sex—all out there, fucking, fucking, fucking. Kabir and I were different, our love truer than any. I needed to be back home.

I left Europe with some regret. I had enjoyed the freedom and the sense of enterprise that I had experienced there. When I arrived in Italy, I had found myself in a world that seemed normal and healthy for a free-thinking human being, and it was like a diver's sudden ascent to the surface of the water from a great depth. Culturally, psychologically and temperamentally, the difference between the East and the West was too great. To me the greatest freedom, and the only kind worth having, is the freedom to be wholly true to oneself. A society as layered as ours with its family loyalties, religious divisions and political mismanagement, is hostile and cruel towards anybody who attempts to live a life true to one's nature. Freedom of the spirit is the product of maturity, of intelligence, of true knowledge, and Indian society still has a long way to go in this respect.

And it has always been easy to shock Indians. I was always scandalizing people. In Europe I'd bought myself a vibrator. The man at the customs at the Bombay airport spotted it as soon as he'd opened my bag and made a fuss about my bringing in banned goods.

'What do you mean I'm not allowed?!' I protested, raising my voice. 'My husband is out of town most of the time, what do you expect me to do? I'm trying to be faithful. Are you encouraging infidelity?' The vibrator was for my personal use, I said. Why should he have a problem with that? He was being bigoted, a rotten, bigoted male, I shouted. The man got so nervous about my flap that he quickly put the vibrator back and shut my suitcase, asking me to shush up.

It is a most marvellous invention, the vibrator. No emotional hang-ups, no games, no diseases, no guilt, and quick orgasm. Armed with it, a woman can work out her relationship with 'the man' coolly.

O

Shortly after I returned from Europe, I became the subject of a major controversy. A film magazine printed photographs of me streaking, and word spread that I had streaked down the busy road outside Jehangir Art Gallery in Bombay. Actually I had done no such thing.

The so-called streaking had happened in Goa. I was spending a lot of time in those days with the hippies on Anjuna beach. Everyone walked around naked there. If you were in a swimming costume, you looked and felt odd. So I was a nudist like everybody else on the beach. Somebody must have taken pictures of me there, and what the magazine did was to superimpose these pictures on a photograph of a Bombay street. And people were so gullible, nobody even questioned it. Wouldn't there have been crowds in the picture if I had really done this in Bombay? What I had done was perfectly normal, given the place I was in and the people I was with. But when every magazine printed the doctored photographs, it naturally looked ugly because it was out of context. Anyway, the nudie pictures had been printed in all kinds of magazines and there was such a lot of noise and righteous bullshit that there seemed to be no point in denying anything. So I kept quiet. Denials or clarifications wouldn't have served any purpose. I knew the media well. Even when I stayed away from glorious film parties, journalists found me and cooked up entire articles on Kabir and me and put all kinds of words in my mouth or reported things out of context. To the readers the media's version was always the truth.

But I have never regretted whatever I did. Everything has its time and place, and every experience helps you evolve. I was amazed at the media's preoccupation with me. I enjoyed seeing how people ran around and after me if I did this, and how they froze or flopped over if I did that. If I took off my clothes there was a stampede, when I put my clothes back on there was a commotion. The whole phase of playing up to the media, feeding it, scandalizing it, shocking it—it was not done out of any conviction, but simply because I was having a whale of a time.

At no stage did I feel that I was playing with my life or that I was a 'disrespectable' woman. Everybody talked so much about the streaking episode, but what was so disreputable or even different about that? All I had done was walk around naked. That is not the same as streaking, where you take off your clothes to shock everybody. I had been walking around naked for years. I used to walk naked on the beaches in Goa where ten million people had seen me. I walked around naked in my house. To me a human body was as ordinary and natural as anything else in nature. If I saw a man's penis hanging out of his flies, I wouldn't get overly excited about it. So I didn't expect others to get excited like that about me. If I wore a low neckline and people passed remarks like 'Kya cheez hai!' I was quite likely to take it all out and say, 'Here, have a look at the whole thing!'

I dressed outrageously, but it was not to please men. Basically I dressed to please myself. If Twiggy (the famous sixties' model who was fashionably skinny) wore even more daring clothes than mine, nobody would have looked twice. When I wore slit-skirts, open-backs, and blouses with plunging necklines, people stared and drooled. Why starve them? As I saw it, I had to show it when I had it that good!

But as I said, everything has a time and place. I wouldn't go back to that phase of my life, but I am not ashamed of it. Life was faster then. I flaunted my youth and my intelligence. And I was 'falling in sex' all the time. Perhaps I mistook it for love.

finding a purpose

I was a product of modern, westernized India, and I was happy in my environment. On the surface, at least, I had all that anybody could ask for: a handsome, well-off and understanding husband; two beautiful children; a home with servants; a car; an abundance of friends and admirers; glamour and fame. All this without even having worked for it.

I knew that poverty, sickness, old age and misery existed, but these things had not touched my life. I was gifted with immense energy, which resulted in many and varied modelling assignments, interior decoration and designing of jewellery and clothes (I designed Kabir's clothes for most of his films). I was Bombay's youngest entrepreneur, for I had started the city's first footpath boutique in 1968 opposite the Jehangir Art Gallery, only a few months after having opened the first real discotheque in the city. Parties, clubs and car-racing were integral parts of my life.

Everything seemed perfect on the surface, too perfect. Yet

there was a restlessness growing within me. The quest for enjoyment was beginning to seem futile. By 1974, I had reached a stage where everything seemed devoid of colour and meaning, and I took refuge in spiritualism and drugs. I needed the stimulus and I got it. I experimented with acid, and studied Buddhism—spending three months at the Rumtek monastery with Kabir's mother. It was one of the most intense and enriching periods of my life. But the restlessness remained.

Because of Kabir, I had become more involved in the film world than I cared to be. I was trapped in the cocktail circuit, and then in the hippie scene at Goa and Bombay. It was the easiest thing to be attached to those people and follow their patterns. But I wanted release from the bad vibes inside—because my husband was only a husband, no longer a friend.

It was a very dark and confusing period of my life. Emotionally I was a mess. I started smoking too much, drank a hell of a lot. And because it was the age to defy society, to walk around practically naked, to practise free love, I did that too. I did not know what it was to be shy. I would take off my clothes for anybody. It was a pointless existence. I was overcome by extreme depression and acute frustration. All the logic and rationale which I had learnt were of no use to me; I wanted to end my life several times.

Where was the point in going on? What was I doing with my life anyway? I ate, slept, looked after the children, laughed, cried, and wondered why I was alive. And even if I spent all my time and energy searching for the divine truth, the Cosmic Truth, and then found it, what could I do with it? What would it solve? I was wasting my life with silly emotions, the toys that humans are given to play with. Something had to claim me. Unless life made use of me for a purpose, it was all a waste.

And then one day in August 1975, my life changed. It was a stormy day and I ran into the Bhulabhai Memorial Institute in Bombay to take shelter and pass a little time before moving on to a fashionable restaurant where I was to have dinner. I walked into the dark auditorium and saw two young dancers giving an odissi recital. The beauty, grace, sensuousness and lyricism of the dance overpowered my senses. It had a tremendous aesthetic and spiritual quality, and the exquisite music was like nectar to my ravaged heart. I sat there spellbound. It was not that the dancers were young and pretty and danced well. The magic was in the dance form itself: a graceful effortlessness and a quality of 'everlastingness', even though it had very complex rhythmic patterns and sophisticated hand and eye gestures. The movements brought to mind the swaying of the palm trees, the breeze upon the water in a lake, the slow and gentle rising of the sun, the rise and fall of waves in the ocean, the quick darting and flight of insects, the sinuous grace of the snake and the gazelle. In short, it was the very breath of life.

I can't say I was attracted to odissi dance; attraction is too small a word for what I felt. I was consumed by it, as a piece of wood is consumed by fire. It filled me with the kind of passion I had never known before. It was as if I was in a trance. I saw myself as one of the apsaras, the temple dancers. I was Uttara and Amrapali. I was Urvashi. I knew the reason for my existence. Some unknown compulsion had taken possession of me. My soul, long neglected, had come alive. It was not an address, but a call, and I could do nothing but follow it.

After the performance, when the small audience started exiting, I got up and asked for directions to the backstage. There were already quite a few people crowding around the heavily made-up dancers. I had no difficulty catching their attention: I was already taller than the average Indian woman, and I was wearing four-inch heels. What was this wonderful dance they had performed? Both girls looked at me and I saw that they had recognized my famous face. Smiling shyly one answered, 'Odissi dance from Orissa.'

'Who is your teacher? I also want to learn it. Where did you learnt it?'

'Please talk to our guru, Guru Kelucharan Mahapatra. He was playing the pakhawaj, didn't you see him?'

'No, will you point him out to me?' They did. I saw a small old man dressed in the traditional dhoti-kurta, surrounded by admirers. He was being very polite. He certainly seemed very humble and sincere, and also backward. I edged closer to the group. Much clasping of hands was happening and polite, nice words were being exchanged. He seemed to be a trifle tense about the packing up of the musical instruments and kept shouting orders in between being polite to his admirers. As soon as some of them left, I pushed myself in front of him and joined my hands in respect.

'Namaste, masterji. Are you the teacher of these dancers?'

'Ye . . . s.' There was a look of surprise and amused interest in his eyes. From my face his gaze travelled down to my high heels, then slowly up my tight trousers and my halter-neck off-shoulder top, to my long, loose black hair streaked with gold. A smile appeared on his face.

'I want to learn this dance,' I said. Once again the smile and then a nod. He seemed to be waiting for me to spell out everything. 'Can you recommend someone in Bombay to teach it to me?'

He shook his head. 'No, ma, there is no one in Bombay who can teach odissi,' he said, his voice full of sympathy. 'Who is your guru?'

'What?'

'You must have done some dancing before. What is the name of your guru?'

I felt like an utter fool. 'I . . . I . . . haven't learnt any dance before.'

He looked surprised. 'What? Never? Not even a little bit?'

I looked even more apologetic, my eyes downcast. I took a puff of the cigarette which was smouldering between my fingers. 'No, I never had the chance. But I'll learn it now.'

He stared at my cigarette in child-like amazement. 'It's not an easy task to learn classical dance,' he said and turned to mutter some instructions in Oriya to his troupe.

'I'll work very hard. I'll practice day and night.' He turned towards me. I was puffing at my cigarette in agitation. 'One has to sacrifice many things to become a dancer,' he said impatiently. Thinking that he disapproved of my smoking, I flung the cigarette to the floor and crushed it under my foot.

'I'm willing to sacrifice anything.'

'No, no, you have to start training at the age of six, maximum eight. It's not your age to learn now. All right, ma?' He turned to go.

'Please wait, listen to me, masterji. I really mean it. I want to learn this odissi dance . . .'

'Uh, uh . . .' he shook his head. 'Please excuse me now, we have to catch the train.' He started walking away. I was too agitated to be offended, angry or uptight. I click-clacked on my heels after him.

'Masterji,' I said, 'I will sacrifice anything you want me to, I will work hard day and night, I really mean it. Please teach me.'

Impatient and in a hurry, he half turned towards me, putting his pakhawaj into its cover. 'I can't help you, I live in Cuttack and I'm leaving tonight.'

I stared in utter dismay and confusion. 'But then . . . What . . . How can I learn?' I was close to tears. He must have heard the desperation in my voice. He cocked his head to one side and with a shy smile, muttered, 'Only way is to come to Cuttack. Our train leaves in two hours from V.T. Station. You can come with us if you really want to.'

'Now?' I gasped. Surely he didn't mean it! 'I can't come now!'

'Why?'

'I have a husband and two small children at home. I can't just leave them.'

He was smiling, knowingly this time, sort of like, 'I knew this was how it would be.' In mock seriousness he said, 'But you just said you were willing to sacrifice anything to learn dance.' He's just baiting me, I thought, he doesn't want to teach me. Through the desperation, my anger started rising.

'I meant what I said. But you surely don't expect me to simply leave my family without as much as discussing it with them? Without organizing my trip in a civilized way?'

He shrugged and turned to one of his students. 'Ai, come on, are your bags packed? Are you sure you haven't forgotten anything? Hurry up, we have to eat before we board the train.' It was as though I didn't exist for him anymore. How could he ignore me like that? How could *anyone* ignore somebody like me? I was too visual, too 'in the way' for anyone to pretend indifference. But this little man, this weasel-faced, balding old man in a dhoti-kurta had simply turned his back on me and walked off the stage! I stood rooted to the spot, burning with indignation. I must have been trembling with rage. It was only when despair set in that I was able to move.

I rushed outside and saw him bowing and smiling humbly at an elderly man. I strode up to them. 'Masterji . . .' The elderly man turned to me, acknowledged me, but the teacher ignored me pointedly and continued with whatever he had been discussing. He didn't speak to me directly but from the way his body was positioned, I got the message: 'How dare you interrupt me? You are a nobody, and I don't wish to be bothered by you. Go away.' I hesitated, but stayed put. The elderly man shuffled in an embarrassed manner, then quickly said goodbye, nodding at me as he left. The teacher turned and started to walk away.

'Please, masterji, I'm in a very difficult situation. Why don't you understand? Please help me. I want very badly to learn. Give me a chance, please.'

It must have been the voice cracking and choking in my throat which made him turn. 'Our train takes two nights and one day to reach Cuttack.'

Suddenly, the noose had loosened. There was hope. 'I'll reach your home before you reach.' I could easily fly to Cuttack or some place nearby the next day. In any case, who would travel two nights and one day in a stinking train?

'If you reach before I do, then I will teach you. But if you . . . listen carefully . . . if after three months of initial training I feel that you are wasting my time, then you'll leave without any fuss. Is that understood?'

By now I was in tears. I nodded dumbly. How had the humble, docile man suddenly turned into such a dictator?

'Ask one of the girls to give you my address. And you can't dance in jeans, so bring some saris and salwars with you. Oil your hair and tie it up. I don't allow my students to look like rakshasis.'

Wait till I get the upper hand on you, you conceited old man, I muttered to myself. How could he talk to me like that? What did he think of himself! Just because he knew an art didn't mean he could be so arrogant! But the chips were on his side. I wanted something that only he could give me, so I would have to suffer him—until I got what I wanted. Then who'd care two hoots for him? Yes! I would certainly make him pay for bullying me in this manner. I lowered my eyes with gratitude and joined my hands. 'Thank you, masterji. I will be there before you, I promise.' Without another word he strode off to his group, while I dashed off to find a cab to take me home quickly, quickly.

The children were asleep, the house quiet. I opened my cupboard violently, knowing fully well that there were no more than a couple of saris. My wedding sari had already been cut up to make a stylish evening gown. There were silk saris which had been given to me by my mother at the time of my marriage, but except for two of them the rest had been tailored into outfits. Hell! There was no time to go over to my mother's to borrow her saris—and what would I do for blouses?

Kabir arrived home, tired from shooting all day. I bubbled, I crackled, my sentences running away without me. I was so excited.

'Hold it,' he said. 'Let me get this straight. You saw a classical dance performance and you want to learn it. In order to do so, you have to go to Orissa. And you have to, for some reason, leave tomorrow, or not at all. Is that right?'

I tried to relate how it had all happened, but everything sounded so jumbled up that I simply gave up. 'Kabir, I'll die if I don't go. I must learn this dance. Please let me go. Look after the children till I return. Please. This is very important for me. It's the first thing that gives me any meaning for being alive.'

I sat at his feet, my arms over his knees, looking up at him with huge tearful eyes.

'Look, darling, I'm used to your sudden flights. If it's not for a holiday in Goa, it's a holiday in Manali. This time you want to do something serious—so you say. Of course I'll make arrangements for the kids. How long will you be gone?'

'Three months.'

'Three months! That's long. Are you sure? Will the children stay without you so long? Think about it.'

'I've already decided. Now I need your support. Please bear with me. This is going to change my whole life.'

'Well, okay, if that's what you want. I'll find out about air-bookings first thing tomorrow morning.'

'No, do it now. I must leave early tomorrow. I need time to shop for some saris in Calcutta, get my blouses tailored and reach Cuttack early morning the day after tomorrow.'

The following morning, at nine, I was flying to Calcutta. Three hours later, I landed at the airport and took a taxi to Anando, the shop with the most exquisite, expensive Bengali saris. I bought eleven of them. I found a tailor who would make eleven matching blouses and petticoats urgently for four times the money. I could collect them the next morning at eight. They would open the shop early specially for me. I had discovered that the train reached Cuttack at two in the afternoon. My flight from Calcutta to Bhubhaneshwar, the capital of Orissa, took forty-five minutes. I would have to take a taxi from there for Cuttack, which was an hour's drive. I calculated that I could easily reach by noon. I did.

O

Guruji told me that I could not learn classical dance at my age. I replied that I had the will and the energy. Dance was not a passing thrill, he said, but a complete way of life. I would have to sacrifice many things for dance, and only then could I benefit from it. I said I would give up everything—my husband, my children. I fell at his feet and begged to be accepted as his disciple. Had he demanded my life in exchange for teaching me dance, I would have given it happily, for what he did not know was that I had surrendered myself completely to odissi. What did I have in life before that? I went from one party to another, thinking only about what to wear, what not to wear—mostly what not to wear. I was 'India's queen of outrage' and I enjoyed that reputation a lot. Now I had found a purpose in life.

Guru Kelucharan Mahapatra was a very traditional man. To him, I was still too 'modern' a woman, without the right attitude for what was to him a sacred art. 'Dance is something pure,' he would say, 'it has to do with the gods.' But I think my persistence and sincerity must have impressed him, because after a while he relented.

I stayed in Guruji's house, learning from him according to the ancient gurukul system. I had to dance twelve to fourteen hours a day, and often I would be in tears. My feet were sore and painful all the time and the skin was peeling off them. I was already twenty-six, and the entire lifestyle there was something I had never experienced before. But I couldn't complain. I hated

Cuttack in the beginning, it was crowded and alien and though the streets stank, the people did not care to clean them. There were millions of mosquitoes and fat lizards on the walls racing after insects. I had to draw my bath water from the well, wash my clothes, sleep on a mat in the dance room (there were no special rooms for the students). I also had to help in the cooking and press Guruji's feet at night. The food and water did not agree with me and I was frequently ill, which did not help at all—you need tremendous stamina when training to be a dancer.

Because I was with my guru and the other dancing companions, I didn't feel like putting on my sexy trousers and see-through dresses, because I had gone there to work and not to play. So I was always in saris and blouses, with a tikka on my forehead and gajra in my hair. I had to merge with and be a part of the whole scene. It seemed natural to do so.

Guruji was a very religious person. There was a puja every morning and evening which I had to attend. I had to learn Sanskrit verses too. When Guruji was too tired to teach, he would talk—about religion, tradition and the gracious culture of bygone days of which he was a living specimen.

I was not religious. I remember my reaction when I first saw the priests from the temple of the goddess Kali who came on stilts to Guruji's house. Apparently they came every year. Guruji asked me to bow before them and give them money. I refused to bow, but gave them money. I stood there cynically, watching the others prostrate themselves before the priests. Poor creatures, I felt, they are being taken for a ride. I would never succumb to that kind of enslavement. Even during the daily pujas in the house when the whole family and the students would get together and chant and pray, I would stand a little apart from the others and watch it all with complete detachment. When Guruji talked about the Rath Yatra of Lord Jagannath and the miracles that could happen in one's life if one merely touched the ropes, I refused to believe him.

Gradually, however, I found that living that kind of life and working so hard, like I had never worked before, was in fact doing my mind and spirit a lot of good. Being in close contact day and night with Guruji, I began to be influenced by his way of thinking.

Even in those early months I saw what it was to be a great guru. My guru was a true master. I had read stories about great teachers who had limitless patience, understanding and humility and deep affection for their pupils, but of course I did not believe that such people existed any more. But Guru Kelucharan Mahapatra was exactly such a teacher. His sole interest was to breathe the song of dance into the instrument of the body. His mission was to preserve the authentic and the aesthetic, to choreograph flawless movements, to recreate sculptural images and create the right moods.

Dance to him was a way of life. From his waking moment he was totally immersed in his art. He lived, ate and breathed dance and saw it in everything around him. He had no interest in petty, worldly matters; I never heard him speak maliciously about other gurus or other dance forms. If his students all over the country remained so loyal and dedicated to him, it was because he was dedicated to his students, and rejoiced to see us blossom into good dancers.

The intensity with which Guruji created a new composition was all consuming. Food, drink and sleep were forsaken. At such times, students were shouted at, ridiculed, slapped and threatened. Though we cried and suffered and were angry and humiliated, no one held a grudge against the great teacher. Once the composition took shape, the tension eased and he was the benevolent father once again.

I remember one occasion when I saw him create a new composition and understood how a genius can be totally oblivious to external distractions. We were in a small room—basically a changing room, barely twelve feet by ten—cluttered with an old cupboard, a tiny divan stacked with a holdall and clothes, an old table and some chairs, and a loaded clothes line along one wall. I was sitting on the table, a cassette player next to me playing a remarkable song by Laxmi Shankar to which the dance was being composed. Guruji wore a dhoti, a vest and a very rapt, attentive expression. His hands and feet moved suddenly and fluidly as inspiration came to him, along with a succession of coughs and sneezes (he wasn't keeping too well, what with the cloudy weather and the pressure of time on his head).

Suddenly, the music was drowned out by the sound of a plane approaching, passing overhead and then away into the distance with a deafening roar. The reverberations shook the room and everything in it, including me. The music had to be stopped briefly, rewound, and played from the beginning. But there was a whole procession of planes flying overhead that day. As soon as Guruji got into the rhythm of the dance, another plane would roar above us, shaking everything, and again the song would have to be stopped midway and replayed.

I was there two hours on that Monday evening and at least eight planes went overhead. Not only that, but in the midst of a very gripping abhinaya piece, with Guruji sitting on the floor enacting a lovelorn Radha in distress, two happy, bouncing children rushed into the room, giggling and shrieking, stepped over Guruji's legs, ran around him and banged repeatedly into the old cupboard, before rushing out. Five minutes later, the maid walked in, pulled down a towel from the clothes line and dusted it noisily near him before flouncing out with it. Two minutes later, someone yelled from the next room that there was a phone call for me and I charged out of the room—and of course, just then, a plane went overhead . . .

Yet, amazingly, in those two chaotic hours half the dance was composed—and brilliantly. I have often since wondered at the snob geniuses who need to retire to the mountains or some quiet countryside in order to be creative.

It was impossible not be changed after being with such a person. The only time I've been a cheli is in front of my guru, Kelucharan Mahapatra. He is the only man whose feet I have touched. Despite the differences we had many years later, I continue to respect and worship him.

When I came back after my first three months of training, my mind was made up. All the hardship I had experienced meant nothing compared to what I had gained. There was no doubt in my mind that dance was what I had inadvertently been searching for. The commitment and the dedication had come naturally to me. I was like a puppet; someone else was controlling the strings.

To continue practicing in Bombay all that I had learnt in Cuttack, I had to change my lifestyle. Before I went away to Orissa, Beach House was an open house, with the Juhu gang dropping in all the time. Now I needed the privacy to practice. I would meet my friends only when I was free to see them. There was no question of late nights because the only time I could practice properly was early in the morning. I couldn't do riyaaz in the flat because the people staying downstairs would be disturbed. So I would get up at four in the morning and go to the beach and dance on the loose sand till about seven, after which the beach was no longer a private space. Those three hours of early-morning practice helped me a lot. For dancing on the loose, soft sand you need to have more energy and power than you would normally need, and I think because of that I learnt the dance much faster.

the split

I returned from Orissa after my first intensive dance course. Kabir came to pick me up at the airport. He still had his make-up on and I was thrilled. 'He's so anxious to see me that he's rushed to pick me up straight from a shooting!' In the car I was full of stories about Guruji and my training and a man called Jadhav who had chased me through a field, intent on molesting me. Kabir went back to his shooting after dropping me home.

We dined together that night, and as I was getting ready for bed I saw Kabir sitting at his desk in the bedroom, looking very uncomfortable. With great effort he said, 'I'll be going over to Parveen's, see you in the morning.' My heart thumped. I refused to believe I had heard right. I knew he was having an affair with Parveen even before I'd left for Orissa, but his wanting to go to her on the very night I had returned shattered me. I couldn't understand. Calmly I said, 'But I've only arrived today. Won't you stay at home tonight at least?'

He shook his head slowly. 'No, I want to be with her.'

I sat on the desk before him, my mind in a complete whirl. I said again, in a voice nearly breaking, 'Wait a moment, tell me about it. What's happening?'

'I'm going to spend the night with her, and I want you to know that in future I will be spending all my nights there.'

'Do you love her?'

He nodded yes, and I asked, 'Does she love you too?'

'Yes.'

I kept quiet. What was there left to say? He came round the table and stood behind me, held me by my shoulders and turned me towards him. I clung to him and burst out crying. He held me gently for some time. Then I sat down on the bed. My mind had cleared a bit. I was now play-acting. I looked despondently at the pillow on my lap. He stood there silent, not knowing what else to do. In a very low voice I said, 'Please leave me alone now.' He came to my side immediately, sat down and put his arms around me. It suddenly occurred to me that he might hear me say, 'Don't leave me alone now,' so I repeated, a little frenzied, 'Leave me alone, please go.' Reluctantly, hesitatingly, he walked out of the room. I dug my face in the pillow and howled uncontrollably, a little louder than was necessary.

But my mind was active, thinking furiously. Perhaps he thought I was going to kill myself! Perhaps he was feeling sorry for me and would walk right back. He didn't really want to go, but had decided somewhere that this was probably the best way to act. He'd probably been planning it for weeks, if I knew him. He and Parveen would have sat down and decided on the course of action. The bitch! She must be sitting at home, smoking, waiting for him to come, a little nervous herself, because she'd probably be feeling guilty.

Just then I heard his car start and go down the drive. It was like a button. The sobs and the dejection vanished completely. I went and looked out from the balcony, and stood there for quite some time, realizing that if this was a movie, I should be standing out much longer, thinking thoughts of my man and singing sad songs to the moon. I got tired of standing in the balcony, because no one was watching me and I didn't particularly like the mood that I was trying to be in. I came back into the room and went to bed. I was asleep in ten minutes!

In the morning I decided I'd play it cool as though nothing had happened and let him bring up the topic if he dared. I loved seeing him uncomfortable in front of me, it gave me a great sense of power. I also wanted to show him how understanding I was, how I had been thinking of the problem all night, that I too had reached a few decisions. I remember putting black eyeshadow under my eyes to produce the effect of sleeplessness and unhappiness. I wanted him to see how much I was suffering, how unhappy I was because of him. But this I wanted him to gather for himself. The attitude I was projecting said that for his sake I was pretending to be calm and self-assured; I would do anything for his happiness because as far as I was concerned, he came first, and even though I was miserable, I would not stand in his way. I'd gain his respect as a sensible, strong woman, even though he could see from the dark circles under my eyes how much I had suffered all night. He would admire my attitude, would be grateful for the act I was putting on for his sake. He would, in fact, feel guilty for his actions.

I think he did. He must have felt like a dog crawling out of the gutter. In a fit of bravado, I gave him an ultimatum. I was so carried away by my own act, so pushed by my emotions, that I said, 'I've been thinking about the situation all day and I don't think that it's fair on me, or on you, or on her. You both love each other, you should be together. As long as it was only an affair it was all right, but since you yourself say that you're in love, then something must be done. Either I'll leave or you leave.' Even while I was saying it, I only half believed it, for it was not my intention to have given this ultimatum. I didn't really mean it. I was hoping he would be so shocked by it that his interest in her would wane. I wanted to make him realize that I had taken this situation seriously—though I hadn't really.

'Are you serious?' he asked. 'Think carefully, don't rush into a decision.' Aha! That's shaken him, I thought. 'No!' I said, 'I've thought about it, this is my decision, you just let me know.'

'How many days do you give me?' he asked.

'Three days to think it over,' I said.

'Give me a week or two,' he asked.

'No, I want to know within three days.' I wanted to laugh at the seriousness of the whole situation. It seemed like a farce, I was not really involved in this ridiculous drama, but I kept a straight face and managed to get through my scene.

Of course, as the days and months passed, I realized that I had been an utter idiot to have given him that ultimatum.

o

Parveen had been a good friend of Kabir's and mine for two years before he decided to go and live with her. I remember how lonely she was when she first moved into our neighbourhood. She was living with Danny Dengzongpa then, but they weren't getting along too well and she used to be on her own quite a lot. She didn't have any relatives she could go to and since she was new in Bombay, she didn't have any friends either, and somehow she became part of the Juhu gang. I and others of the gang—Neelam Johar, Anju Mahendru, Ketan Anand, Satyadev Dubey—felt quite sorry for her because she had to go back to an empty house and I would often tell Kabir, 'Why don't you take Parveen for a swim before reaching her home?' So they got to spend time together.

Parveen was grateful to me for being kind to her. Eventually we became close and she would even ask me for advice. She would come over after her shooting, with her make-up still on, and yell out for me and we'd talk a lot. As a matter of fact, she used to sort of hero-worship me. She admired everything about me—my personality, my style, the way I carried myself, my bold, offbeat views. She even admired my living room furnishings.

I remember the time when her flat was being done up (she had just split up with Danny and had decided to live alone) and she'd bought big leather chairs for her living room. She was quite friendly with the Khans (Feroze, Akbar and Sanjay) then, and because they all had leather furniture, she wanted to have the same stuff too. Anyway, when she'd arranged it she found that she didn't like it at all. I told her to throw out those heavy chairs because they didn't go with her personality, and she did. Only, she went and copied my living room next. Exactly like mine, except that the things she'd bought were a little more expensive.

Parveen and I were very friendly till she started getting possessive about me, and if there's one thing I can't stand it's anyone being possessive about me. We were on the beach once and she started complaining that I was more friendly with Neelam than with her, and that I never told her any of my secrets. It was too silly for words and I tried to tell her that she was behaving like a schoolgirl. But she didn't take it very well and that evening marked the start of our drifting apart.

After that, whenever we met I could sense a sort of silent war going on between us and one evening when we were at Neelam's house the vibes between us were so bad that I decided to sort things out with her. When I went over to Parveen's the next day, I found her in tears and the whole house in a mess. She had been trying to find a shirt of mine which I'd left behind, just so she could throw it out. She disliked me so much that she could not bear to have anything of mine in her house.

Later Parveen fell out with the rest of our crowd. Someone had told her that it was the Juhu gang which was responsible for spreading gossip about her in the industry, and that we had gone around saying that of course we smoked hash and had orgies and that Parveen was part of it all. Parveen publicly denied all this and said that she had nothing whatsoever to do with us. To hear her deny any connection with us and to be dismissive and disparaging about us after all those evenings she had spent with us, hurt us all. We didn't see much of her after that and shortly afterwards, she and Kabir got involved.

It is true that I encouraged Kabir and Parveen to have an affair. I was then busy trying to untangle complications in my own life and I wanted Kabir off my back. Besides, as Kabir and I were no longer attracted to each other sexually, I didn't see why I had to be a dog—sorry, bitch—in the manger. Kabir needed a sexual outlet. In fact, it was at a party in our house that I had first seen the two of them giving each other those special vibes and then I went out of my way to encourage them.

When they finally got serious about each other, Parveen came to me and told me all about it. Kabir had never really kept it a secret. In fact, almost every night he would kiss me and the children goodnight and say, 'I'll be back in the morning, darling,' and we'd go to bed and he'd go off to Parveen's. I never tried to stop their affair. I didn't want to. Besides, I could see that he was happiest when he was with Parveen.

Parveen once asked me if I was unhappy about their affair and said that if I was she'd put an end to it, but I assured her that it didn't matter. And at the time it really didn't. They were more made for each other than Kabir and I ever could be. I was the exact opposite of Kabir. But Parveen was made like him. There were so many things that Kabir wanted in his woman which he found in Parveen. As for Parveen, she was lonely and she found in Kabir all the things she needed in her emotional state. Parveen was a one-man woman. Kabir needed such a woman—someone secure, someone he could depend on. I suppose it would have been stupid if they hadn't lived together! I am not a petty person and I don't believe that people should tie each other down just because they are married. Still, it was not as if I had given Kabir away. Nor that he had been taken away from me. It was just something that happened because it had to. I respected their relationship and wanted to ensure nothing went wrong in it.

About a month after their affair started, I had to go to Guruji's house in Orissa, so I asked Parveen to look after my kids while I was away. I must say she looked after them very well, and they loved her. When I came back, of course, Kabir had decided to leave me.

O

Soon after I had given Kabir the ultimatum—that either he left or I did—I realized that I'd been a fool to have presented the option of separation to him. He must have been happy that I had brought it up myself. Of course he must have talked to Parveen about it, going about it gently, and would perhaps have given himself a few weeks to do it, but my attitude had changed the picture. When I saw him taking my words seriously, and no sign of any change in his behaviour towards me no extra gush of love, I got a bit worried. He did tend to take the business of love very seriously. I didn't see him for some days after that. He simply didn't return from Parveen's. I realized that he had kept a few clothes of his at her place and had not found it necessary to come home at all.

When he came two evenings later, I was gentle and a little sorrowful. This time there was quite a bit of fear. 'I take back my ultimatum, Kabir. I realized that I'm happy to be with you, even if you only come home to bathe and change your clothes. Please don't leave. Treat this as your home, as it's always been. Don't break up the unit. Do whatever you like, go wherever you want to, no questions asked, but please come back home.

I suddenly knew from his expression that it was too late. He shook his head and said, 'I accept your first ultimatum, I think it's much wiser. No, you will stay in the house, with everything as it is, I will just move out with my personal belongings.'

'No, Kabir, please don't go, I love you, what about the kids? I can't live all alone!' I was now really getting hysterical and afraid.

'You gave me the ultimatum,' he said. Swine! How he used my emotions. He had probably planned it this way and was overjoyed when I asked him to choose, and now he was blaming me! I cried, I pleaded, but I knew that nothing would penetrate anymore. He could be very cruel at such times, because he would become completely selfish.

After that he came briefly, a few evenings or mornings, to sort out his mail, take a few clothes, attend producers' sessions. This carried on for two or three weeks. Meanwhile I'd packed all his clothes in suitcases, gathered all his personal belongings, and would send off parcels with him every time he came. It was now a new game for me. This extended departure from the house kept me busy, and I didn't delve into it emotionally. I would go out at nights, dancing and dining, but only for the first few days. Then, because I wanted to show him that I was all alone and suffering, I stayed home all day and night, so that just in case he dropped in suddenly, he'd find me mooning at home, complete with the traditional sari and tikka—the ideal wronged wife. Unhappily for me, and my little game, he hardly dropped by.

But we kept in touch. When Kabir's mother arrived, we both went to the airport to pick her up separately in our cars. He took her with him. She stayed with them, and I was hurt. She would come over almost every day, talk to me about us, but I couldn't communicate my feelings to her. Whenever Kabir came over I'd make a point of hugging him, holding his hand, and generally fooling around with him, just to show him that it wasn't so bloody serious, and why the hell shouldn't we be pals? He was so uncomfortable in the house, so uncomfortable in my presence, that it used to hurt. I hadn't given him permission to break the friendship. I'd only permitted him to leave me as his wife, which he'd done years ago, anyway. He was so bloody uptight, so serious about a situation in which *I* should have been the serious one. I was doing my best, what fucking right had he to play with my emotions? That was simply not demanded of him . . . I hated his being serious and petty.

Actually, everything had happened so quickly that I don't think I quite realized the gravity of the situation. In fact, I didn't entirely believe that it had all happened and that it wouldn't all fall back into place. It affected me gradually. I remember New Year's night, 1976, when I sat on the beach at night, alone, crying my heart out for Kabir. I knew he was dancing, drinking, making merry just a few bungalows away at Parmeshwar Godrej's party. How I longed to see him, even if he was in Parveen's arms. Caught up in my own little game, I was refusing to accept the hurt and the pain. The truth was that it was over. Reality was just dawning on me and it was bleak. I still loved him and I knew now that no matter what direction he went in, I would always be there, waiting for him to realize my worth.

Normally I would have been at that party at Parmeshwar's place. But now Parmeshwar, like Zarine Khan and some other people who were my friends, had changed their loyalties—they would invite Kabir and Parveen to their parties and not me. After all, he was Kabir Bedi, the film star, and she was Parveen Babi, the famous film actress. I couldn't see why these people whom I had known so well had to make this kind of choice. It hurt.

Parveen did not bother to come and talk to me and the kids at Beach House even once, but I guess it was because she was feeling guilty. I went to her flat one day. If Kabir's happiness lay with Parveen, I thought, I'd try and reassure her and make her feel secure about my man. She and Kabir were fast asleep in the bedroom. I banged on the door and then sat down with a cup of tea. I thought my casual attitude would relieve any tension, but Kabir came out looking nervous and panicky. Parveen came scuttling out behind him and the two of them huddled together. It was ridiculous. They looked like they expected me to create a scene.

'Kabir is yours,' I told Parveen, 'yours completely. I don't want him back ever, you are absolutely made for each other. In four months you've managed to give him what I couldn't in seven years.'

Parveen was so shit scared that she kept stuttering 'Yes-yes'. Looking at them acting so suspicious of me when I was being so damned nice, I couldn't control myself anymore. Tears started rolling down my cheeks and when they saw that, they drew together again. It was like they were supporting each other. I told them not to worry, that I was crying only because I was overwhelmed by emotion and that I would be okay in a few minutes.

Two months after Kabir and I broke up I gave my first dance performance. Since it was such a big day for me I wanted to share it with both him and Parveen. After all, it was Kabir who had first encouraged me to take up classical dancing. Just before the show started I peeped out through the curtains. I was really upset and disappointed when I saw that neither of them had bothered to come though I'd specially invited them to the performance. After the show everyone told me that I had danced beautifully but I knew that my heart hadn't been in it. The next day I asked Kabir why he hadn't come. He said that both of them had been shooting till late. I couldn't believe that this was the same man who had taught me not to be petty about anything.

Later when Kabir was away I met Parveen and asked her the same thing. I told her that since Kabir was the father of my children, surely we could share him. But she was very hostile. She snapped that she didn't believe in sharing.

I think she knew she was doing the wrong thing by trying to act possessive. Once Kabir had come home to play with the children and she rang up. I tried to be friendly, but she was rude and demanded that I put Kabir on the line. She resented Kabir spending any time with us. No woman should try to keep a man away from his family. Kabir was very understanding in the beginning—'She feels insecure,' he'd explain. But soon, I think, it must have started irritating him. He couldn't have been used to such behaviour. I was jealous of him, I competed with him for attention when he became a star, and I resented being pushed into the background. But I was never possessive about him.

Kabir insisted on sending money for me and the children every month. Harbance Kumar, one of Kabir's film producers and a close friend, used to come over with the monthly instalment. I felt ashamed taking Kabir's money, but I knew he would be annoyed if I did not. Besides, I was not in a position to earn that kind of money. I hated having to depend on him. But if I went out to work the children would be neglected, so I accepted the money. Anyway, he was doing well financially. Harbanceji had told me that *Nagin* was a super hit and that Kabir would make a lot of money. He had already signed hordes of films; 1976 was the year of the Bedi! He was also investing his money very wisely.

Parveen and I never met each other after the separation. Whenever Kabir came down from one of his foreign shootings, he would take Pooja and Siddharth out. They always came back full of what they had done and where they had gone and how sweet Parveen was. The kids adored Parveen, and I take the credit for that, because I could easily have poisoned their minds against her had I wanted to. Everytime I was away from Bombay, in Orissa or on tour, she looked after my children and for that I have always been grateful. Because I made sure they got to spend a lot of time with their father, the kids were not really affected by Kabir's going away. I don't think they quite realized what had happened. Occasionally they would ask why Daddy didn't come home to sleep. But finally, home was where Mummy was, and they got to visit Daddy anyway.

But Parveen could never accept this arrangement. She wanted Kabir only to herself. She was paranoid and neurotic. Kabir could not come to Beach House to see the kids because she would say to him, 'I feel insecure if you go near her.' Kabir would obey; his excuse for being unreasonable and not doing the things he should have done as a responsible human being was always 'Parveen doesn't want me to do it.'

Then Parveen started pestering him to get a divorce. Eventually he asked me. I will not say that I felt no pain when Kabir told me that he wanted a divorce. If you don't brush your teeth for two days you feel uncomfortable—it's a small thing but you are used to it. A husband is more than just a habit. He's a whole person with whom you sit, talk, eat, bathe, sleep, have sex. When he goes, it hurts. In fact I went through a bad time for over a year after Kabir left. It was not so much because I had lost him but because of the way in which he had gone. After all the understanding, after all we'd shared—and we were the forefathers of the whole new permissiveness in India—he walked out saying, 'I want a woman who is faithful to me, who will cling to me. I want a cloying relationship.' To me it was a negation of all that we had talked about and shared.

He had left me, because he wanted to spend 'all' his nights with Parveen, and now he wanted a divorce—for her sake. I could not understand it. The bloody fool. He had it so good with me. I gave him everything, plus his freedom. He could have had his affairs, he could have done anything. I wouldn't have objected. I hadn't been uptight when he had that affair with the beauty queen, nor when he fell in love with Parveen. Where was the need for him to have walked out on the kids and me? We could all have been one big family.

I refused to give Kabir a divorce. Parveen was the right thing to have happened to him at the right time, but marriage was different. I knew she would not have made the ideal wife for him, and I told him so. But Parveen wanted the divorce badly and Kabir would come asking for it and try his best to hurt me. 'I can't be your friend! Parveen is so insecure,' he would say. Once he said, 'Remember that trip of mine to Bangkok? I'd told you that I had picked up some infection in the massage parlour. Well, it was a lie. I said it because I just didn't want to sleep with you anymore.' He said many such things but I refused to be hurt. I was not going to let him win. Then Parveen started asking me through her secretary to sign the papers and set Kabir free. I knew the relationship could not last. It would have been a mistake for Kabir to marry her. So I withheld the divorce.

Meanwhile Kabir went to Rome for the release of *Sandokan*, and Parveen went with him. I felt a little disgusted—would he have taken me to Rome? I doubted it. He had resented being a married man. I think somewhere he held it against me that I was his wife. It was glamorous and scandalous to be with an actress, a girlfriend. It had so much colour. And of course he also believed at the time that he was in love. I could see why. She made him feel secure. She was faithful to him and made it known by her entire personality. I had never made Kabir feel secure. In all other ways I was terrific; he hated me only so far as my relationships with other men were concerned.

When he returned from Italy, I gathered that he had been terribly successful there. He was a rage. There were *Sandokan* and Kabir Bedi shirts, brocades and scarfs being sold in Italy. The great success he wanted was finally his. Perhaps he would now make it big in Hollywood, I thought, and I could see him proud, happy, fulfilled, rich and lonely. Would he at any time want to patch-up with the family? Perhaps. I heard that he had cancelled all new films and was planning to shift to Italy. I wondered what would happen to the 'Babi'. She had her own contracts in India. If he did shift, it would definitely mean bye-bye Babi—unless, I thought, Kabir with his sense of justice did something stupid like marrying her.

I felt happy for Kabir. His success made me happy. I still

considered him *my* man. He and I both knew that greater things were to come for him, but the waiting was killing him. It had killed us. I wondered how I would have related to his success had we still been together. It would definitely have gone to my head, and I could see myself in a grand villa in Italy, being Mrs Kabir Bedi, poised, elegant, with no aim in life except the Italian men. Perhaps it was good for us both that we had split. We had each found a direction in life.

But I wanted him to know how much I loved him, even if he had been a bastard. I wanted to say sorry to him for the hurt I had caused him in our marriage. I wanted to be his most special friend. But I knew that until he approached me himself, I could not go to him. A part of me wanted his fame, his success for myself. I had stood by him and shared so much for so long and now that the fruits were coming, someone else was enjoying them. I felt deprived of the limelight, of the whole damned bag of success. I wanted to be the wife of the famous *Sandokan*. It hurt that in the midst of all this, he wouldn't even think of me. How cruel of him to be happy on his own! And I was angry that he didn't need my friendship. If only he could understand that I didn't want to interfere in his life, that I didn't want his body or his care, just an acknowledgement that he needed me and that I was there for him.

When Kabir rang up sometime after his return from Rome to say that he wanted to meet me, I was excited. I tidied up the house, dressed the children, had a quick bath, wore my beautiful cotton saree, put bangles on my wrists and a big tikka on my forehead. My hand reached out for the golden necklace I had borrowed from my mother a month ago, and suddenly a thought raced through my head. He was bound to notice the necklace and wonder who had given it to me. I couldn't bear to have him think that I was having an affair with someone. The necklace remained in its box. He came with Harbanceji and started talking about money and separation.

'Regarding the flat,' he said, 'I've spoken to the landlord, it will have to be in Guli's [*Kabir's sister*] name because the housing society will not accept you as a landlady and a member of their committee.'

'The disadvantage of being Protima Bedi!' I said.

He gave me a funny look and added, 'And about the divorce, can you go somewhere next week with Harbanceji and sign some papers in the court? Will take you only fifteen minutes.'

'I've already discussed it with Harbance. We've fixed it for the first week of March because I'm terribly tied up with my dance performances,' I said.

This was not how I had expected the meeting to go. There was no need for Kabir to have brought up the topic of divorce again. We'd already discussed it and I had agreed to the divorce, but at the right time. Why was he so impatient? Did he really want to marry Parveen, and this quickly? Or was he worried that perhaps I would get too greedy later on when he would clearly be earning too much money. It angered me.

He left after a few minutes. I felt let down. I went to the kids' bedroom. Siddharth hugged me tightly and I him, for I needed the love. Then my emotion got the better of me and I rushed to my bedroom, locked myself in and cried hysterically, the kids banging on the door, wanting to come in and play with me.

The divorce finally happened after Kabir and Parveen parted company. Kabir did not want the divorce now, but I gave it to him. I had always said that Parveen was wrong for him, and now I had been vindicated. 'It was wrong for me,' Kabir admitted, and I said, 'Now you shall have the divorce.'

The Kabir-Parveen split was inevitable. With Kabir ambition has always come first, and no woman can deter him from that. Kabir is not an emotional man, nor does he get mushy; his head rules his heart. A woman must accept him for what he is. Maybe Parveen couldn't remain just the girlfriend, maybe she wanted more of his time if she was going to give up films. She was wrong to get so possessive about him. And I think Kabir was also being bigoted with her—'I wouldn't stand you talking to anybody, smiling at anybody,' and that sort of a thing.

Parveen definitely gave all of herself to Kabir. She was faithful. She would never two-time a man. She hadn't done it to Danny and she wouldn't do it to Kabir. But that kind of fidelity is great only for some time. I mean, dogs are the most honest, faithful creatures, but they do get pushed around, don't they? A man tends to take a woman's faithfulness for granted once it ceases to flatter him. Then he demands more. Too much emotion and too little intellect was never the right combination to hold Kabir.

I felt very sorry for Parveen when they broke up. I even wanted to ring her up, but what does one say in such circumstances? I asked Kabir about it when we spoke to each other over the phone. He had shifted to Hollywood by then, and he only said this about their split: 'My work is here and her work is in India. You can draw your own conclusions.'

o

After the divorce, I made things very easy for Kabir. I stood up in court and declared that I didn't want any alimony, that I could look after myself. Kabir put the house in Pooja's name and decided to give Rs 3,000 every month without fail. After two years I had asked him to pay a little extra, as prices had rocketed, so he paid Rs 5,000 for two years. Then when he was going through a bad patch I told him to stop sending money, I could manage on my own. Later we worked out that Ranga [*Kabir's brother*] would pay the school fees directly and send me Rs 12,000 a year for incidental expenses.

Looking back now, I realize just how good I had made it for Kabir. I had taken full responsibility of the children. I supported them pyschologically, physically and emotionally, and I was paying for more than half their expenses. I didn't even have a house to my name. When Pooja came of age, Beach House would be hers. If she wanted me, I could stay and if not, I would lose everything I had invested in it—I had spent more than a lakh on just doing up the place. The kids' school admissions and related things had cost about a lakh and I also took care of their medical bills, shopping and expensive enjoyments.

It was quite a raw deal, actually. I should have consulted a lawyer and worked out legal details. Kabir had made so much money on *Sandokan* but he had not shared it with us. Instead he had bought a golden Mercedes and a house in Beverly Hills. He had been left free to make a home and family for himself, to pursue his career and give it all his time and energy. I struggled to establish my career and order my emotional life, but always had to compromise. I had to live with the guilt of 'neglecting' the kids, and with their resentment whenever I wanted something for myself which they felt mattered more to me than them.

The hardest part was being both mother and father to the kids and at the same time having to cope with my own desires and ambition. I remember writing a very poignant letter to Kabir describing how every time Pooja was unhappy, I sensed it—it was a gut feeling—and then I would suffer pain because I did not know what was making her unhappy. If she fell and hurt herself, I felt helpless and as if I was dying. But because he was the father, he wouldn't suffer like that; he could leave them to take care of themselves, take them for granted. I was bitter about that.

Some years after the divorce, I decided to take some time to order my personal life (I had fallen in love with Mario) and asked Kabir to look after the kids while I went to Switzerland. 'No problem,' he said, 'you've done such a wonderful job with them. I'll look after them.' When during the month I phoned from Switzerland, I was told that they had all gone off to Bangalore. When I spoke to the kids in Bangalore, they told me that he was always out. Then he sent them off to Goa for a week on their own (everything paid for, of course!) because he could not afford to miss the opportunity to compere the international film festival in Delhi. The children begged me to come home, so I flew from Switzerland to look after them.

But there was no guilt or apology. The man always goes scot-free. That is what I resent.

O

Kabir and I remain the best of friends, though of course there is nothing personal in it anymore. He is no longer my possession. Sometimes it seems like he has moved next door. If I were to fall and get paralysed today, I know the first person at my side will be Kabir. He will look after me. And I would do the same for him. Kabir and I were never husband and wife in the accepted sense of the term. Rather, we were 'yaars'.

If there's any blame to be taken for the failure of our marriage, I will take it all. It is easy to lay the blame on another, but the truth is that no matter what he did, I am sure I must have done worse. Anyway, it is ridiculous trying to prove whose deeds were blacker.

Basically, I think Protima was too much for Kabir Bedi. It was my whole attitude towards life, my very nature that became too much for him. I was impossible! It required a lot of patience on Kabir's part but he coped with me for seven years. I can only admire him for it. Basically he is a very conservative man. I am surprised he took so much from me. He allowed me to do all the things I've done, which no other man in the world would allow. It was because he tolerated me that we managed to stay together for seven years. Maybe if he had just accepted me, we would have been together for a lifetime. I'm the kind of person who needs to be accepted, and not tolerated.

In a way, I was the wrong thing for Kabir (of course I was right for him for some time). Showbiz is such an insecure world that Kabir needed a woman who was dependable. I was not that kind of woman. By nature, I'm too free in my spirit and soul. Kabir could never be sure of me. He would come back home and find me throwing tantrums or absolutely 'high', or simply not find me there—I could be in Goa! I found out that being married was too binding and I rebelled against it, and against Kabir. I used to hurt him. I used to hurt him terribly. And he once told me that it was as though I were tearing the skin off his body.

Somewhere I feel that I didn't do enough to be a good wife to him. But I don't know how to be a good wife. He tried too hard to become the kind of person that he thought I was. It was out of character. It kept hurting him all the time. If I had known that, I would've been a little more understanding, tried to be a little like him. It was too late when I realized that he was a very orthodox, straightforward, honest man who was wearing the mask of freedom. He had an admiration for the free, liberated lifestyle of the hippies but he couldn't live up to the tensions of such a life. So the first opportunity he got to run, he went to Parveen. When she came into his life, Kabir had been desperately trying to escape from me. She was right for him then.

Finally we had to split because we weren't appreciating each other and each other's values. It's like having a diamond and not knowing its value. But when Kabir left home to live rent-free with another woman, he may have ceased to be my husband, but he didn't stop being my children's father. What's a divorce anyway? As much of a piece of paper as marriage.

I've never held Parveen responsible for breaking up my marriage. When Kabir finally left home to shack up with her (actually I'd left Kabir so many times during the seven years we were together!), I had felt almost relieved. Our marriage had ended long before she entered the scene. We had stopped being man and woman. Sex had finished between Kabir and me. My body was not his. But I never stopped loving him with my heart, my soul, my mind, not even after all the things he said in the press about wanting to block me out of his life.

It is peculiar that even after our divorce, though we have remained the best of friends, I have never desired Kabir sexually. Instead I feel a great warmth and affection and would like to hug him and hold him close to me. When sex did happen after the divorce, it was full of self-consciousness, and was possible mainly because we smoked hash. I remember one time when we met after his second marriage and he started to make a joint. I got a little excited because I knew that he was going to make sexual advances. It was not the sex I looked forward to. I was excited by the knowledge that he desired me. I wanted him to want me feverishly, to be consumed by desire for me, and then I would refuse.

When we were together, Kabir was my King and I was his Queen. Even when the King was around I had many Jacks around me, but never another King. There cannot be another Kabir Bedi in my life. I'm mature enough to know that. And I also know that Protima will remain his one Woman, in the ultimate sense of the word. There will never be another Protima for Kabir.

a new direction

The time Kabir left home was also the time that dance arrived in my life. I could only be grateful for this intervention of fate. I had a new direction in life, a new passion. My complete dedication to odissi was to keep me stable—and happy, for happiness is essential for me to live; I breathe in happiness like I breathe in oxygen.

The most immediate problem now was money. When I started learning dance, I was a married woman and I hadn't really had to worry about money too much. But after the separation, I had to find the money to pay for my dance—for the training, the travel and my musicians. This, of course, was in addition to running the house and taking care of the children. Fortunately, with the help of friends like Shanti Chopra and Vimla Patil, I returned to modelling and fashion shows.

But I had to be careful about the modelling. I couldn't be too public. The classical dance world was a very low-key world and for them I was like a meteorite in the sky which came hurtling down to create havoc in their lives because they were religious, traditional, highly orthodox and deeply dedicated and devoted to their art. They could see the devotion and dedication I had, but my background was something they could not accept. Guruji had made it quite clear that I had to forget my past life because now I was an artiste and devoted to God. I couldn't afford *Stardust* and *Cine Blitz* now. When *Mid-Day* printed an old photograph of mine in the 'Sunday Mate' section, I went through a terrible time with my guru.

In fact, after Kabir and I formally broke up, there was a brief period of estrangement between me and Guruji. He wanted me to remarry 'and come back as a decent married woman.' After much persuasion he accepted me again as his student, but insisted that his name should not be associated with mine in public performances.

So while I continued to model in Bombay and do many of the things I used to do before, I had to be very discreet. I couldn't ruffle any feathers. This did become easier because with Kabir out of my life and living abroad and my dance and my children claiming me entirely, I had no time to socialize. I had to practice early in the mornings, which ruled out late evenings. I saw very little of my old friends. My circle now included great artistes like Pandit Jasraj, Pandit Hariprasad Chaurasia, Shivkumar Sharma, Girijadevi, V.J. Jog and Zakir Hussein. They were my cultural family, they took me into their fold. Whenever I stayed at Girijadevi's place, she would say, 'You have to sleep in my bed.' We were like old friends.

In many ways, I had changed the day I made the decision to take up odissi. It had meant a whole reorientation of my personality and a different lifestyle. It was like starting from scratch, learning Indian music and Sanskrit, going back to an almost Sanskritic existence, to many of the things I had always fought against. Though actually this was not really a decision; there just was no alternative. I knew I had to do it.

Once I left for Orissa to live at Guruji's place, there was no coming back. I had to give up smoking entirely. And because I was not going for late night parties, I automatically cut down on drinking too; there used to be a time when I was drunk almost every night. My wardrobe had no sexy, short dresses any more, only simple cotton saris. Of course this continued for a long time even after I returned to Bombay. I had to create a new image. Before, it was all very well to be rebellious and modern because I had nothing to lose. But now that I was serious about classical dance, I could not afford all that.

I did not feel like a hypocrite changing myself like that; I felt a part of that world, I belonged to it. Sometimes I did feel like wearing my other clothes but I would always worry about people who were concerned with my dance seeing me like that. I respected them and I wanted their respect, so I went out of my way to make sure that I did not antagonize them. And I did it very successfully for five or six years.

In classical Indian dance, the metamorphosis that your personality goes through is remarkable. I'm not saying that I conformed totally and became a traditionalist in my way of thinking, but it certainly did give me a weight and balance and then I couldn't be flippant and frivolous. With the dance I also had to study classical literature, religion and mythology, and I came to understand faith. Dancing out the lives and exploits of the gods—Vishnu, Shiva, Ganapati, Sita, Radha and Kali—I became a believer. I could now understand the finer nuances of different feelings: Meera's love for Krishna differed from Radha's love for him. It is the dance that makes you think, for dance is not just movement and aesthetic beauty, it is an intellectual pursuit. The entire philosophy of our mythology, of our classical and religious arts is so liberating, so large and all-encompassing that it is a shame to narrow it down to simple caricatures of the gods, as is common.

When the Kali priests came to Guruji's house this time, my

cynicism and pride had gone. I felt the energy and the power they were able to communicate with their rituals. I decided to sleep up on the terrace that night and took the mosquito net and my chatai upstairs. I dreamt of a magnificent snake with a jewel on its hood. 'No one can harm you so long as you have this within you,' it said, as it stung me and vanished. I woke up shivering and bathed in sweat. I felt I was in the power of Kali. The fever continued for days. It was malaria.

In those early days, I remember returning from the Kali temple and dancing the Kali tandav. I felt the most powerful waves shaking my body, like a strong waterfall cascading over me. I trembled violently. Tears flowed copiously and I thought of the saint Ramakrishna, the greatest devotee of the Mother. He was in a permanent trance and cried half the time. Now I understood why. I was to have a similar experience on stage some years later after a great performance. It was an overwhelming feeling of being one with the energies that spring from complete devotion. There is something about devotion that belies everything intelligent. It is a strange form of energy, like a wave inside you; it builds up slowly and then, reaching a tremendous peak, comes crashing down, leaving you helpless, weak and dazed. It can be frightening to feel so much so soon, and that is why there are always tears.

It is very difficult to accept these things if you are a non-believer. I know because I was one. But when you start believing, it's another story altogether. The idols, images and mantras simply provoke you to reach that space within where everything is sensation and feeling and you connect with the energies around you. And if you really come into contact with yourself, you face God. Then life brings you everything you need. We don't allow life to work for us. The moment you just 'let go' and 'flow with it', amazing things start happening all on their own. That was what was happening to me. Dance became my dialogue with God. I was a medium for God to express His divinity. How else could my body get into all those postures?

My priorities had begun to change. The world of odissi was now my world, its ways, my ways, its energies, my energies. I might have given it up if I felt that the kids needed me, if they were going through some emotional trauma. Yet, on the other hand, I might not have been able to give it up even if they needed me, because at that moment I felt that my dance wanted me more. For the first three years it was just dance, and when I got a few moments away from my dance, it was my children. Nothing else came in the way. Of course I took care to practice when my children were away at school or at play or asleep. They did feel a little left out. In fact they hated it when they were young.

In Bombay, my first real public performance was at the Kal Ke Kalaakar festival which was held at Rang Bhavan every year. It was the first stage for a new dancer to be presented on if the organizers and the guru thought that you were ready. I was paid Rs 700 for the show, and it was so successful that I started getting invited for many performances. In the beginning there were a lot of people who came just to laugh and giggle because it was Protima Bedi who was performing. When I began to dance they sat up a little straighter and took some note of me because I wasn't what they thought me to be.

My past image did to an extent come in the way of my being accepted as a dancer: Dance was serious business; who did this 'startlet' think she was? But at least my notoriety ensured audiences for my shows and many were impressed, perhaps because they hadn't expected me to do even ten per cent of what I finally did on stage. But it took much longer to convince the critics. In fact, the very orthodox and religious pundits, specially in the South, still write me off and never invite me to dance because for them it is the whole image, the entire personality that matters. Even Sonal Mansingh, because she has had a broken marriage or two, lives alone and has an unconventional lifestyle, rarely gets invited.

I am proud of what I achieved as a dancer. Eventually even the critics were forced to recognize me. I started learning odissi at twenty-six and in three years my name was being mentioned with the names of dancers like Yamini Krishnamurti, Sanjukta Panigrahi and Sonal. I travelled all over India and people came in droves for my performances. The pundits also sat up and took note of me because nobody had ever become so popular and good at dance in such a short period.

When I look back, I feel that I was really not all that good then. I have been dancing for two decades now and I feel quite ashamed that I had the audacity to go up on stage after just three years of learning. But I can't help admiring myself for having had the guts to do that. People would have come for one performance out of curiosity, they wouldn't have come a second time if I was not good.

My strength as a professional dancer, I think, was my stage presence and my personality. Having been in the public eye for long and with my experience as a model I had the confidence to face large audiences without batting an eyelid. And the larger the audience, the more I enjoyed dancing—I was always a bit of an exhibitionist. Also, I had a natural grace and a tall and slim figure—attributes that, unfortunately, are rarely found in our dancers—and large eyes, which are very essential for a classical Indian dancer. So when the audiences saw me on stage their first impression was of something very pleasing and attractive, and that was half the battle won. What also helped was that I spoke quite well. I communicated with my audience between each item, explaining the mudras and lyrics to them. I developed a rapport with them immediately and they felt a part of my performance.

Besides, dance had become part of my being, it was in every nerve fibre. Even when I had just started dancing, I was convinced that it had been with me for centuries, through many past lives. I had discovered love and I had glimpsed God through it. When

I was so involved with my dance and so intense when dancing, how could the audience remain unaffected?

But I still can't believe how quickly I managed to make it as a dancer. It has given me tremendous respectability. There have been times when people have come and touched my feet, saying 'Namaste Protimaji' and all. In the early days I was aghast. I was the same girl about whom people used to say, 'Ah, she's the one who streaked,' or 'Voh to nangi-phangi phirti thi, and now she's in a sari!' But public memory is short. I'm a living example of that.

To perfect my dance, I started studying abhinaya from Guru Kalanidhi Narayan of Madras, though I never lived with her in the customary guru-shishya parampara way. As a teacher she was very learned, had a tremendous knowledge of mythology, and was extremely creative and open-minded in her approach to creating new dance compositions. Whether the composition was in Hindi, Tamil, French or German, her mind came alive with a hundred possibilities of interpretation. Her abhinaya had a very refined quality and I was fortunate to have found a teacher like her.

Once I had established myself as a professional artiste, I started giving many performances all over the country, but this did not improve my financial position. Dance as a career was not worth all the hard work. The organizers of programmes and festivals used to grumble about my fee being too high. But they did not realize that at the end of the day I was left with very little, if anything at all. What I had to pay my musicians alone accounted for more than half of what I got. Besides, there were all kinds of other costs I had to bear: each costume was expensive, and I had to have around ten costumes at a time; my make-up stock had to be replenished every year (I used foreign make-up because that was the best—and also very, very expensive); the jewellery had to be polished and re-threaded every year; my costumes had to be laundered each time I used them, and I could use a costume only six times, after which it had to be discarded and a new one stitched.

[*Around this time Protima started her own dance school at Prithvi Theatre in Juhu, with an initial group of twelve students. The youngest was four years old and the oldest was thirty-two. It later became the Odissi Dance Centre, affiliated with the SNDT Women's University in Bombay.*]

O

After the separation from Kabir, I was looking for an emotional anchor. It was through my dance that I found it. I got involved with a wonderful musician and a saintly man. Pandit Jasraj and his wife were producing a ballet on *Geet Govind*, Jayadeva's twelfth-century erotic poem, and I was selected for the lead role. I was thrilled, though it made many people bitter and jealous. During the preparations and rehearsals, I heard Jasraj's voice and it had a tremendous effect on me. I had never been moved by something as greatly as I was by his music. I craved the spirituality and serenity I had sensed in his voice. Because we were part of the same group, creating *Geet Govind* together, we were in close proximity in any case, and I fell in love with him.

It was the beginning of a very close and intense relationship. We both travelled a lot, giving performances, and in every letter we professed our love for each other, over and over again, impatient to be back together. I remember one time when on an impulse, because I missed him so much, I had gone to Durgapur from Calcutta only to see him. I wanted to surprise him. Jasraj also accompanied me for some of my performances outside Bombay. He would say that I could take him anywhere, he only wanted to be with me. It was also, of course, because he was extremely possessive. He would get irritable and angry and say unreasonable things if I stayed away too long, and then write letters apologizing and saying how much he loved me. My absences disturbed him, he would explain, because he kept imagining the worst—probably that I was with another man—and that was what led to his outbursts.

Sometimes it surprised me that we should be having that kind of a relationship. In many ways we were completely different people. How had a man like him accepted a woman with the kind of image and personality that I had? And how had I accepted a man with his attitudes and limitations? Looked at objectively, it was an unlikely bond; it could not possibly last. But with both of us it was the heart that ruled, not the head. Besides, though he was not young, rich, handsome or modern at all, he was gentle and saintly and innocent. He was simple and uncomplicated—just the kind of man I needed after the separation from Kabir and when my life had taken a different turn after odissi.

I went with Jasraj to his foster father's home in the kingdom of Sanand. He was an intriguing man, very well read and a very devoted bhakt of Goddess Kali. He would get up at four every morning and do his drim-zing-dring ritual to Kali for three hours or so, and then would walk about with his silver-knobbed stick. I was told that he had been a great womanizer in his younger days and had indulged in excess of every kind. But today, they said, there could be no greater devotee of the Goddess. What a fantastic personality he was—flowing white beard and eyes that bored holes into you. He always told Jasraj, 'Protima is no ordinary woman.' He would give me food from his silver tray, a privilege that no one else had. He favoured me in front of everyone. I had invaded his home and won his heart. Before dying, he had asked Jasraj about me, and again repeated that I was no ordinary woman. Jasraj was very impressed by these things, and I became more precious to him.

Jasraj taught me the intricacies of artistic expression. I learned from him about aesthetics, the art of listening to music and enjoying it, the art of refining each sense used in the performing arts. In large measure, he was responsible for my dance being what it was and for the friends I had in the art world. When with Kabir, I used to dress and behave like a hippie, with Jasraj I became the typical Indian woman, with sari, bindi, gajra and bangles.

I had only recently discovered the goddess Kali through my dance, and Jasraj was a great devotee of hers. He used to talk to me about Kali all the time, and I would go to the temples with him and sing the matakalika.

He took me to the Kalibari often. On one of these visits I was overcome by an overwhelming sense of devotion. I shook and I wept. It frightened me. I asked him to take me to Dakhineshwar after that, where She would not be so fierce, as the deity there was reputed to be a gentler version of the same goddess. We went, and I sat there taking in the serenity of the place, relaxing in the presence of the gentler Mother. But there was something very attractive about the fierce one, because there was something terrible and horrific about Her. A year later, I went to the Kalibari again with Jasraj. This time it wouldn't be the same, I thought. After all, that was the first time, and I must have been worked up. But the moment I entered the narrow dirt-filled lane leading to the temple, my heart started pounding and my eyes filled with tears. I started shaking like before. I bowed down, and on an impulse, knelt and put my head through the grill and touched Her feet. A great sob broke out within me, like a storm at sea, and I cried uncontrollably. That was the first time that I spoke to Her.

On our first visit to the temple, the priest had thrown a garland of flaming red flowers around us both. He put the red tilak on my forehead and on Jasraj's, and as I walked out, with the symbolism of the action still sharp in my head, a lady ran up the steps and fell at my feet. She was crying and pleading for something. She wouldn't let me walk. When I asked one of the paandas what she wanted, they expressed surprise that she had fallen at my feet. She was saying, '*You* tell Her about my plight. I know She will listen to you because I can see that you are Her daughter. She is within you.' Apparently, the woman had lost her husband and then all her children, one by one, within three years. All she wanted was to die, and she had been sitting at that temple for almost four years, begging the Mother to take her away. This was the first time she had spoken to anyone. I was naturally quite moved by it all. Maybe I did have the energy of the Mother in me. I saw Jasraj looking at me with admiration and love, and I felt very special. I was filled with a sense of pride.

I thought about the Kali connection in my life so far. People used to call me Kali when I was a child. Through college, too, the girls and boys had called me Kali. Some said that I looked like her—big eyes and jet black hair. Shortly after I moved in with Kabir, he had taken photographs of me with pictures of various gods in the background. The picture that came out the best was the one with Kali in the background. Kabir had blown it up and had it mounted. It really was a beautiful photograph and he even won some prize for it. I remember the photo well—black-and-white, with me in the foreground, eyes closed, face relaxed completely as though in a deep trance (I had been sleeping at that time of the night when the photography bug had bitten Kabir) and fierce Kali behind me.

When I danced on stage, it was not to Lord Jagannath that I offered the flowers when I began my recital. It was the Mother who was always in my heart. Even with the gods you cheat, I would tell myself. But it must be okay with the ones above, I would reason and use Jasraj's favourite line: 'It is all the doing of Ma. It is Her will.' (Jasraj, of course, used this line only when the mistake I had made did not concern him or did not bother him too much. But when it was something that hurt him or made him angry, it was not the Mother's will, it was entirely my doing, my fault. I could never understand that, especially since he said he loved me and was also a great devotee of Ma.)

Through the constant visits to the Kali temple, I cemented a bond between the Mother and myself. I even went there alone on many occasions. My dance performances became more meaningful and deep. The spirit with which I danced became forceful and the audiences were touched. The dance was not perfect in technical terms, but then, wasn't dance essentially the expression of the soul? If one was perfect technically and had no soul, the audience would sit for half an hour, then they would get up and go. As I saw it, Indian dance was something more than just aesthetic pleasure. It was a communion with God. The dancer was only a medium. I danced with an intensity that I had not known existed within me. I danced with complete involvement. I was Radha, and I was Krishna, and I was responsible for the creation and destruction of everything that existed. And yes, I was Kali.

My dance became my prayer, my communion with Her. I had a small temple made in my bedroom where I installed Her idol, specially bought from the Kalibari. Jasraj and I prayed to her every morning when we were together.

Gradually, as my relationship with Panditji deteriorated, I stopped praying at my little temple. When the relationship snapped completely, I pulled down the temple and kept the pieces away in the storehouse. I didn't feel guilty at all. It was only for him that the temple was there in the first place. My temple was within my heart.

For four years, Jasraj was the man who was closest to me, whom I loved with a passion. In my own way I was loyal to him. But there was a lot that I could never share with him. It was also a very demanding relationship, and very taxing emotionally. The fact was that I was the other woman, and I wondered often how long I could go on being one. Jasraj could not marry me, he would never be entirely mine, but he was possessive and jealous. He wanted all my time.

My feelings for him fluctuated. Later, when I got involved

with Rajni Patel, Jasraj suffered greatly. When he had a heart attack after that and was in hospital, I went to the Kali temple and cried bitterly and asked Her, 'What do You want from me? Why do You put me through all this pain? Just give me one passion, pure passion for something, someone, and let me be faithful to it.' We had both let each other down, but the burden of guilt was mine alone.

Over time the relationship lost the power and the vibrancy it had in the beginning. The objects remained the same, but the magnetism was lost. I remember Jasraj singing one of Ameer Khusrau's compositions to me, choked with emotion, begging me to give him one more chance, to forgive him and take him into my embrace. I had been proud on that occasion, and haughty, but the resistance broke, and I melted in his arms. That time the reconciliation lasted another few months. The relationship dragged on a little longer. Then there came a time when no endearments worked, neither from his side, nor from mine. Eventually it was only my dance that I could rely on to awaken me to joy.

finding a balance

'Kabir is getting married on the first of February,' Guli said.

'No! Really? I don't believe it, who to?' I said, quite composed.

'To an American girl . . .,' and Guli went on.

I listened quietly, taking in every detail, thinking how Kabir really did require someone to look after him. Guli expected some emotional upheaval, but I said I felt nothing whatsoever. She would not believe that.

I left for a fashion-show rehearsal immediately afterwards. By the evening I had a chill and a fever. I finished the rehearsals at 9 p.m. and drove homewards. Suddenly at Haji Ali I felt a great surge of energy rising within me and an unearthly, animal-like cry rose out of somewhere deep inside and out into the traffic sounds all around me. Then a moan, and then tears streamed down my face. There must have been a great ball of unhappiness within me. Pathetic! I thought. 'Cry, Kiddoo,' I told myself, 'pull it out by the roots. You're absolutely miserable and you won't show it to anyone because you don't even want to show it to yourself.' I cried all the way to Juhu.

I slept peacefully that night and the next day I left for Nagpur for a fashion show. It had come at the right time, it would keep me busy and my mind steady. Through the three days in Nagpur I wasn't alone for a single minute. When I returned, I put my head in Pooja's lap and burst into tears. I did not tell her or Siddharth why. I wanted to share my pain with someone. I thought of Jasraj. Yes, I would tell him. He was so simple and serious. He would share and suffer my grief. But how could I expect him to understand my sorrow over the loss of the other man? Hadn't I myself wanted to marry Jasraj and take him away from his family?

Kabir phoned early the next morning and I talked to him freely, full of love and warmth. 'Of course I'll stand by you,' I said. 'Don't worry, I'll never allow the children to feel anger or unhappiness on account of this. I'm happy that you're happy. Don't worry. I love you. Go do your thing. You'll always belong to me.'

Susan Humphreys. I could only visualize her as tall, thin, straight, without vivaciousness, and rather plain. A steady woman, one hundred per cent together and very warm. It was simple. After Kabir had been in the gloss of Hollywood with all its pretensions and tensions, it was a natural rebound to be with someone honest, practical and simple. The home life was so important to a man whose work lay in the tension-ridden field of movies. Love was not the only reason why Kabir had married Susan, there were many others—his green card in America, a housekeeper, good food, and other such comforts and conveniences. And why not? Wouldn't I have done the same in his place? It did not make him any less beautiful and warm a person. I could only think of that marriage as a contract of convenience. I wouldn't let it hurt me. How on earth could any person come between Kabir and Protima? It was a special union.

Kabir had said on the phone that he would be coming in

March to visit India and would stay with me for a few days. I looked forward to the event, curious to see how their relationship worked.

Would he have children? I found the thought distasteful, the thought of his being father to strange little foreign children, the children of another woman. But I could never hold grudges against petal-soft babies. I wondered whether I could hold any grudges at all. Kabir was happy and that was all that was important.

I had offered to come to his wedding and help out. But he was silly and still immature. He felt it would cause tensions, and had almost ordered me not to arrive.

o

The Odissi Dance Centre at the SNDT University was inaugurated two days after Kabir's marriage, on 3 February 1979. The mahurat went off wonderfully. Soli Batliwalla, Pandit Jasraj, Pandit Maniram, Nargis Dutt, Shashi Kapoor, Shabana Azmi—they were all there. And Guruji himself! I could have cried for joy, and yet I knew that it was not really my doing. What spurred me on? What energy drove me? I had not visualized an Odissi Dance Centre for the next ten years at least. But there it was! I also had a teacher to take over the responsibilities of the dance school.

And then Soli Batliwalla offered me a grant to do a biography of Guru Kelucharan Mahapatra. Which meant that I got paid to be near the man I needed to be close to for the furthering of my dance. It was a great opportunity to come closer to him. I needed him to give me the treasures he had, because I was convinced that I would be the one student who would perpetuate the form and keep the tradition alive as he wanted it. The Mother had chosen me for this task. I knew I was not the master of my own destiny. I could not change it, could not sit in one place for the rest of my life, because I had been blessed with this incredible energy to do things.

I sensed the pattern: the school had come to be, the book on Guruji would happen, and I would become a renowned dancer. Naturally, they would make films on my life, I felt, and write books on me. People would marvel at how wonderfully I had shaped my destiny and what courage I had, but only I would know that I had done nothing. It had all come as part of a plan. We were all being used.

Would the Odissi Dance Centre finally have a hundred acres of land? Just like Kalakshetra in Madras? Would I be a grand old lady, completely responsible for the birth and growth of a vast, famous and important institution? Would I also be a great dancer? I was sure it would happen. I could see that I was going to have a good time, and I savoured the feeling.

Kabir and Susan arrived the following month. They were staying at Holiday Inn. Kabir rang me and said he was coming over to pick up the kids and wanted to see me as well. I wondered whether I should go and meet Susan at Holiday Inn or not. She ought to come and meet me, I thought, and suggested it to Kabir. They arrived at 8.30 p.m. Susan turned out to be a nice, charming woman without any complexes whatsoever. Kabir was lucky to have her.

I fixed a dinner-and-music evening for them a couple of days later at Beach House. Jagjit and Chitra Singh would sing ghazals. I invited all of Kabir's friends. I wanted them to see how wonderful I was being to my ex-husband and his new wife. I hugged and greeted Susan and I genuinely meant it. It was a wonderful evening, and they both moved into Beach House the very next day. I was going off to Ahmedabad, so I had my room prepared for them. The three of us lay around, talking about everything under the sun, totally relaxed. But by the evening I had a heavy headache, and so did Susan. I noticed that Kabir was smoking too much.

I brought back a beautiful red ghagra for Susan from Ahmedabad. She was thrilled and I liked her even more for that. They left, the day I arrived from Ahmedabad, for Guli's. I lay alone in my bed (which was now a single bed once again) and could not sleep. They had been sleeping on that very bed; I saw them before me, kissing and embracing lovingly, unembarrassed and uncaring of my feelings. I had sent them an exquisite brass lamp as a wedding present, but they hadn't brought even a tiny gift for me. How utterly thoughtless of them! They would continue to drop in, sleep in my bed, have lunch or dinner without any formalities, and there'd be not so much as a flower for me.

Why the hell did I have to be the 'understanding woman' in everybody's life? Didn't I have the right to yell and shout, to seethe with anger and jealousy and show it? But I only felt a great self-pity. I would never be the only woman in anyone's life. Sometimes I hated Kabir so much that I wanted to hurt him deeply. But how could I? I loved him. 'When he comes to see the kids tomorrow,' I would think sometimes, 'I'll erupt, or I'll be totally cold, so that he can start wondering and worrying a little bit.' Yet I knew that by then the anger and resentment would have passed. I could not bear to be petty and small. But I resented having to be 'big' all the time. I wanted Kabir to appreciate my stand and to say it in so many words. I wanted his appreciation. I wanted him to love me madly, to care for me, to put every single thing he owned at my feet. Whenever I sensed this need, I felt ashamed of myself.

Kabir and Susan had been in Bombay for barely a week when Manu arrived from Delhi. [*Manu was a prominent Union minister whom Protima had met at the Khajuraho dance festival the previous year. They had been seeing each other regularly since then.*] He was staying at the Centaur Hotel and asked me to spend the night with him there. Kabir, Susan and Johnny Bakshi had come over for dinner. Late that night, after dinner, I changed into my jeans and red Chinese jumper and said, 'I'm off. See you folks in the morning.' I got a cheap thrill watching the expression on Kabir's face. He smiled, coughed uncomfortably and said bye. Susan smiled too, eyes a little lost. She must have felt happy seeing me go off, at least she'd know that as far as I was concerned, her future with Kabir was safe. I did not want her to think that I carried a need for Kabir deep within me.

I drove off to Centaur and walked into the lobby. How I hated it. The receptionists must have known that I was going to meet the minister. Why couldn't they have private elevators to the rooms in five-star hotels? The security guard was outside Manu's suite. He looked at me suspiciously. I tried to appear nonchalant and looked right at him as I knocked on the door. Manu opened the door.

'Let's just talk today, I don't feel like sex,' I told Manu.

'Okay, if that's what you want.' He was always ready to fall in with whatever I wanted. He had put me on some sort of pedestal.

'You know, Manu, I felt so good telling Kabir that I was spending the night out. It's odd how the marriage contract can make such a difference. When I was Kabir's legally-wedded wife, he could not bear even the thought of my being with or thinking of someone else. But now it's as though I have earned all the rights of giving vent to the emotions which were always there.'

Manu agreed. That was how marriage was. But it wasn't just the men, he said. The marriage contract worked for women too. 'It is a question of security,' he said. 'They cannot afford to have their husbands feeling free to do what they want. My wife, for example, is a very ordinary woman, completely devoted to house and family. That's her whole world. To her, it is of utmost importance that her social position is protected. She is the wife of a minister and that has its perks. That is all that gives her happiness. Can I deny her this? She has looked after me and the home to the best of her abilities. She doesn't ask for much. Is it fair to deny her that little facade which ensures that her world is safe?'

'No, it isn't, Manu, but is it an honest life? Do you really think that she's happy living with a lie? Do you think she does not sense that there is someone else? She must be suffering. Better to know and live honestly than to pretend that everything is all right. I'm not blaming her, I'm just questioning the basic morals of the society in which this is done. I'm not talking about her, personally. It pains me that there is no understanding between partners. If she was your real companion, your comrade, you would tell her. The fact that you can't means that she's not your companion. She's merely your housekeeper.'

Early morning, at five, I left the hotel. Manu had to catch the morning flight. I slipped away quietly, so as not to disturb him. And I forgot to take my bangles. At 6.30 he called: 'Listen, you forgot your bangles in my room. What can I do with them? I can't leave them in my hotel room. I'm taking them with me to Delhi, you can take them when you come there.'

I was in Delhi two weeks later.

'I forgot to get your bangles,' Manu said when we met.

'Where did you put them, Manu? How dangerous to carry them with you. Didn't your wife find them?'

'I put them in my office drawer. She never comes into the office. And the drawers are always locked.'

'What if she finds them? What would you say?'

He thought a while and then shrugged. 'I'll just pretend that I don't know how they got there.'

'No, Manu, whenever your back is to the wall, take an aggressive stand. Don't just deny or look upset. Get angry and yell—"What are these bangles doing in my office? This is an office, not a ladies' dressing room. I won't have this sort of thing in my office, understand? Take them away and never let me see this sort of thing again!" Mutter to yourself about ladies' fashions etc, etc, and warn her again and again about this.'

He laughed uproariously. We giggled about it for long. One week later, he came in excited. 'Guess what? Just as you feared, she found the bangles. I did exactly what you said I should. I fumed and yelled. She said that they were not hers, and I said that if that was true then it was worse. How dare these things get into my office drawer! She took them away quickly, saying that perhaps someone had brought them as a gift for her and I must have forgotten about them.' I laughed.

'And she said the bangles were so beautiful, especially the black ones with the silver lines! I was so relieved when she walked out with them. It worked! You're a real crook, Pamo. Oh, I love you so dearly.'

The next day there was a concert at my friend Reggie's place. I was tempted to wear bangles similar to the ones Manu's wife had found, so that she could put two and two together. But better sense prevailed. What could I gain by exposing the affair? After all, he was right. She didn't ask for much. So why hurt her? Better to let things be.

O

My dance had become the single most important thing in my life. With my dance, my students at the Odissi Dance Centre and Guruji's biography, I was up to my neck in work. It surprised me that I could be so dedicated to my dance. My legs were getting muscular and my feet often hurt badly. But the Mother had a plan for me and I was grateful for that. I wanted to devote all my time to Her plan and serve Her to the best of my abilities. I decided to send the children to boarding school.

I wrote to Kabir about this, explaining that I did not have enough time to run a proper house. He wrote back saying that he was dismayed. He wrote that 'faced with a choice between having the children around you, in the house, or another man (most probably Jasrajji), you are choosing to send the children away. You are employing new cooks and ayahs in the hope of creating a more inviting environment for him, in the expectation of radically shifting the balance of that relationship in your favour.' A lot of my travelling, he said, was so that I could have the freedom to be with Jasraj outside the constraints of Bombay. That hadn't been good for the children, but at least they weren't being 'uprooted' from their house. Now, according to him, what I proposed to do would be very bad for them. He reminded me of the time when I had protested vehemently when he had suggested once that we send Pooja and Siddharth to boarding school. He could not see how I could have changed my mind now. 'What is damaging for the children,' he wrote, 'is to know that now even their mother pushes them out of the house to make room for someone else.'

Kabir suggested that I take time off from everything and arrive in America with the kids to spend some time with Susan and him. I should not take such irreversible decisions in a hurry. The children had already had a rough life, he said, having had to 'bear the brunt of parents who chose to go their own ways, even if for the noblest (or craziest) of reasons'. We would find solutions 'as friends in the Californian sunshine'.

[*Pooja and Siddharth were finally sent to a boarding school—Blue Mountain—in the Nilgiri Hills. They were there for less than a year. They were in Bombay for a couple of years after that before being sent to Lawrence School, Sanawar.*]

Through 1980 I lived like a gypsy, performing in Bhopal, Baroda, Hyderabad and many other places, and going to Cuttack to be with Guruji. I spent much of that year inside trains. I wrote to the children regularly from wherever I was and went to meet them in school whenever I was free. I had chosen the right school for them and I wanted them to be happy. I tried explaining this to them, telling them that change was wonderful, like new blood in one's veins. They had to learn to be independent.

Siddharth hated boarding school and would write to me saying that he was miserable and wanted to be back with me. It was difficult convincing him that it was best that way. I was rarely home, and my work was going to get more demanding. Guruji came to Bombay and I was dancing all day, working very hard at what I enjoyed most. But I had to be careful with Siddharth. He thought a lot about things and worried too much. His unhappiness made me unhappy. Pooja, fortunately, was adjusting well to the new environment.

In the middle of all this was the anxiety about my mother. She was getting old, and I worried about her living all alone. My brother Bipin, who always said that his friends valued him more than his family did, did not care for her. I had asked her many times to come and live with me, she would have company and the servants would do all the work. But she chose to live on her own. I would go and meet her often and got Jasraj to bring me a taanpura for her, so she could sit and sing for hours.

O

Pooja and Siddharth went to California to be with Kabir whenever they had long holidays. Kabir invited me too, on more than one occasion, but I could not bring myself to go and live in his house. What had I got from him for all the trust and reasonableness that I brought to our relationship? I still considered him mine in a very special way, but none of it mattered to him. I remember meeting a 'chhaya shastri', soon after Kabir and Susan left, who had told me that my ex-husband and I would never be together again, and yet would never be separated. I had believed that completely. It was true, as far as I was concerned. I still felt such a loyalty for Kabir that I had recently rung up a magazine and fired them for having dared to print unpleasant things about him. In return, I received no love or understanding. Kabir dismissed my aspirations as insignificant, and had the gall to say that I was being an irresponsible mother to the children, the children whom *he* had abandoned.

I was angry and hurt and wrote Kabir a long letter to get the load off my chest. I was sick and tired of smiling sweetly and being a 'yes' person in his life. I had to tell him how things seemed to me. I had to let him know that he had caused a lot of pain and never given a damn. Having done that, I thought, I would be at peace with myself and therefore happier.

I had painted Kabir as almost a saint, defending all that he did, because he was the father of my children. Tainting him would have affected the children and their relationship with him in a negative way. I cared too much for them to let my pain and anger show. But I was doing myself an injustice. Kabir had done much wrong in the marriage but had never thought twice about making me suffer all the guilt. The only decent thing he had done was to have provided for us, unasked. He paid me a measly Rs 5,000, and that took care of his guilt. I did not need his support anymore. Besides, could that money compete with the care and attention and love that the children were getting from me? I was quite certain that he was incapable of making the kind of sacrifices I had made in my personal and professional life for the sake of the children.

Did he know what it meant to cancel a show which gave me my month's income because my daughter needed my presence at home, or to cancel a significant tour of America because my child was psychologically upset? Pooja was going through a hard time emotionally and needed a parent who belonged only to her. She meant more to me than the fame, the money and the marriage I ought to have had. And it upset me that Kabir could sit comfortably in his posh Beverly Hills bungalow, shelling out a tiny part of his income and feeling he had done his bit.

I wanted him to feel the guilt of having deserted his children and causing a void in their lives. They hadn't felt it before, they were too young, but now things were different. Pooja was almost twelve and extremely sensitive. Kabir had never had to handle the kids' emotional crises. If they felt any security in his house it was probably because of Susan; they would never be able to tell him about how lonely and afraid they felt inside. They could say all that to me, they could even be mean and nasty to me because they knew that I was with them and would always accept them. I felt that it was time for them to work out their own relationship with their father, without my being his PRO.

I had done enough to keep Kabir together and happy. He had Susan now—and I told him that he did not deserve her—and I too had a man whom I could trust. Jasraj, for all his faults, mattered a lot to me because he loved me dearly, even when I did not always love him as much. He was willing to give up even his music for my happiness. When Kabir came to Bombay just before his marriage to Susan and tried to revive our relationship, I could not go along because of Jasraj. I could not cheat that man, even when it was my own husband who was trying to seduce me. Perhaps it was Jasraj's love that had made me write that letter to Kabir, not to hurt him, but to cleanse my soul of him.

Some months later, Kabir came for three weeks, this time without Susan, to spend time with me and the kids. We slept in my room on two separate mattresses with long pillows separating the beds. Six nights went by without anything happening. We would drink every night, laugh, joke, and would always end up snoring in our separate beds.

And then one night he asked me to press his back. I did, and then he sat up and stroked my head ever so gently. I said, 'I don't care if you misunderstand, but I must lie beside you.' And then we were together. How wonderful it felt to be engulfed by such a large body. But so long as it was protective and warm, it was all right. Then the sensuousness took over, his lips on mine, and it was a strange feeling. He was a total stranger to me. We went through all the motions but I was above and beyond the physical senses, trying to fathom what I felt for the man and who he was to me. All that came to mind was the gentle, beautiful Jasraj and my love for him and his love for me.

Only when I was closest to the man I had shared so much with did I realize how deeply I loved Jasraj. I could not share him with Kabir in any way. Jasraj was still my heart and my soul. And yet, though I saw the depths of my love for him, there was always a distance between us. There were times when it seemed that our relationship was over, and then some plea, some need would bring us together again and we'd blunder along for a little longer. Jasraj loved me without a thought. I loved him with realization. There were so many important moments of life that I could never share with him—moments of intellectual discussion, philosophical debates, having fun. This hunger had to be quenched elsewhere, and he would never understand that. Perhaps no one would.

The more successful and rich I became, the less men were interested in me romantically. They did not know how to approach me and with what line to start a conversation. I could afford just about anything, I was not impressed by expensive dinners and gifts. Men knew that they had to meet me on a one to one level and it was very awkward for them to do that. Men bank upon their good looks, their money and power. But when the woman has all these and has had a partner who has had it all too and shared it with her, they are complexed. I was a rich, famous, influential and popular woman and I had all the freedom I wanted. What could they offer me?

I have realized that men always feel that they are offering something besides themselves, as if by themselves they don't amount to much. A woman only offers herself; a man offers all that he stands for. Perhaps that is the reason why intrinsically a woman is stronger than a man. The man's ego is the cause of all his failures. He needs his ego to prop himself: without it, he's just his mother's little boy who never grew up, and is afraid of what the world is up to. He must keep up pretences, for he is truly defenceless without his ego. There's nothing solid backing that.

a beautiful relationship

I was living in with Pandit Jasraj when I met Rajni Patel. I had gone to meet him with Jasraj to sort out a small legal matter with regard to my car. Rajni was his usual flirtatious and charming self, and whenever we met after that he tried very hard to get me to visit Cuffe Castle, his office. Of course I was hugely charmed by the attention of such a powerful and famous person but I kept a safe distance for a long time. Then I started using his office along with a bunch of my dance students from the Odissi Dance Centre. When I was doing a show at the Nehru Centre in 1981, I used his secretaries, his phones and other office equipment. I also asked him to help me financially, but he told me to collect money on my own steam first and he would double whatever I managed to receive. I was thrilled.

Except for the flirting there was nothing else between us till that point. Then one afternoon I was in his office, dying to pee, but both the bathrooms were occupied. It was around 3.30 p.m. He was usually asleep at this time, but I heard sounds from his closed room and thinking that he was awake, I knocked and entered, so that I could use his bathroom. I saw him kneeling on the floor with his head on the bed, crying. The great Rajni Patel was crying! He was sobbing his heart out, and it was the most natural thing for me to quietly hold him from the back and hug him tight, trying to share whatever pain it was that he was suffering. He told me that he had got his medical report and it had confirmed that he had cancer. He said he was afraid, and we held each other for a long, long time. There was nothing sexual about it at all. Just a need to reach out to another person. I felt very close to him after that, and he would tell me about his deeper feelings, his fears, and his dreams for the future. We shared a very deep bond for the simple reason that I had shared his grief.

He delayed going to Delhi for his first operation only because of my dance festival which was held in Bombay. He wanted to see me dance before he died. He was convinced that he was going to die. He asked me to come to Delhi with him. To me it was the request of a dying man, a man whom I cared for deeply. Of course, if I went to Delhi with him we would enter into a deeper relationship. In hindsight, I wonder if he had manoeuvred the whole thing, but at that time I believed every word he said.

My mind was in turmoil: I wanted to be with Rajni; but I had been loyal to Jasraj for five years, I couldn't cheat on him. Finally I told Jasraj that I was going to Delhi with a man I knew and who wanted me to see him through a difficult time. I did not know how it was going to turn out, I said, and begged him not to ask me any questions right then. When I returned I would have all the answers.

Poor Jasraj, he suffered for two days in my absence, wondering what was happening and fearing the worst. On my return I told him that I had gone with Rajni and that I was committed to be ng with him for a year as he was dying and he needed me and I felt deepey about his pain. Jasraj had a fit. He went to Cuffe Castle and blasted Rajni. 'Just because you are dying, you have no right to ruin my life,' he shouted. Rajni tried to reason with him but he was inconsolable. He said some very nasty things about me to Rajni—that money had finally bought me over, that I was not a woman who could be trusted—and strode off. He was thereafter admitted to hospital with a heart attack.

That was a period of great suffering for me. I still loved Jasraj, but I also felt a deep commitment to a man who was dying and who depended completely on me for his happiness. (At least that is what I thought at the time. Perhaps I was naïve, too soft for my own good, but I was certainly not conniving.) My thyroid problems began at this time, caused no doubt by the deep anxiety, the guilt and the stress.

I was not allowed to see Jasraj. His wife had cordoned off the ICU with her relatives; there was a strict vigil being kept to ensure that I did not get anywhere near him. Rajni phoned the hospital, where his friend was in charge, and requested that I be allowed to go secretly to visit Jasraj. The doctor, whose name I forget, did a very daring thing. The plan was that I was to wait in the doctor's office while he asked for Jasraj's wife and close relatives to come into his office to discuss an important development. Just before they entered, a nurse would secretly whisk me away through the back door and into the ICU to talk to Jasraj for exactly five minutes. The plan worked. I saw Jasraj on his hospital bed, looking helpless and frail and lonely. He cried and whispered that he loved me and I cried too. He asked me to give up Rajni and I promised that I would do so. I just wanted him to get okay. Even after he was discharged from the hospital, I was not allowed to see Jasraj for three full months.

I gave up a lot to be with Rajni. I had to be secretive and guarded in my relationship with him, and not just for Jasraj's sake. He was a public figure and could not afford to let anything damage his image. It may not have been in keeping with my philosophies of life, but he was dying and that made everything else unimportant. I put aside my friends, my freedom—everything—just to be with him because I knew we didn't have long. Yes, I knew he was married but I have never viewed these things in terms of simple right and wrong.

The best time my Da (Rajni) and I shared was two days in Cuffe Castle. It seemed to me like a dream come true, the two of us staying almost as husband and wife—waking up in the morning and reading the newspapers; sitting together at the dinner table, being served by the servant, Janoo; lying together in the bed which had been his for years and which I now shared. They were two incredible days full of all the everyday, trivial things that make a house a home.

Of course, it was a world of make-believe. We were being children. I was playing at being his wife; in reality I would have been a disaster as one. But I knew that I could be his complete woman, and I was. I had discovered much about him in those two days that very few could have known—so many odd things which endeared him to me even more.

It was a great feeling to be desired and needed by a man like Rajni. I saw his performance in court one day and was convinced that he was a genius. I have not encountered a more remarkable brain. Even at his age, despite the illness, he could muster enormous will and stamina, and his mind was exceptionally alert and alive.

Of Rajni's political connections I didn't know much, nor really cared to know. But I did know that he had enormous clout. One day he said to me, in all seriousness, 'I'd like to make you the mayor of Bombay. Would you like that?' I was already aware that Rajni could make and break politicians. His protégé, Sharad Pawar, owed his chief ministership to him. 'I made Antulay the CM,' Rajni had said once, 'and look at what he has done to me!' Of course Rajni had fallen out with Mrs Gandhi by then and did not have unlimited powers any longer, but he had enough goodwill and influence because of all the favours he had done numerous industrialists. Had I really wanted to become mayor, he would have forced his friends to part with the money needed to make sure that I won. They would probably have paid the workers to vote. Datta Samant had a strong labour union and could have used his men to get all the votes for me if Rajnibhai had wanted it. Of course it was very thrilling and exciting to think about all this, but I could not see myself being in a responsible position. But I did wonder that if some godfather could make me, a nobody, a mayor, how many of the existing official seats must have been filled in a similar manner?

When his illness became worse, Rajni had to go to Hawaii for an operation. He made me promise that I would phone every day from the office. I did. When I called on the day of his surgery, his wife picked up the phone; Rajni had been taken in for surgery a day early. After that it was sheer hell for me. His family and friends made sure that I was not able to contact him. I continued to tour and perform, but my heart was rarely in it. I remember one very successful performance I gave in Baroda around that time after which I was completely exhausted, not by the physical effort but by the emotional stress and the sadness. I could only think of Rajni. I did not sleep for two nights. I tossed and turned, worrying about how he was, fearful of the final parting. I wanted him back; I ached to be with him. I came home with a high fever and stayed in bed for days, banking on my children to take away some of the pain and loneliness.

Even when Rajni returned to Bombay, his family continued to have him tightly guarded. Both his secretaries were told that no information was to be given to me, no calls were to be taken, no messages, nothing. I was completely cut off from him. A mutual friend used to carry my letters to him and his letters to me. Even Sharad Pawar was used to try and arrange some sort of a meeting between us. Nothing worked. I was going through hell—I was still being kept away from Jasraj, and now everything was being done to prevent me from meeting Rajni as well.

It was a lifetime before we could meet at Malavika and Vir Sanghvi's wedding. He was sitting with Bakul, his wife, by his side, looking ill, a glazed look in his eyes. My heart wept for him. He saw me from across the room but made no gesture. My heart missed a few beats as I approached him, unafraid of how Bakul would react.

'Hello Dada, how are you?' I said and smiled. He was non-commital and distant and did not even offer me his hand. It seemed like only yesterday when he had wept uncontrollably in my arms and I had wept for him. Now I just wanted to get away from him, and quickly. He obviously did not need me anymore. I was convinced he loved me deeply, but was this love only for his own private pleasure? What did it mean to me? He did not have the courage to stand up to his family. He did not have the courage to even phone me. What was I supposed to do? Wait? For how long? And for what? For his death? He was dying. He knew that, as did everybody else—you could see it in his eyes. Did he not realize how little time was left and how precious that time was for us? Would he deny me those few moments of togetherness? And if he did, should I still believe that he loved me more than life? I felt then that I was merely another episode in his life; Bakul was his wife, the whole of his life. She would always matter more to him than I ever could. I left the place thinking that perhaps it would be best for me to say goodbye to him before he bid goodbye to life. It would be another love lost. My search would go on.

When he was shifted to hospital again, I begged his family to let me see him just once. I said that I would only stand near his bed and listen to him, saying nothing myself. But they were adamant. I could not see him. I wondered then what love was all about. If they had truly cared for him, would they not have thought about his happiness first? Perhaps they genuinely believed that they were doing him a favour by keeping him away from me, but I could not understand this.

I never saw Rajni after that. There were just a few brief, strangely gruff phone calls in a low voice that I could barely recognize. 'I love you,' he would say. 'I am dying and I want to die soon as I don't want to live without seeing you.'

I will never forget the morning when a friend phoned and told me that Rajni had died. My Da was dead. It sounded so final, so utterly ridiculous. His body lay at Jaslok Hospital. It was difficult to imagine him like that. I hated all those who had deprived him of my love, the love that he needed in his last days, and yet I knew that his wife had taken great care of him. I wondered how she felt, now that it was all over.

The thought of the pain he must have suffered in his dying moments tortured me; I should have been there by his side. But I *was* with him, sitting at home, looking at his photographs, caressing them. And then I had run down to the beach, into the waves, with the wind blowing in my hair and a great laughter in my being. I had said to myself, 'I haven't been so happy in a long time.' It was probably the moment when he passed away. I had talked of past lives and rebirth when I was with him, and though a non-believer, he had encouraged me in my belief. I wondered where he had gone to and where he would reappear. For the brief period that I had known him, he had given me hope, comfort, security and balance.

At five o'clock on the morning after Rajni's death, Sharad Pawar took me to Jaslok Hospital so that I could spend a few moments with my beloved in death before the family came to claim him. I will always be grateful to Sharad for that. At the Jaslok Hospital morgue I saw Rajni's body surrounded by ice, covered with a white sheet. I touched his forehead. It was ice-cold, not like his touch at all. Gently I stroked his head and all the memories came rushing back—of him smiling, talking on the phone, lying in bed, caressing me. 'Wolfy', I would call him, and 'Foxy', and he would laugh. He had promised me another sixteen years of his life and we had made many plans for the future, well aware that they would perhaps never materialize. Now I stood before his corpse—that is all that remains. I put mogras all over his body. They were his favourite flowers.

Was his family happy now? What had they gained by keeping me away from him? He used to say that what disturbed him was not the thought of death, but the thought of being parted from me. I could not then understand how he could have allowed people to bully him and deny him my love when he needed it the most. Perhaps he was too decent to create chaos in his family life.

I sat in the car outside for three hours, till the world gathered around the hospital. The family arrived at about half past eight and took charge. Bakul was in a white sari, just like me. Her face was swollen. I felt sorry for her. After all, she must have loved him too, in her own fierce way. But I knew that I had won. I could feel his presence, as if he had returned after his death to hover over me, wanting to embrace me. In death he was mine. After death a person will only return to where his heart and soul belong, and Rajni's heart and soul were with me. I had kept them with me under lock and key, just as those others had kept his body. I knew Da was sitting next to me in the car, looking out at the world. The hearse pulled up and his body was put in it. Sharad Pawar and Bakul sat in front. Everyone went up to Bakul to comfort and console her. I watched it all. No one would bother with me; I was only the beloved, not the wife. Only Rajni's driver and servants gave me a respectful nod. I was sure they understood.

They carried his body away. They did not know that he had returned to me, that he would come home and stay with me now.

I went back home and sat down to an interview with Binoy Thomas for *Society*. I talked almost non-stop for four hours. I tried not to think of the cremation, of his body being reduced to fumes and ashes.

I re-read all his letters to me and later in the day I was outside Cuffe Castle, a little surprised to find myself there. Janoo opened the door to let me in, quietly led the way to the bedroom, unlocked it and left me there. I lay down on the bed, and then the tears came. I cried my heart out into his pillow. Suddenly I felt his hand on my shoulder, caressing me, soothing me. 'My child, my beloved,' he said in Gujarati in that gentle, patient, loving voice of his. I sat up. The tears stopped. He was with me again. I had to be content with whatever he gave to me of himself and in whatever form.

Janoo handed me the keys to Da's cupboard and said that he had been told that I should take from it whatever I wanted. I made Janoo stand in the room while I took the packet of letters I had written him. I also took two sets of his kurta-pajamas and his pillow on which I had cried. I showed Janoo all that I had taken and he started sobbing, talking about Rajni. I listened to him in silence, making a bundle of the things I had taken.

'Is this all you want of his property?' Janoo asked, still sobbing.

I smiled. I was taking my Da with me. I finally had him for myself for ever. I had no need for anything else.

I had a terrible pain in my chest that night.

o

Rajni and I used to write letters to each other even if we were apart for a day. He would read and re-read our joint letters which he kept in his cupboard—both my letters to him and his to me. He had made me promise that after he died I would publish them, as he thought they were the most precious treasure of his life. He had even had a new typewriter sent to me before he died so that I could type up the letters for publication. That typewriter is still with me.

I worked day and night to get the book ready as a tribute to

Rajni. I believe that after forty days the soul returns to this world and is reborn. The book, to be titled *To You, My Da,* was to be released on the fortieth day after Rajni's death.

I took the letters with me to Delhi, where Reggie would help me select and put them together. As I read the letters again I felt the vacuum that Rajni's death had left in my life. When Manu came to see me, I talked to him about Rajni, but couldn't tell him exactly how I felt. I looked at Manu and felt that at that moment of my life he was perhaps the only man left whom I could lean on, who would give me strength. If only he could be my Da, I thought—his touch was so much like Da's, and his kiss so gentle and full of love, and for a moment it felt almost as if Rajni would live through him.

'Pam, I was supposed to be at the doctor's this afternoon,' Manu said. 'I have been having so many problems with my stomach and the doctor advised me to have . . .'

'A scan?' I interrupted.

'Yes. How did you guess?'

'They suspect cancer?'

'Yes,' Manu said, still a little surprised that I had guessed. 'And suppose they find it, I wondered—and I thought about what I would do if I did have cancer . . . and do you know what I would do?'

'Yes. You would pack your bags and come and live with me,' I said.

'How do you guess these things? That's exactly what I had planned! You see, many things change when people know that you're going to die. In the ministry people will react differently. Most people who would normally go out of their way to be nice to me will stop bothering. I wouldn't have the job for long, of what use could I be to them?'

'And what about your wife?' I asked. Rajni had been loyal to his till the end; he could not allow a scandal, or hurt her. I knew Manu was loyal to his wife too.

'I would tell her that I have spent thirty years of my life with her, shared the good and the bad, and now she should give me my one year of freedom to be with whoever I want, to do whatever I want. And I think she would.'

'I don't think so. To her, this one year before you die would be very precious. She would want to be near you always.'

'Well, she would have to think that I was dead for her already. I would live for a year or six months or for whatever time I will have left, in your house. You would be out dancing, I would be at home, writing, reading, and then you would return and we would go for walks on the beach and watch sunsets and play in the sand.'

'Manu, it sounds wonderful. Please have your scan done tomorrow. We must know immediately. And suppose it is negative—how awful. All these dreams will come to an end!' I laughed. It was so ridiculous. But I was also a bit frightened. I had lost Rajni to cancer. I could not afford to lose Manu as well.

It seemed to me as if Rajni was responsible for this. He had decided to live through Manu and would give him the fatal disease too. That evening I met my friend Popsi and said that I had to go to a temple and do a puja for Rajni's soul, otherwise he would hover around, always unhappy.

I needed a Calmpose to help me sleep that night.

In the morning I left for Sanawar; I needed to be with my children, where there was always love. At Chandigarh I met a young man whom I had met at a party on Holi a couple of months earlier. He smiled and came over to talk. He said he was going to Vaishnodevi with his mother. On an impulse I took out fifty-one rupees from my purse. 'Please give this offering of mine at the temple,' I said, 'and here's a photograph of the man who died. His soul must rest in peace. Please do this for me.'

I met the young man on the flight back to Delhi from Chandigarh. 'What a relief to find you here,' he said. 'I wondered how I was to get in touch with you. Here's some prasaad from the temple. Please eat it when the sun is high, auspicious days are Wednesdays. Here's some money. Keep it where you pray and give a coin each to the members of his family.'

I smiled to myself. This was really too much of a coincidence. Da wanted it this way. I would eat the prasaad on a Wednesday. I also wanted to give Bakul some, but I knew I couldn't approach her.

I had done what I thought would help bring peace to Da's soul. But I needed peace too. I only wanted to live for my children. It was pointless looking for a man to replace Da; no one, it seemed, could ever fill that vacuum. Even when he was alive, I had looked for sexual excitement elsewhere, though I hadn't really enjoyed the encounters. I wanted none of that now. I was even losing interest in my dance. The only thing that helped me keep my balance was the mission of publishing our letters. But that became a complicated and dirty affair.

I was working at a frenzied pace to have the letters ready as a book to be released on the fortieth day after Rajni's death. Then quite by chance I met Sunil Sethi, an old friend of Kabir's and mine, who was then writing for *India Today*. He saw the photos that Mitter Bedi had taken for the cover and asked me what they were for. When I told him, he asked if he could use a small fragment from the manuscript in his magazine and I let him. I had no idea that it would become such big news. I can honestly say that it never struck me that people would misconstrue my motive for publishing the letters and react as violently as they did.

I was in Bombay when the *India Today* article came out. They had sensationalized the whole issue, making it sound like a secret love affair, the kind of scandalous thing you see happening in the political world every once in a while. I was upset, but there was nothing I could do. No matter what I said, people were sure to misunderstand. Even my closest friends were uneasy. People would phone and ask why I was doing it. I would say that it was a very personal thing, very emotional, and I couldn't really explain it. The book was not about me, not even about us; I was immaterial. The book was about a very special phase in the life of a sensitive man with a wonderfully alive mind. The letters were simply about love—a dying, unhappy man's letters to a woman he loved. But no one understood. I was told repeatedly by acquaintances that now that Rajni was dead, I should leave it all alone. Bakul would be very hurt, they said.

A close friend came home one evening, very anxious, and said, 'Has anyone come to see you?'

'Who?' I asked, wondering what he was so worked up about.

'Look, I was on the train going home and these labour union types, about thirty of them, were abusing you in Marathi . . . their tempers were high and it was very ugly. They were saying that this woman should be found and beaten up for trying to malign the name of such a good man. This article has done such mischief. Protima, please look after yourself. Don't go out at night, remain indoors. Can't you leave town and go away for a couple of weeks? You don't know how dangerous it has become.'

I was shocked. It only got worse with every passing day. There were articles and letters in the press against me, full of incredible hate and nastiness. I was being accused of bringing Rajni's name down! I was told that the Shiv Sena was planning to kill me; I should lie low. Datta Samant's men called up and said they would throw acid on my face, my children would be kidnapped and all that kind of trash. I took off with my children to Simla for weeks, frightened out of my wits. When I returned, I instructed the authorities at the boarding school in Sanawar that no strangers should be allowed to meet the children. It was a terrifying time.

Ayub Syed desperately wanted me to give him the letters so that his papers could carry the story. Various publishers phoned me saying that they had received queries from Rajni's family asking whether they were publishing the book. Then I received surreptitious offers from people who wanted to buy the letters off me. A veteran film star sent feelers through his nephew, who pretended to be a friend of mine. He asked me how much the letters would be worth and I laughed and told him, 'At least ten lakhs!' It was an arbitrary figure, given in response to a preposterous query—there was never any motive to make money from the letters. Besides, I was being offered more than this amount by publishers desperate to publish the book!

I wondered whether I should change some names in the book and leave out things that would hurt people who were close to Rajni. I had no desire to cause anyone any pain. But what meaning would the book have had then? People I had known so well and whom I respected were calling me publicity-crazy. This troubled me greatly.

Russi Karanjia wrote in *Blitz* that Rajni Patel was a magnificent human being, given to an extravagance of love, sympathy, compassion and friendliness for everyone, that his language reflected the generosity of his heart, and therefore such letters to me. He said that the deep and abiding love that I claimed, Rajni reserved for his wife Bakul till the last moment of his life. The book I was publishing was an attempt at blackmail.

The fierce reaction from a man like Karanjia, a man supposed to be liberated and constantly fighting for every just cause, astonished me. Hadn't he himself had relationships with many women in his life? Obviously even men of his stature lived by double standards. It upset people like him that their great and noble friend had loved outside of wedlock. But he had done that even during his first marriage. No one had made such a noise then.

Rajni's family and friends really had nothing to fear from me, but they continued to do their worst to me. They talked to the press and I had muck thrown at me almost every day. After so much dirt and nonsense, nothing seemed to make a difference any longer. I was amazed at the reactions of Rajni's friends and loyalists. What were they really afraid of? That I might talk about all the money transactions that each one of them had been a part of? Now that Rajni was gone, who would say who took how much from him? I'm sure they felt that I must have known about all that and about Rajni's political connections too. But I was never interested in that aspect at all. It had nothing to do with me. I had edited and re-edited the book five times till I was convinced that it could hurt no one. Beyond that I would do nothing.

The affair of the letters began to intrude on my other relationships. Manu was always tense about the door not being locked when we were together and he would sometimes scrutinize every inch of his surroundings. When I met him around this time, I wondered whether he thought that I had a tape-recorder or camera hidden away somewhere to trap him. Perhaps he thought that if I could publish Rajni's letters, I was capable of anything.

He too wanted to know why I was publishing the letters. Was it revenge, he asked. 'Why don't you give the book to a publisher with a clause saying that it will only be published after ten years, or in case of your death, within forty days of the death?' he said. 'That way the ones who feel maligned, who may suffer, will be reassured. And it will be the first time that such a thing will have been done. It's a great idea, think about it.' I said I would.

In September 1982 I read out excerpts from the book at Reggie's house in Delhi. Apart from Digvijay Singh, Anees Jung and Jatin Das, there were about fifteen young people gathered there. At some moments my voice broke, and by the time I came to the epilogue, I could not go on. Nor could Jatin, who was reading with me. We stopped. Nobody said a word. Composing myself, I asked for feedback. The women felt emotional because it was too personal. Anees said that some passages were exquisite but the book needed to be rewritten to hold the readers' interest. Many agreed. And then there were the inevitable questions: 'Why are you doing it?'; 'Don't you think it's too personal to be shared?'; 'Why should you show it to the world? People are not going to understand and will only belittle it.'

After listening to everyone, Manu cleared his throat and said, 'Now I want to say something. I want to ask cruel questions. Why is Protima doing it? The press has raked up much and said all kinds of nasty things about her. This is her only defence now. She wants to show that her relationship was actually not what everyone thinks, but something beautiful. Also, it sounds a bit like revenge: I'll teach Bakul a lesson—you didn't let me see my Da, now suffer the consequences. Moreover, what will she get out of it? The man is dead and gone. Won't she tarnish the image of the man she loved?

'And what about her own image? She has worked hard to earn the reputation of a serious and good dancer, and now people will say all kinds of things about her. What will she get out of the book? This is only bravado. Yes, we know she has the guts to do anything. Tomorrow she'll say, "Okay, I'll have sex with the man I love publicly in Connaught Place." That's all very well, but some things are best kept private.

'Also, there's another point. I'm a lawyer, you see, so I think from all angles. Suppose Rajni had also written such letters to others. After Protima's book is published, someone else might decide to publish the letters she has. What happens to Protima's book then, to this beautiful and rare love with the moon, clouds, birds and what not? And Protima must have written to others too. What if someone stands up and produces beautiful letters written by her to him? She will become the laughing stock of the country.

'I've told her that the best thing to do would be to give the book to Reggie and let him make an announcement that it is in his custody for the next ten years, after which it will be published, or immediately after her death. That alone will create a sensation. And everything will be safe.'

I noticed that it was the older men who were most upset about my book. Somewhere they all felt threatened that I would set a precedent for others to speak out. They saw it happening to them and so they condemned me. 'But Protima, why?' they all asked. 'Why not?' I replied flippantly, then with more seriousness: 'I don't know why. I wish I knew. It's like my dance. It possesses me.' And when everyone was attributing all kinds of reasons, I related to them too, and saw that there was a bit of everything in my venture—revenge, defence, publicity, money. But that was not all of it. In fact all those things added up to maybe twenty per cent of the real reason. The greater truth was different, and even I could not see it clearly.

Manu said he felt envious that the letters were not written to him. I was amazed that he had had the guts to say all that he had said in front of so many people. He was so open, so charming, so concerned, so utterly beautiful. I stared at him and wanted to embrace him. Why couldn't I feel for him the love that I felt for Da? Perhaps it would happen on its own sometime.

Finally at the end of the evening Manu said, 'Okay, publish it and get it over with. Get it out of your system. Then promise that you will do nothing dramatic again. Just stick to dance.'

'Yes,' I said, 'I promise that.'

A few days later I was in Udaipur, spending time with Kabir, who was there shooting for *Octopussy*. He read the manuscript and said unreservedly that I should publish it. He even agreed to write the foreword. When I returned to Delhi, Manu showed me a copy of *Sunday* where Rita Bhimani had written a very positive article about my book. He was impressed by the article and endorsed every sentiment of it.

I heard Manu out, then told him what I had decided during my Udaipur stay. I had decided not to publish the book. I'd use it as a chapter in my autobiography, whenever I wrote it. He was amazed, happy and laughed uproariously. 'Why?' he asked.

'You know, Kabir read the letters in Udaipur. After reading only four letters he said that I should publish them. He himself volunteered to write the foreword. With all that has been written and said against me, the noise, the scandal, I was becoming quite sick of it. Then there was your opinion that I shouldn't publish . . . But I think it was Kabir who helped me decide. Somewhere, just to know that I had his support was more than enough. I quite lost the intense desire I had to publish the book. After I had shared it with him and he had supported me, I didn't need to do the damn thing at all.'

'You've done right,' Manu said. 'I know that it's difficult to have the kind of love and care you and Rajni shared. It is rare, and it should be preserved.'

It was a relief to finally have the burden of the book off me. The scene had become too nasty. The press had painted me as some kind of scarlet woman and a greedy publicity-monger after I had announced my decision to publish the letters. People were still calling up and abusing me, threatening me and my children. Sensationalists and hypocrites were hounding me to sell them the letters. All this had completely ruined the reason for which I was making public the very special words of love that I cherished deeply. Everything had turned ugly. It was not the right atmosphere to put a sensitive work of love out in the world. My own friends had turned against me, thinking that I had written some sort of kiss-and-tell trash. Things had reached a stage where I was tired.

I did not feel the need to explain or defend myself anymore, nor the need to share with the world the beauty of Rajni's and my love. Besides, no matter what I said or did, people would never understand. They had an image of me as a flighty, immoral woman. It was my word against the the words of honourable editors, columnists and the dutiful wife. Respectable society was their territory, not mine.

I remember a party at Powai that Dr Dayal, my ancient family doctor, took me to around this time. It was the silver anniversary of a couple he knew. It was a very boring affair, terribly respectable. I could see that the rich Gujarati hosts were stunned to see me there. I could sense their discomfort. They were probably thinking of how they were going to explain my presence to their respectable guests. No doubt they and their friends knew about my relationship with their Rajnibhai and about the letters I had intended to publish. They must have discussed the 'scandal' for days. What on earth could the venerable Dr Dayal be doing escorting Protima Bedi?

Sitting there in that party I felt resentful. What was so scandalous about being me? That I publicly acknowledged all my relationships and made sensational statements which went against standard norms? That I wore revealing clothes and smoked, drank and laughed with men in public? I tried to see things from the perspective of those respectable, smug, boring and murderously ordinary Gujarati ladies. I could imagine how scarlet I would appear to them.

I felt hurt and a little humiliated. Not that anyone said anything, but the disdain and rejection was there in their eyes, in the way they turned their faces away. I tried to be as gentle and sweet as I could. I smiled innocently and really tried to behave. I wanted them to see that I was not as bad as people made me out to be. I wanted to be accepted. If only the Rajni Patel scandal had not happened—how much goodwill and respect I had earned for myself as a dancer! It seemed then that I had made a terrible mistake in life.

Some men had video cameras and were filming the party. They kept focusing on me. I felt important, also a little amused. These were the same people who condemned me, who wished I hadn't come there. Why did I want so desperately to be accepted by this boring, hypocritical lot? I was not a freak. What gave them the right to brand me as a fallen woman and feel superior and self-righteous? Did they not have any secret longings, any desires? They would never have the courage to go out and take what they wanted, and they hated me because I had that courage, because I was not a hypocrite. And why was there this wall, a total non-understanding, when it came to a woman having more than one lover? Every woman I knew secretly longed to have many lovers, but she stopped herself for so many reasons. I had the capacity to love many at a time, and for this I had been called shallow and wayward, a good-time girl. I had had many beautiful relationships. They didn't ever die when their time had run out. I carried them with me, always, like the relationships I had with Kabir, Jasraj, Manu and scores of others. Most people perhaps did not have the capacity to love so much, to give so much. But why did they hold that against me? Besides, there were so many other aspects to my life. Everything had its time and place. Why didn't people see that?

We finished eating our food and I asked Dr Dayal for a cigarette. He ignored my request. I realized that it was not proper to smoke in such a gathering. There was a foreign lady there who was puffing away at a cigarette, but that was all right, she was a foreigner. If I smoked now, I would be endorsing the image they had of me. It was strange how I felt like smoking and drinking especially when I was in places where such things would be misunderstood. What was I trying to prove? In social gatherings like the one I was in that evening, I felt impelled to rebel. It was to prove that I was not afraid, that I was not bothered about my image. Yet I was doing precisely that. I fuelled the image that had been built of me. I went to absurd lengths to protect that image which caused me so much embarrassment, humiliation and pain.

Time passed. I kept Rajni's letters with me for use in my autobiography, if it ever happened. Many years later I heard from my friend Lillette Dubey that Amit, Rajni's son, believed that I had sold the letters for a large sum of money to Bakul and with that money I had started Nrityagram, my dance village. This was in 1996; much had changed in my life by then. Yet what Lillette told me threw me back into the turmoil and agony of all those years ago and it troubled my soul no end.

It was time to give up my precious treasure which I had kept safe all these years, and it seemed only right to give the letters to Rajni's son so that he could see for himself what Rajni and I had shared. It did not matter to me what the world thought. It never had. But it did matter what Amit thought because he was my Da's flesh and blood. It was important for Amit to know that despite all the talk of intrigue and politicking, his father was a good man. I had never been part of his political life and I knew nothing about his work; all I knew was that he was vulnerable, soft, frightened and in need of my love and my strength. Perhaps it was an act, perhaps he actually felt quite differently. Who is to ever know? In my heart and in my mind I felt completely clean and pure. That was all that mattered to me. So I made a packet with all of Rajni's letters to me and sent it to Amit. 'Here are the originals,' I told him. 'They were never sold and they're never going to be published. You do what you like with them.' He could burn them if he liked—perhaps fire would be best.

moving on

In the winter of 1982 Kabir was in India with the unit of the James Bond film *Octopussy*. We met in Delhi before he proceeded to Udaipur for the shooting. We sat in the Taj coffee shop and talked of the children, of friends and work and money; of future holidays and family reunions. I had hoped he would have grown up, matured in a way which would have been exciting. But it wasn't so.

He was the same old comfortable 'fatty', so protective, so brotherly. He had always been a big brother to me. I could not remember my feelings towards him as a lover. Had he ever really been my lover? Had I ever ached and longed to be in his embrace? I could not remember having pined for him the way I had pined for Da, the way I pined for Jasraj. It seemed a pity.

I joined Kabir at Shiv Niwas Hotel in Udaipur some days later.

He introduced me to some members of the unit as 'my ex-wife'. Roger Moore and some others from the *Octopussy* clan were in the swimming pool. Kabir had arranged my dance performance that evening.

We went to his room. I noticed the double bed immediately and smiled.

'I'll rest this afternoon,' I said. 'Which side of the bed is yours?'

We stretched out side by side. We talked, about the family, about other things, and I tried to sleep, but I was disturbed by his presence.

There was a massive turnout for my dance performance in the evening. Kabir announced the programme and said, 'We've had a great marriage, a great divorce and now a great friendship.' Everyone clapped. I danced for forty minutes, there was much applause, then a lot of Hollywood talk over wine and dinner with Roger and Louisa Moore, Louis Jordan and wife, and then Kabir and I returned to the bedroom. I was still a little tense and so, I could see, was Kabir.

'Can I come and sleep with you?' I asked simply. 'Of course,' he said, so I moved over to his side of the double bed, held him lightly, put one foot over his legs and closed my eyes. I did not want him to know how exciting this was for me. But the fact was that even with the warmth of his body next to mine, I did not feel sexy in the least. I tried to remember if he had ever really turned me on. Those early days at Mrs Delph's came back to me, when we made love five or six times a day, but I could not remember feeling any great sexual need for him even then. I must have felt it, but I could not remember. I wanted to feel all that with him now. And then, lying there with him at Shiv Niwas, I asked myself—Why? Is it really necessary? Must I be a woman to every man? Wasn't it terrific that I could lie with him like this and just feel comfortable after all these years? My breathing became normal. He, too, had made no pass. After an hour or so, he turned to the other side. For a while I wondered whether I should cling to his back, then rolled over to my side of the bed and fell blissfully asleep.

The *Octopussy* girls were all over the hotel. Beautiful English and Indian girls romping around in bikinis. Kabir eyed every one of them and I could sense that he was looking for opportunities. I wondered whether I was in his way, what with all those luscious beauties around. That evening Kabir and I got stoned. It is strange what a little weed can do. I sensed all his reservations and mine melting away. We gazed into each other's eyes and smiled shyly, talked and laughed. I remained in my bed, not wanting to make the first move. He touched my arm, I caressed his and he moved into my bed. There was a quick scramble to take off our clothes, and then the bodies met. I still did not feel aroused by the man at all. It was just a feeling of being comfortable. I knew the man within that body; the body itself was completely unfamiliar. The sex wasn't bad, but I would rather have cuddled and talked.

The next four days are indelible in my memory—the laughter, the understanding we shared. It was the closest I have ever been to Kabir. He even read the manuscript of *To You, My Da*—all the intimate letters to another man whom I loved better than him—and urged me to publish it. And I lectured him on how to be a good husband.

'Susan's a wonderful girl and Adam's so adorable,' Kabir told me, 'but I get the feeling that being a married man I'm at a disadvantage as an actor. You know, when I was in London there were so many invitations for parties etc, and I was made to feel so wanted, so popular, but the minute Susan came to London, everything just stopped and I miss all those moments of creative discussions and one thing leading to another—you know, just plain free and available.'

I understood what he was saying, I'd felt the same way when I was married or in a demanding relationship like the one I had with Jasraj. Now I was free, still attractive, still young, and that was so precious to me that I could not and would not be bound again. Kabir had to run away from me, he needed to be free, and Parveen was only an excuse. Now it seemed to me that he would do the same with Susan.

'You can't hurt Susan just because you don't need her now,' I told him. 'We'd all be very upset with you. You need that stability and you need a house. Don't destroy it, just because your ambition is so great. You will make it. Have patience. And learn to say "I love you" more often. You're a thoroughly unromantic man and I have suffered terrible neglect at your hands as your wife. You have to become less of yourself to have a happy family.'

'You're right, Kiddoo. I've been so confused in the years following our split. I wish I had never entered some relationships. Some of them were real mistakes, like Persis Khambatta, for example. But I was so tired of all the games one has to play as a bachelor. The same lives, the same act, and then the wretched things become attached to you and want you permanently! How do you handle that? You just run! And it is a pity because you can't have them as good friends because you're so suspicious about their motives and their getting hurt and all those things. So it was one after another after another, and I was so disgusted and tired and lonely that I wanted a family life and now that I have it I feel trapped.

'Of course it's not as bad as it sounds. Susan knows that I'm not a saint. I'm away for weeks at a stretch on shooting stints and there are wonderful women everywhere and she knows what I'm like, but I hate that accusing look and the questions. Susan's been wonderful, mostly . . . And she feels insecure about you too.'

I confess that I was happy to hear that. 'Why me?' I exclaimed, 'I'm no threat to her marriage. In fact I'm supporting it.'

'Yes, that's all very well, but you made statements in the paper that as far as you're concerned I am still your husband. She didn't like that.'

'I'll put that right,' I promised. 'But let me warn you about honesty. Our relationship based on some kind of honesty and large-heartedness and freedom—did it work? Slowly, so many doors closed one after another, merely because we were honest. Now you can tell me about Persis or Parveen or Susan and I can share it with you, there's an empathy, and I can feel closer to you. We can both have our freedom without hurting each other. The only thing which will affect me, as far as you're concerned, is if you are unhappy. I feel like a mother! When I'm in bed with you, I'm your woman, but the love I feel for you is that of a mother. I would do anything for you, and you know that.'

He looked embarrassed, and happy. I knew he wanted to say something gentle and sentimental too, but he had always been incapable of being soft. It embarrassed him.

One afternoon I told him about my old fantasy—he and I and Susan and all our children would live together in a large house. It would be like a commune and I'd be the mother. He could screw around as much as he liked. He smiled again. We actually bathed together that evening.

During dinner on my last night there, Roger Moore's wife, Louisa, remarked, 'You two are like a little girl and a boy. So happy together, laughing all the time. Why don't you live together if you are so happy being with each other?'

I laughed. 'It's because we don't live together that we laugh. Once we stay together, the laughter goes. I prefer it this way.'

'Yes, I see,' she said, 'but after seeing both of you so happy, I won't let Roger visit his first wife anymore.'

I returned to Delhi and Manu came over that afternoon.

'No marks on your neck?' he said.

'No, he doesn't care to make you jealous, like you do,' I said, then asked, 'Manu, don't you ever feel possessive about me?'

'Yes, sometimes I do, but I know that it is wrong and so I dismiss the thought. I do think how wonderful it would be to merge with you completely. But I know that it would be disastrous for both, in terms of society, our own professions, our very relationship.'

'Suppose you were free to remarry one day, and if we became husband and wife, how would it be? You busy with your politics and I busy as a dancer. And I wonder whether my nature could take that kind of responsibility. I don't think so. I couldn't be your wife and control my fickleness. I'd make a lousy wife.'

Manu laughed gleefully. 'You know, Pamo, I had the same thought myself. I know that you would have to give up so many things which are integral to you. As a minister's wife you may even have to give up dancing. Then I thought, I'll resign from ministership and free myself from all this hassle. I have enough for two meals a day and a roof over my head. I don't care for many things. Then I can be free. Free to be with you and do all the things we want together. But, then again, we have our destinations.'

'You think dance means a lot to me? No, Manu, not anymore. Dance is only a medium through which I'm coming closer to where I'm going. Dance in itself is not all, and sometimes I suspect that its work, its purpose in my life is coming to an end. I've been feeling like this ever since Dada died. It does not hold me completely anymore. I can do without it. Don't laugh when I tell you this, but I see myself with my head shaved, wearing robes and sitting on the peak of a mountain, meditating. I see myself as a guru; giving knowledge, healing wounded souls.' It was the first time I was telling anyone about the change that was overtaking me after Rajni's death—the loss of interest in dance, the desire to give everything up.

Manu laughed. 'Really? You'll be a bhikshuni, a godwoman? I'll become a godman, then. We'll be like Shiva and Parvati, living in a cave, with the whole world at our feet. It will work.'

I looked at him and wondered if I could actually spend the rest of my life with him. It was clearly impossible! It would never work with him. But what was the harm in letting things be as they were, in listening to him and not disagreeing?

Again, as always, I was relieved to see him leave. And again I questioned myself as to why I was with him, meeting him whenever I could, when I did not love him. Was it because he was a minister? Perhaps it was the power that attracted me. But I knew that even if he did not remain a minister I would still see him. His spirit and his mind were the true attraction.

After Rajni I could only connect with Manu, however imperfect the connection. We met more often now, and one day I received a circular that some members of the Youth Congress were passing around to the press and to many government officials. It was about Manu having had an affair with 'Mrs P. Bedi' and his current affair with Popsi. The circular also said that he was involved in all kinds of shady deals and had bestowed favours on Popsi and her father.

I gave the circular to Manu when he came to see me on his way to meet Antulay. He read it and I could see that he was quite upset. The first thing he said was, 'I'll give it to Madam tomorrow morning.' Obviously, he had an enemy in the government in his own ministry who was also part of the same social circuit and also of the inner circle at the Prime Minister's office. We discussed all the possibilities and Manu was sure he knew who it was. A year ago, a similar circular involving Manu with Uma Vasudev had been circulated in Delhi. The object clearly was to have him removed from the ministry. 'Did you speak to Madam?' I asked him when we met next.

'No, I thought about it and decided not to. After all, what could I say? That all this was untrue? Why should I defend myself unnecessarily? Like that famous story of the yogi, which Madam tells so often, I also should smile and say, "Oh! Is that so?" No matter how much the denial, people will believe what they want to believe. So, each to his own mind and its games. I tore the circular up and decided to forget about it.

I admired Manu for his maturity. In his position, I would

have reacted impulsively and done something rash. I told Manu that we should not meet at Reggie's house again, for obviously his enemies were well informed and were keeping tabs on him. And poor Popsi had already had to bear the brunt of my meeting Manu at her place. I did not want Reggie to get involved in any complications with the government. We would only meet in Bombay now, at my place, I said, and Manu agreed.

After I had said all this, for a moment I wondered whether he would be driven to desperation by his inability to see me in Delhi and then perhaps he might think seriously about buying that small flat for me in Delhi which I had been talking about. But Manu was honest and straight and I knew he would never have that kind of money. I wondered whether I would like him to be corrupt, just for a little while, so that we could have that flat. It didn't sound like a bad idea, but I felt slightly guilty thinking about it.

Manu was not like Dada. I had heard that Dada was dishonest and corrupt in his business dealings, but even if he was—and I had no way of knowing—it was business, its laws were the laws of the jungle. Each man had to survive and survive well by all devious methods. So long as the heart remained sensitive, did it matter what he did in business? They were all sharks out there, he had to be tough. I always defended Dada because he never directly hurt the poor and the gullible. In fact he helped them. Being in charge of an important portfolio he was dealing with moneyed crooks, but I liked to believe that he himself did nothing wrong. I didn't care what people said, for who really knows the truth about anything?

I did not seriously want Manu to be corrupt and make some money for the flat I wanted, but I found myself trying to pressurize him emotionally. There were not enough opportunities in Bombay as a dancer, I kept saying. Besides, I said, I also needed to be in Delhi to see more of him. I knew it was wrong, I didn't really want him to do all that for me, but some devilish energy drove me on relentlessly to say all that I didn't really want to say. Perhaps I was doing it because I wanted proof of the intensity of his love for me. To what lengths would he go to have me near him? He had said some time ago that we kept intellectualizing and philosophizing only to cover up the real issue—we were falling in love and refusing to accept it. Now I told him that he was right, that I couldn't bear to live away from him any more. 'Either I leave you completely, so that I'm not disappointed because I don't see you often,' I said, 'or I move to Delhi, so that I can be close to you.'

'Hold it a moment,' he said, 'if your moving to Delhi is because of me, then you must set right a few misconceptions. I have worked too hard to be where I am . . . You are my Jonathan, my Seagull. You cannot crumble and be ordinary and talk of ordinary things.'

'It's not fair to put me on a pedestal and make me suffer,' I protested. 'You mean, I don't even have the right to be vulnerable, to love in a human way and to cry, just because you think I'm your Jonathan? Don't, for heaven's sake, do this to me. I love you and that's all I know.'

'You have the right to feel and do exactly as you feel,' he said resignedly, 'but you cannot stop me from placing you where I want to.'

I realized how much harm I was doing to our relationship. I was trying a kind of emotional blackmail to make him feel responsible for my lodging problem in Delhi. I had hoped that if he couldn't use his position to get me a government house, then he would pay for the rent of an apartment. That way I would be sure that he meant to look after me. I also felt guilty about asking directly because I hated to be thought of as a materialist. But the devil was busy within me. I wanted him to make some commitment, a substantial material commitment which would bind him to me physically. And now, seeing his reticence, I was insecure and afraid.

Why did I have this need to have my men prove the extent to which they loved me? I drove them all up the wall with my insecurities. With Rajni I was super-secure and therefore controlled and calm. But even there, had we the time, I would have egged him on to leave his wife at least in spirit, just to test the intensity of his love for me. Jasraj had been like that with me, he had driven me round the bend with his insecurity and insane jealousy. And now I was destroying my relationship with Manu. I felt horrid, mean and small.

I told Manu that while he was an important reason for my decision to shift to Delhi, there were many other reasons as well. One was pure economics. I needed money to survive. If I gave up my place in Bombay for a year, I'd get about Rs 8,000 per month as rent. I could pay upto Rs 3,000 in Delhi as rent, the rest would be pocket money for me. The children's fees would be taken care of, and I could earn a decent amount by having just one performance every month. I would also be closer to the kids. I could see them every fortnight in Sanawar. Besides, professionally Delhi was good for me.

Manu reasoned with me. 'Let me tell you that in Delhi there is a tremendous groupism. If you are favoured by one minister you automatically get vetoed by the others. So long as that minister is in power, it's fine for you, but the moment his star is eclipsed, you're finished as a dancer and all patronage stops. Look at what's happened to some dancers here . . . You'll have to keep aloof of all political support. Being sponsored by business houses is more feasible. And that you can do in Bombay. It's very difficult to keep away from political pressures if you live in Delhi. I think you should stay in Bombay and visit Delhi more often.'

Why was he so adamant about my not shifting to Delhi? I had always believed him when he said that I was the only woman he had had a really complete relationship with. Now, I wondered about him. Was he afraid that I might ruin his political career? Was he afraid that someone more important than him would claim my affections in the ministry?

He didn't seem to need me physically, or even emotionally anymore. I was hurt by that, and confused. What exactly did he want from me? Perhaps he had tired of me and wanted to end the relationship. I'd been in Delhi six days and had met him for only half an hour, over tea one evening. 'Just knowing that you're there is enough for me,' he had said. In my deeper moments I understood that phrase. But in regular moments it had other connotations. It said: 'I will not be responsible for you. I cannot give you all of myself, my time, my energy. Whenever I need contact, strength, the need to know that I am loved, I shall get in touch.' This made me angry. I wanted him to drown in love for me. My ego wanted to captivate him and be all powerful. I could see that. I saw also that what I had with Manu was a selfless, perfect relationship, something I had always dreamt of. No giving or taking, just total understanding and the knowledge that the other person was always there. Passionate love and this kind of friendship were incompatible. I wanted everything in one person, which was impossible.

But 'friendship' and momentary thrills had gone on long enough. I'd had more of all that than most people do in a lifetime. Now I wanted absolute commitment. I wanted a man to love, whom I could give all of myself to and who would give all of himself to me. That had never happened and I was beginning to despair. I had neither given nor received one hundred per cent commitment, and I had glorified my attitude by saying that it was the most mature and evolved thing to do. All that now sounded like a lot of bullshit.

Perhaps I was going mad. Yes, I was sure I was going mad, what the world called cracked up, loony, crazy. Actually, they covered it up by saying that I was different, bold, didn't care for the world, etc, etc. Some said I was 'a warrior'. And that sounded so right to me—you had to be a warrior to survive in the so-called sane world which seemed to me to be so full of deceit, bullshit, fake manners, 'gentlewomanliness' and charm. The outward charm of cowards: 'How wonderful to meet you, Mrs Bedi', 'Heard so much about you as a dancer', 'How are you, Mrs Bedi?' They all appeared frauds and liars, because no one dared to bare their teeth and say, 'I hate you, Protima. Who the bloody hell do you think you are?' Not one wife dared to come and say, 'Keep your filthy mind off my home.'

But did they know that such madness was a gift? It was not a punishment. It was a priceless gift. What had logic and reason given me? When Kabir left, logic and reason were my weapons. 'You must be strong,' I told myself, 'you must be brave, you must understand, for the sake of the children, for the sake of sanity. Be good. Be a martyr, without being one.' And all I had *really* wanted to do was to tear my hair out, scream and cry. I wanted to punish Kabir for his shallowness, for his weakness, for his unfairness. He was wrong, wrong, wrong.

That was where it all started, the whole bottling up. They said I was strong. Actually I could not bear to be strong enough to show my real feelings. It was camouflage all the time. Sometimes I felt sure that Pooja sensed it. It must have affected her the most. She would complain of a strange buzzing in her head, and I would think—'She's neurotic, all right. Like mother, like daughter.'

There is a very fine dividing line between sanity and insanity, they say. Perhaps I had been walking the tightrope for quite some time, afraid to go all the way in either direction. But I didn't see why I had to choose. I wanted to be with Pooja and Siddharth. They were all that meant anything to me. And yet sometimes they seemed part of another world, as though I had imagined them mine. Did they really belong to me? They were strange. Beautiful, but strange.

I wanted to punish Kabir. But punish him for what? For not loving me to distraction? For not suffering on my behalf? For being able to live without me? I admired Parveen, at least she had the guts to be mad.

O

The year 1982 had been disastrous as far as my dance was concerned. From the beginning of the year, I had seen dance slip away from me. It was leaving me. The body still moved to the rhythms and knew all that it had learnt, but the soul had vanished. And if the spirit had gone, then what use were the technical aspects of dance alone?

I tried to understand why my art no longer brought magic into my life. Perhaps the fault lay with the manner in which modern performances were conducted, I thought. Classical music and dance had lost its traditional spirit in the modern auditoriums. The essence, it seemed, was being corrupted and diminished in the halls. I had to keep my dance clean—if I intended to keep dancing—by opting out of the urban performing circuit. I wasn't entirely sure if I could do that, though. I wondered if I would miss the glamour, the publicity and all the other things that went with being a professional dancer. But if I continued the way it was, it would be pointless. It seemed pointless already, and false. I could see myself quite clearly being a fraud, intellectualizing my dance, talking about the religious flavour, the rituals and the aesthetics of the terribly ancient dance form from the land of Konark. Bullshit. What the hell was I doing it all for? I could make money doing other things, and I already had enough fame.

Where was that heady excitement which I felt as I learnt new, intricate odissi steps seven years ago? Where was that flutter I felt in my heart when I walked into parties, knowing that I would meet interesting people? Where was that total joy and abandonment which let me surrender myself to life, unbothered about what the next moment might bring? I had lost it all, lost it perhaps to discipline and dull routine.

At Prithvi Theatre after an Odissi Dance Centre programme, with Nargis Dutt (extreme left), Guru Kelucharan Mahapatra (third from left) and Pandit Jasraj (extreme right), May 1979.

In Khajuraho, sometime in 1980, with Vasant Sathe (third from right), Dr Sunil Kothari (extreme right), Vijay Kichlu (third from left) and Protima's lead singer, Ashit Desai (second from left).

Pandit Jasraj helping Protima make it through a gruelling performance.

The big family—Protima and Susan with Pooja, Siddharth and Adam.

With Rajni Patel and his wife.

A happy moment with Mario.

Gerard da Cunha and Protima shaping Ntrityagram.

With Ramakrishna Hegde at the inauguration of Nrityagram, May 1990.

Protima (right) with a friend at boarding school.

Seeing Jalal off at the airport.

At
O. P.

Protima and Kabir when they were 'living in sin'.

The Juhu gang at Beach House in the early seventies.

Protima, Kabir, Pooja and Siddharth with Ooggee Dadi.

With Jean Jacque's Lebel, her young French lover, Pooja and Bobo the dog. In the background is the famous picture of Protima that Kabir took against a painting of Goddess Kali.

Protima, the wild model, posing for a glamour shot in the mid-seventies.

Protima, the committed odissi dancer, only three years later.

With Pooja and Farhan shortly after their wedding.

The two families at Pooja and Farhan's wedding.

With Kabir at Siddharth's funeral in Los Angeles, July 1997.

Adam carrying Siddharth's ashes into the sea.

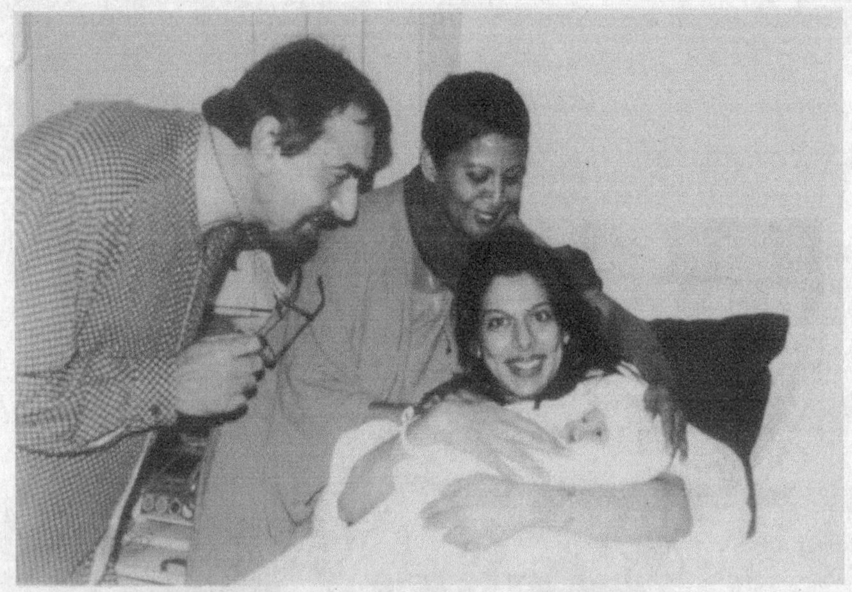

Protima and Kabir with Pooja and their newborn granddaughter, Aalia.

Protima after her last public dance performance, her first after seven years. Little Aalia was the chief guest.

Nrityagram, Protima's magnificent dream.

At Nrityagram with Guru Kelucharan Mahapatra.

Protima in her tent at Nrityagram, getting ready for a long walk.

At Nrityagram with (R to L) Kalanidhi Narayanan, Kalamandalam Guru Krishnan Kutty and Kalamandalam Kalyani Kutty Amma.

Tribal drummers performing at the Vasantahabba festival.

At Nrityagram with her mother, who was at the time undergoing treatment for cancer.

The Nrityagram Dance Ensemble in New York. Back row (L to R): Peter Bogyo (producer), Rima Gorben (publicity manager), Lynne Fernandez, Protima, Jonathan and Jennifer Soros. Front Row (L to R): Jaya Mukherjee, Surupa Sen, Bijayani Satpathy, Anitha Nair, Pavithra Reddy.

With Siddharth in 1994.

Kabir and Siddharth at Siddharth's graduation in May 1993.

Siddharth in Bombay, in late 1996, shortly before he was diagnosed as suffering from schizophrenia.

And then when Dada died, I lost interest in life itself. Nothing seemed to matter much, and I did not want to dance at all. But what else could I do for a living? I knew only dance as a profession, and it ensured not just money but also the attendant perks and the public attention.

So, with a heavy heart I went to a dance workshop in Calcutta in August that year, hoping to revive the passion for odissi. There were small stirrings, yes, but nothing more. It seemed like the end of the road, the fatal seven-year itch. I thought of taking to writing full-time, starting with my autobiography. But I hesitated. I was not yet ready to give up my hard-earned position as a dancer.

I had performances scheduled through all of 1983, and I knew that I would not refuse any, but at the same time I didn't really care if for some reason they were all cancelled. The desire to move to Delhi and the desperate need for the ultimate love were all because the magic of dance was gone from my life. At one level I also knew that none of this would help, I had to find all the strength within me.

My life was changing, and I felt this clearly at Shekhar Kapoor's birthday celebrations at Shabana Azmi's place. Marc Zuber was there—strong and handsome—and out of old habit I tried to seduce him all evening. I think I succeeded with stupid talk, cheap, easy, clever talk. There was no soul in it, no heart, no warmth. Kunky, a friend, said that I should have taken Marc home for the night. It would have been easy, and I wouldn't have thought twice about doing it some months ago, but now I couldn't bring myself to do it. I didn't want another one-night stand. Panditji's song from the Ameer Khusrau album came on and my mind went back to him. I had really loved the man.

I told Kunky I needed a fulfilling, permanent relationship, and she said that I was suffering because of Kabir, that Kabir was still my man. And I wondered about that. As far as I could see, consciously I had never pined for Kabir. In fact I often felt guilty that I hadn't cared for him enough. Subconsciously, though, all kinds of things could have been happening. Of course, I had always thought of Kabir as my man. Perhaps I hadn't really flushed him out of my system. I was always talking about him, as though we were still living together.

But the truth was different. It was the loss of the love I had with Rajni that was doing this to me. I longed for him. 'Dada, Dada, Dada,' I would say over and over again and often break down. I longed for his care, his concern and the intense love he felt for me. I needed to know that someone cared madly about me. It made me feel secure. Rajni had made me feel secure like no one ever had. He was like a father.

In my letters to Kabir at this time I wrote things that I would never ordinarily have written or said. For so many years my ego would not let me say to him that I was hurt when he left. I now wrote to him that I needed him. This wasn't entirely true; I was just making myself believe that I loved and wanted him. It was because after Rajni's death I felt completely alone and at sea. Rajni had taken with him my other great passion—odissi.

In those heady days when I first started learning and performing, every time I danced, it was for the Mother, for Kali. I was possessed. I became Her. The audiences everywhere loved the last number the most. They said that they caught a glimpse of the great goddess in person. My faith in Kali was a reflection of my faith in my dance.

When Rajni came into my life, with his Marxist views and attitudes, I had to keep defending my faith all the time. He would mock me and laugh at my old-fashioned beliefs. There was no God, he said. I would tell him about the chain of events that had led me to believe in Her, and he would use logic to pooh-pooh everything.

'But Dada, logic is such a small part of illogic,' I would protest. 'Whatever the scientists and doctors have been able to prove is called logic. But think of how much illogic there is.

How so many things can't be proved. How so many other things don't need proving.'

Talking to him, trying to stress my point and convince him of my point of view, I became more involved with devotion. The more he resisted the stronger became my faith. He *had* to see, and I would show him, that Kali was there as much as he was. I talked to him a lot about Kali, Her origin, Her ways, Her strength. But as far as he was concerned I was his Kali. He became a sort of disciple by proxy.

Shortly before he died, Da had come with me to the Kali temple. I prostrated myself before Her, and when I stood up, the red-flowered garland came through the air and encircled us both. I looked at Da, and with his shining eyes and the red tilak on his forehead, he was Kali for me. I saw Her face in his. Tears came to my eyes.

'Mother,' I cried silently, 'what is it that You want from me? Why do You put me through all this? Where has the love for Panditji gone? Where has this love sprung from? What is my fate, what is required of me? Why must I always be on the move? Please let me be . . . I am tired. I am exhausted, emotionally. Yes, I will love this man with the devotion You want, with the devotion *he* wants. Yes, I will promise him that I shall stay by his side and do whatever makes him happy. You have spoken . . . and I am only Your loved daughter. Whatever be Your will . . .'

Then we had gone back to the Oberoi Grand and had a bath together. And we had cried, uncontrollably. We never knew why.

Now even he had gone away. Kali too had abandoned me, even in my dance.

I visited the temple a year after Da's death, and the priest asked me where the old gentleman was this time. I could only smile. 'He is in there,' I wanted to say. I went in, as usual, and knelt before Her feet to cry, but the tears did not come. There was no shaking, no quivering, no tears, nothing. I stared at Her for long. There was a feeling of strength, of being together with everything that was. I can't say that I was joyous, or sad, or anything. I just was.

From the temple I went straight to the class where I was trying to get back the connection with dance that I had lost with the death of Dada. It was the last effort I was making. Nothing changed. In fact the distance between dance and me seemed for some reason more formidable. But I wasn't worried that day about where the attachment had gone, why it had gone and how I could get it back. I was filled with the strength of the knowledge that it had stopped mattering to me. It was okay if I never reached the top, didn't get the Padmashree. The critics could keep saying that I was technically imperfect; it did not matter.

At the moment of his death, what had mattered to my Da? Not his success, his wealth, his position, his friends. Not even his wife and children. Only I had mattered, I was sure of that. And I mattered not because of bodily charms, not because of the love I was giving him or the understanding, but only because of a perspective that I had brought into his life—of life in its raw form, without labels and logic. He had taken nothing tangible with him. It seemed pointless to want this and that and everything. I thought of all the trappings we involve ourselves with throughout our lives, they all seemed pointless.

Life was making fun of our greed, wasn't she? The feast was all laid out in front of us, and everyone was invited. It was a buffet. You chose what you wanted. The payment was the same—whether you took large helpings or ate only a slice of cucumber, you paid for it with your life. When the Lord had given with a hundred hands, how much could you take with your two little hands? It was all up to you. My perspective changed. I saw the spread before me, the temptations in front of me, but the greed which clouded reason had vanished. I would take only that which I wanted and needed for survival. I didn't need the fame, the success, the glamour or the wealth. No, I would not move to Delhi to consolidate my position through foul or unfair means. I didn't need it anymore. I would do only that which mattered. I would get some land and grow my own food, and live close to where everything came from—the earth.

O

In January 1983 Kabir, Susan and their son Adam arrived to stay with us in Beach House. I was at the airport with Pooja, Siddharth and Johnny Bakshi. I was on tenterhooks. Then the family arrived. Susan looked gorgeous with her golden hair. Kabir, as usual, looked extraordinarily handsome. Adam was a surprise. I had expected him to be big and fat and cuddly. I had built him up in my mind as the most beautiful baby in the world. And here he was, small, lean, golden-haired and blue-eyed—a good-looking average American baby.

In the days that followed, Susan and I got closer to each other. I did everything to convince her that my relationship with Kabir was now almost that of a brother and sister. I wanted her to trust me completely because to me we were all one big family. Early the first morning, while Susan and Kabir were still asleep, I picked Adam up and went down to the beach for a walk. I wondered what Susan might think. Did she fear that I would drown him in the sea, or drop him, or feed him something bad? But when we returned Susan was awake and not at all worried. She was sitting with Siddharth and Pooja and showing them how to play some games. I marvelled at how normal she was. I liked her very much for that. Slowly Adam got used to me. He called me Mataji, and we became inseparable. I felt flattered by the attention.

I would watch Kabir changing Adam's nappies, powdering him, playing with him, and I wanted to laugh. Obviously Susan had made him do all this before. I regretted not having made him do those things for our children. He didn't talk or behave with them like he did with Adam. Obviously, it came from living in the States. You were forced to work, to do things for your children which you normally left to servants in India. But Kabir did seem to enjoy being with the older children. The most wonderful sight was of Kabir lying on the chatai, with Siddharth on his back, and Pooja by his side watching Adam doing his tricks.

Kabir was a better husband to Susan than he had been to me. But he was still quite impossible. He created a mess with all his toiletries in the bathroom. The floor was always full of powder, the brush full of hair, there were wet towels on the bed and clothes everywhere and I wondered how Susan coped with him every day. She had to be a very patient, understanding woman.

I saw the negative emotions too. The tensions, the feuds which happen in any marriage. I asked how she felt when Kabir went away for long. She said she knew why he did that—if she was with him, his work as an actor suffered. People related to him better if he was seen as single. But who were all these people who wanted him single? Women on the make, obviously. 'Why should he only want to be wanted as a male?' she said vehemently. 'I know all about his affairs. He doesn't need to tell me, I just know. So long as it doesn't come into the house, it's okay. But what normally happens is that when he's been involved elsewhere, the guilt is within him and so he finds the smallest reasons to explode. Then he yells and says that he is suffocated by marriage and that his career is affected . . . I don't care if he fucks around, but I certainly don't want him to take it out on me and the home.'

I understood exactly what she meant. 'It always happened in the same manner with me too,' I said. 'The worse thing was that he used to genuinely make me feel guilty and rotten, and I always believed it was my fault.' I got carried away and told her about his affair with Gita. She had tears in her eyes. So did I.

Some days later I was in Bangalore with Kabir, having

dinner with some friends. I started talking about my dance—the deep inner satisfactions, the money, glory and whatnot, and my recent feelings about it. Kabir made some unintelligent remarks about my dance, and I resented that.

'You're a great guy, Kabir,' I retorted, 'but as an actor you're a ham. A first-class ham. So long as the camera concentrates on your good looks, it's okay. And don't talk of creativity. You may have ideas but they're unoriginal. What creative thing have you done?'

His eyes flickered and I saw the anger that I knew so well and feared. 'What are you talking about? Have you read my scripts? You haven't seen any of my latest movies, either. You have no right whatsoever to make that observation. I think I have great talent and I am a very creative person,' he said.

'So you have always thought. Well, you're wrong. Everything you have done up to date is middle-class. There is nothing deep or meaningful in any of your works. And until I feel or see something that is good I will maintain that you're mediocre.'

I could see that I had really hurt him. 'Well, you're entitled to your opinions, but that does not make it necessarily true or valid and I object to your saying these things in front of other people.'

Later I apologized for having been insensitive, but insisted that I stood by what I had said, and that if he really was a sensitive artist, the sensitivity should also reflect in his relationships with those closest to him.

The next day Kabir and I went to his brother Ranga's office and discussed money matters. Ranga would pay for the upkeep of the children. The school fees would go directly from his office. A big burden was lifted from my shoulders. Now I had only myself to look after. That was easy.

I was scheduled to perform in Bhopal a few weeks later and I invited Kabir and Susan to the programme. I was apprehensive about how it would go and found some inspiration in Kumar

Gandharv's concert at Bharat Bhavan. I had never really cared for his style and yet, that day I heard in his singing a cry from within, a heart-rending plea, as if he meant to shake up God Himself and make Him pay attention. That was what I needed to do to re-establish my connection with the Mother. I had to dance with the spirit of Mahakali, seek to merge with that great something out there.

Kabir came to my recital with Susan. I saw them sitting right in front. Manu and his wife were sitting there too. Two wonderful men with their spouses. My men. Kishori Amonkar had come specially for me. I would dedicate my dance to her; if I danced well tonight, she would sing for me. She would sing of longing . . . I too had longed for my Krishna. Many times it seemed that I had found him and I embraced him, but, alas, it was never my Krishna. I could only find Krishna in my dance. This I was saying through my dance to Kabir. I wanted him to know that he wasn't what I was searching for. Why did I always want to put him down?

Susan hugged me repeatedly after the recital. It was a good show. But Kabir said that the first two items were tense and unsteady. He always found some fault with my recitals. In Bombay at the ODC festival two years ago, he had said that I had taxed the patience of the audience!

Kabir's niece, Ami, was getting married that month and the whole Bedi clan had gathered for the event. I liked Susan, but the fact that she was the present Mrs Kabir Bedi bothered me a little at the wedding. There was no faulting her at all, but the attitudes of the family in various situations hurt and upset me. It was Susan, Susan, Susan all the time because she was Kabir's present wife.

Parveen was there too. She had come to attend the wedding on her own. It excited me no end to know that she was there. Somewhere inside I gloated over the fact that I was family and she wasn't. Kabir's family was fond of Parveen, but they couldn't make her feel as special as they did when she was Kabir's wife-to-be. The women were singing and each member of the family had to get up and dance. When they called for the bride's chachi, I got up and danced; Parveen was merely part of all the bride's friends and had to dance in a group. I made no bones about the fact that this was my home, and I was courteous and hospitable to her, which put me in a superior position.

She sat quietly at the sangeet session. I was loud, laughing too much and ordering people around—it was only to tell her in so many ways that this was my family and it would always be because I was the mother of Kabir's children. And all this while I was trying to stop behaving and feeling the way I was. I tried to do this to Susan too. It did hurt somewhat to see Kabir holding her hand in his special way in front of me, fussing over her all the time and fondling Adam. He had never fondled our children like that. He had never fussed over me in public when I was in a bad mood. He always left me to sort things out on my own.

Susan and I kept Kabir busy, staying around him so that he didn't get a chance to be alone with Parveen. Anyway, he did manage to sit with her at the dining table and discuss his money matters. Poor thing. I felt sorry for her. But she really did deserve what she had got.

Before they returned to America, Kabir went to Sri Lanka to discuss another film and Susan and Adam were in Delhi. I met Susan there. They were in Popsi's house, where I used to meet Manu and Rajni. I talked to Susan about many things, and she came across as self-righteous and rather moralistic. Obviously she thought of Popsi and me as scarlet women. Respectable, rich people appealed to her—secure homes, well-behaved womenfolk and solid family bonds. She was always tense and nervous whenever I was around.

On the third afternoon Kabir joined us. Susan got busy packing and Kabir as usual got to a state where Susan snapped and he snapped back. He made a great effort to be nice, polite and patient in front of me. I shrugged my shoulders and smiled, raising my false eyebrows I had been through all this myself and it hadn't been pleasant. Susan was pregnant again and nauseous and fed up with all the travelling. Kabir, of course, had no idea that she was pregnant. She would have an abortion, of course.

Finally, Susan, Kabir and I got stoned. It was strange. Kabir talking and Susan trying to trip him all the time. Her voice had desperation in it. I saw myself of eight years ago in her. She was so desperately wanting to be a person, to have some say, make some important or clever observation. Meanwhile Kabir was only talking to me and at me. I was his yaar, the one who didn't want or need anything from him. I couldn't be his 'woman' in the sense of mistress or wife. Nor did I want to be. I knew he had his destination. I had mine. Whatever negative things I felt about him had vanished because I was with him. He had an honest, childlike quality. He was a nice boy who was naughty behind his wife's back. A boy who meant no one any harm. He was a dear boy, but a lousy husband.

o

After Kabir and Susan left, I stayed on in Delhi for a while. I met Jeevan Pani (of Kathak Kendra) and he spoke about my Krishna, or what ought to have been my Krishna—my dance.

'Why, Protima,' he asked, 'why do you create so many misunderstandings about yourself? You're warm and sensitive and I want everyone to talk of you well. Why have you drifted away from dance?'

I gave him so many reasons, none of which were the real ones, but each sounded plausible and I believed each one of them, for I myself did not really know which was true.

'Where has that passion gone, Jeevan? And will it ever be the same for me again? This feeling came upon me suddenly and took me by surprise. It has left me confused, I don't know what to do with myself.'

'Have you thought of what it would be like to embrace it again? If you have, then go and search for it. You took it for granted, you didn't realize how precious it was and now you feel deserted and confused. Remember how you shuddered with ecstasy? You were happy, lived intensely, and now you will allow it to just fade away? How do you know that it is not waiting for you, hoping that you will come back? Don't hesitate. Go, it's waiting.' He made it sound so real and poignant. He really made me believe that dance was my Krishna. Jeevan was the 'sakhi' who soothed Radha, scolded her to put sense into her head.

'Krishna said to Radha, "Place your lotus feet on my head." Do you know what that means? That's what dance is saying to you, Protima. Give it a chance.'

And I immediately thought of Jasraj singing those lines to me, begging me to give him one more chance. Now I was going to cajole my dance and bring it back into my life. With fingers crossed, hope in heart, I would wait to feel the joy once again.

In April 1983 I gave an odissi recital at Premabhai Hall in Ahmedabad. The show was sponsored by *Gujarat Samachar*. The hall was packed. It was strange to be in Rajni's home state. During the scandal only a few months ago, people had threatened that 'the disgraceful Protima Bedi' would not be allowed to set foot in Gujarat. They would boycott me. *Aas Paas* had written four pages of all kinds of shit against me. Every allegation was put down for lakhs of people to read all over India, and I had been so low, so unhappy. And now, because of Vijay Kichlu, because of the ITC Sammelan in Ahmedabad in February and my good performance in it, the leading state daily had asked me to dance for their charity trust. So many ministers and VVIPs came to see the scandalous woman in the flesh, and went away defeated and changed.

The next day, magic happened! I was exhausted after the

previous night's recital and had gone to bed at 4.30 a.m. I hadn't been able to sleep, and at 7.30 a.m. the alarm went off. I rushed off to the TV station. They filmed first in colour and then again in black-and-white, so I had to dance for almost five hours. At 7 p.m. I was at the hall again. I decided to do only slow dance items because I was exhausted. 'O God,' I prayed, 'just let me get through this performance. Keep up my strength and I'll be grateful. I don't want anything more.'

Ashit, my vocalist, began with the usual invocation. I was standing in the wings. My heart heaved suddenly and my eyes filled with tears. There were flowers in my hands, which I was going to shower at the feet of Lord Jagannath. A great feeling of bhakti overpowered me and it was difficult controlling the muscles of my face. The chin quivered. 'Calm yourself,' I told myself and started the dance. I don't know how I finished the mangalaeharan, but I do know that no one in the audience could have remained untouched by the electric charge I felt in the air.

As each item finished, I became more and more confident, joking with the audience, talking to them, dancing with complete abandon. Then the cramps began. It was time to do the strenuous Kali tandav. 'O Mother, give me the strength to finish this today.' I stood in the darkness, back to the audience, waiting for Ajit, the light man, to put on the red light, not daring to lift my right foot for fear of the cramps. So long as the foot stayed down, firmly, it was okay. The moment I raised it off the floor, it would trouble me. The red light came on, and my foot shot up, toes pointing, heels arched, and I began the terrific Kali tandav. I was infused with a sudden burst of energy and vigour and not for a moment was I conscious that it was I, Protima, dancing.

I sat for the last pose, the meditation. Om, Om, Om, sang Ashit. And I closed my eyes. A brilliant blue light hit my eyeballs. Of course Ajit had put on the blue footlights—but with my eyes closed, such brilliance? I was shaking with some unknown energy and rushed off to the wings. People poured onto the stage. Excellent performance, they said and all the rest that I had heard time and again after my performances. That night all of it seemed unreal. Somehow I walked to my make-up room, sat on the chair, put my head on my arms resting on the table and wept. It was uncontrollable grief. Why was I crying? I just had to. People gathered, anxious, upset by my tears, and someone said, 'It's nothing. It happens sometimes. Too much bhakti bhava, she is only experiencing that emotion.'

'Yes, yes,' they said, 'We too felt the presence of Mahakali Devi. She has the blessings, sure enough.'

State ministers, the governor, the mayor were all eager to invite me for breakfast, lunch and tea. I met Madhavsinh Solanki over breakfast. Many other ministers were present there, and also the journalist Kuldip Nayyar from Delhi. I talked about politicians and why I detested their coming for my recital. The next morning I was on the front page of *Gujarat Samachar*, my photograph over and above the Chief Minister's and Indira Gandhi's! How had this come about? In a state where everyone was so hostile to me, I was a heroine. At least eight papers wanted to interview me. There were people who wanted to send their daughters to live with me, the guru!

Less than a month later was Rajni's first death anniversary. I had been disturbed during the days leading up to it, wondering what was to emerge from within me and frightened to let go. I spent two sleepless nights, and then early morning on 3 May I awoke, put on my dance clothes and drove to Da's office. I felt strange and self-conscious and also a little apprehensive standing near the lift again. I reached Rajni's office and stood outside the door. It was a new door, with a new nameplate—'Bakul Rajni Patel'.

I rang. It was 8 a.m. Janoo opened the door. No smile, nothing. Just an unspoken acceptance. I walked straight into the office room. Everything was, mercifully, the same. Except that his wife's chair was there now, and the photograph of Indira

Gandhi had been removed. I turned to look at the dining table, and there on his chair was Da, smiling brilliantly at me! It was the large photograph he had wanted me to have. I walked up to him and offered the mogras in my hand. As I sat in my chair, opposite him, I couldn't help smiling. It really was a good photograph. 'My Fish, Wolfy, my Tiger,' I said, and the smile broadened. I didn't notice that Janoo had brought in agarbattis, a garland and a diya and placed them on the table. It was time to do the little things which would please Da. I put the garland around the photo, lit the lamp and smiled at him. Gently, of course; it had to happen this way.

Then I turned my attention to Janoo. He complained bitterly about his position, his housing problems, the money. I was sorry for him and promised to do something for him. I said goodbye to Da and left. That evening I went to the beach, where I had been at the moment of his passing away exactly a year ago, and sat there till after dark.

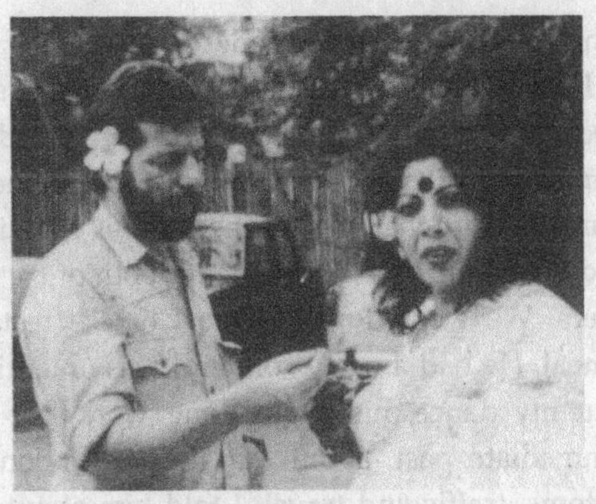

blind date

The year following Rajni's death was a terrible one. I had no interest left in life. It was at this time that Mario came into my life.

I met Mario on a blind date. I was thirty-five, and it was my first blind date. My friend Vinod Advani had fixed it up because he thought it unnatural that I should have stopped socializing altogether. He told me nothing about Mario. And all he had told Mario about me was that I would meet him at the Taj Rooftop, wearing a white sari and a big red tikka.

And so it was that Mario and I met one evening in May 1983.

I fussed with my sari and my hair in the elevator, a little nervous about the date. Would he be attractive? And would he think that I was willing to sleep with him just because I had agreed to have dinner with him? In any case, I had my periods and I was not up to it. I hoped that he would turn out to be special. I needed something special to happen to me. Dance had lost its hold over me, friends had started to bore me, and absolutely nothing excited me anymore.

Finally I was at the Rooftop. He came up to me, smiling. He was bearded, brown-haired, of medium height, and had a big nose and small beady eyes. On the whole, he seemed pleasant and unassuming. We chatted, laughed about the situation we were in, said it was the first blind date for both of us, that we felt like teenagers. We went down to the Chinese restaurant and ordered a meal. He had a nasty cold and was on antibiotics. We talked about my dance, his engineering work, my immediate past, his immediate past, about the sun, the moon, the stars, society, customs, traffic and travel. I told him about some farm land I had bought and how excited I was about it.

I dropped him at Hotel President and gave him my phone number.

'I'm having a dinner for my sister-in-law's birthday next Saturday,' I said. 'May I take this opportunity to return your kindness?'

'Sure, I'd love to come.'

With that we shook hands and I drove home. I thought about him from time to time, but it was nothing to get worked up about. Mario turned up for the dinner (which was at a hotel) with Sunil Sethi. He had a big spade in his hand. 'You told me you had just bought your land. Well, I thought this would be the right present. I wish you luck.' It was quite funny, having to walk through the hotel lobby with the spade. He had a sense of humour, all right. I liked that. That night, when everyone had left, I asked him if he would like to spend the night at home and then spend the next day, a Sunday, with me and some of my friends. He readily agreed.

'Mario, you're welcome to sleep in this bedroom with me,' I said when we reached my house, 'or I could make a bed for you outside.'

'Up to you, makes little difference to me,' he said.

'I would like to add that I'm not asking you to share my bed in a sexual manner,' I told him. 'I'd like to be comfortable with you, to know you. Can you understand that?'

'Sure,' he said. 'I'll sleep in this room, if it's okay by you. Don't worry about me. I know how to control myself. It won't be easy, but I can do it.'

We chatted for long, then went to sleep. I cuddled up to him, put an arm around him and dozed off. I knew how attracted he was to me, but I was playing with him, having fun, leading him on. Mario wrote with his fingers on my back, he stroked my head, he caressed me, he kissed me, but that was as far as he got.

I kept him on strings for three weeks or so, and then when I couldn't wait any longer myself, I said, 'You must think I'm frigid. I'm not, you know,' and then I went on to prove it. One thing led to another and soon I was seeing him almost every evening. He went away to Switzerland for a month and I wondered whether he thought of me at all. He had an English wife, Caroline, and four children. I had never heard him complain about his wife. I tried not to take our relationship too seriously, but I kept thinking about him. Of course we had not spoken about deeper feelings. Instead, we had made it quite clear to one another that while what we had was a great relationship, we had our own lives to live. And here I was, driven crazy with longing for this man.

He phoned the day he returned from Switzerland. I had to go to Sanawar to see the kids. On an impulse, I asked him to come along. The kids were happy to see him. I thought they got along pretty well. It was while we were playing hide-n-seek one day that I realized how much he meant to me. When the kids were home a month ago, he had spent hours helping Siddharth build a radio. How cordial he was to my servants, how committed to his work. He had never spoken ill of his wife. He was mature and down to earth and always dismissed my melodrama with a laugh. Suddenly I saw the wonderful qualities of this man. It was shameful the way I had been leading him on.

He had to leave a day before I left. I had to stay back in Delhi to meet Manu. The meeting was like all our other rendezvous. Manu came for an hour. We chatted and then he wanted to make love. Normally I would have given in and let him, because he was a wonderful friend. I never desired him, ever, but I didn't resent it either. But that day was different. I was tense, evasive, odd. I couldn't bear the thought of being touched by him. 'I don't really think one should,' I said. 'Your heart problems frighten me. I can't bear the tension . . .' and so on and on.

I flew back to Bombay, and Mario was waiting at the airport for me. He loved me. Day by day the longing became more intense and I was frightened. I didn't really want to be involved deeply. I didn't want to break any more homes.

We were lunching one afternoon at Hotel President and he told me that his wife and children were arriving in a fortnight to spend three weeks with him. It disturbed me greatly. It was disturbing him too. But what did I want from his man? Did I want to be his life partner? Could I love him for ever? His wife would never share him. What if he gave up his family for me and then, a few months later, I tired of him? Who could tell where love flew and why?

I would never feel free. Yet, I wanted him desperately.

'Mario, I'm going to leave you,' I said. 'I love you much too much to keep you. I'm sorry, but this is the last time we meet.' There were tears in my eyes and my pizza was only half-finished. I saw him stop suddenly. He pushed his plate away. I saw his knuckles go white as he gripped the edge of the table. He pushed the table aside, stood up with an exaggerated motion and said, 'Come with me.' He led me to the elevators and took me to his room. Not a word was said. 'He's going to tear my clothes and rape me!' I thought. I was sure of that. I followed breathlessly, and sat on the bed. He went to the bathroom and turned on the shower. He yelled out to me to come in there. I walked in, and before I knew what was happening, he had picked me up and dumped me in the tub, with the shower full on my face. I screamed, yelled, kicked and pleaded but he held me there firmly.

'You need that,' he said, 'and if you carry on in this vein, you'll get a spanking on your bottom too.'

The drama fizzled out in my head and I started laughing. Then he got into the bathtub, in his safari suit and boots, and stood in front of me, dripping wet. I clung to his neck.

'Now when you are dry you will tell me what's bothering you,' he said.

His reaction had floored me. I love surprises. Here was a man who wouldn't play my games. He was an enigma. He took off my dripping clothes, dried me and tucked me into bed, then took off his clothes too and got in.

○

Manu had a heart attack (in July 1983). I read about it in the papers and went berserk; I knew I could not phone or go and see him. For two weeks he was in the intensive care unit of Willingdon Hospital in Delhi and there was nothing I could do except rely on the news and on mutual friends for information and reassurance. After he went back home from the hospital, Manu called every day. He sounded tired, lonely and depressed, but after some time I felt no desperate anxiety for him; I felt that he was safe where he was and everything was all right. How different this was from what my state had been when Rajni and Jasraj were critically ill. The emotional involvement was too great then. But Manu was different, he was my companion, it was a different kind of bond, a much deeper one . . . or was it because I had found Mario?

Mario Kropf, the blind date. He was fast becoming more important than any other man in my life. There was tremendous passion when we were together, and sometimes there was just peace. But through the many shades of love, the relationship between us seemed like just another illusion. Sometimes the idea of being a wife appeared attractive—to have a man coming home to me every evening. And then the thought appalled me. What about my freedom? How could I have my men friends come over? But why not? Didn't I pride myself for being honest? I hated it, I hated this deceit. Why did my life have to be full of deceit, always because of a wretched man!

It seemed at such times that I had used all my relationships for my own selfish reasons. I wanted to be Kabir's wife so that I could crow about my catch to the world: I was the sexy siren, the beautiful one who had landed the best man, and I wanted everyone to envy me. And with Jasraj, wasn't it a total power trip? Only I could seduce the moral, clean sage, change his ways and his thoughts. With Da it could well have been because he had the power and the money. And all the other men in my life were there because I needed something or the other from them—fun, excitement, sexual pleasure, some cheap thrill. Even with Manu there was the possibility that because of his position he would help me with my dance.

This time, I told myself, I would do things differently. I wouldn't let Mario suffer because of my bullshitting. I would expect nothing, only love.

I had spoken to Mario about how fickle I was and how the brief moments of flirting became so important for me. Those moments made me feel important, cared for and desired, and then I felt the greatest need to be free, and if there happened to be a person to whom I was tied, I started resenting his presence in my life. I wanted all this to end. I wanted Mario to help me get out of myself. His love could do it, and I told him so. I wanted to love him with all my being, but my mind kept wavering.

So it was the old merry-go-round once again. Precious Mario, married happily for fifteen years with four children, and now because of me his life was being thrown into turmoil. How would he tell his wife? I had asked him not to tell her. I wanted him, but I certainly did not want the guilt. He would become my responsibility—what if I found one day that I didn't love him anymore? How could I desert him after he had broken his home for me? 'But it is not your problem,' he had said, 'you don't have to feel guilty. I am decided. And if things don't work out, then we part.' How easily he said all this. How could the guilt not be mine too?

I wanted to marry him. He was the kind of man I had wanted to live with always—the sporty, outdoor man, direct and unspoilt by social graces. It was easy to love him. And we had fabulous sex together, the best I had ever given and got. Maybe it was my age—at thirty-five, I was in the prime of my life. Mario gave me the strength to be myself. I only wished he would find a way to be with me all the time and yet keep his marriage intact and his children happy.

I imagined the future. It seemed challenging, a whole new change. I loved change. If I didn't jump at it now, I would forget to jump at all, and then I would never have the courage. What was the worst that could happen? That it wouldn't work all the time? So what? It wouldn't be for lack of trying; I had decided that I was going to make it work.

When I met Manu shortly afterwards and he tried to kiss me, I kissed him lightly on the mouth and turned my face away.

I told him that I was terribly in love and utterly miserable.

He laughed. 'If you're in love, enjoy it, why should it make you miserable?'

'Because he's not here, that's why!'

'So, he'll come back, won't he?'

He tried again to embrace me, to kiss me. What could I say to this man who was such a wonderful friend? How could I tell him that I did not want any of his physical attentions?

'Manu, can I be your friend, without being your woman?'

'Of course you can. I just want you to love me always.'

'I do love you. You've been a wonderful friend. For a whole year, after Dada died, you were the only one who took his place. Well, I wanted you to take his place but . . .'

'But you love another? Go ahead, darling, enjoy it. I'm with you in whatever you do.'

'Thank you, Manu. But this is the first time that I don't feel like sharing myself with any other person. You know, with Kabir, Jasraj, Dada, I loved them, but I was open to others too, but this time I can't bear even the thought of being with another man sexually.'

He looked at me with deep interest. 'You're lucky. If this is how you feel, then it must be the real thing. I envy you, because I don't have it.'

'Manu, do you feel jealous?' I asked.

'You know, Pamo, I do feel jealous,' he said, 'in many ways it's instinctive. But I also love you deeply, and I ask myself what it means to love you like that. For me, love is seeing you always happy.'

I hugged him tight and covered his face with kisses. 'Will you always be my friend?'

'Of course! And I shall help you to be together too.'

He was a very courageous man, honest and truly in love. I admired him. I burst into sobs. 'I've always wanted a home,' I said, sobbing, 'I've wanted a man to love completely. But I've always had to make do with half a man. It was so painful to be a wife and have a husband who desired other women, and again more painful to be the other woman and have your man go back to his home, his wife and his children. I've just been so deeply unhappy all these years.' He held me tight and stroked my hair.

He looked faraway, thoughtful. I knew he was hurt, I could see it in his eyes. I loved him for not making a show of his hurt.

o

Mario left for Switzerland, to spend time with his wife and children. He said he would be back in three weeks. I was scared. I was sure that I wouldn't see him again. He tried to reassure me, asking me if I really believed that it was possible for him to live away from me. Of course I knew he couldn't, but the fear that had gripped me remained, and it only became worse after he left.

Was it because of my periods? I had felt devastated when I had them that month. For a few days in Madras we had pretended and hoped that we would have that one-in-a-million baby that is conceived despite the (woman's) tubes being tied. I even had the symptoms, and we spent three days dreaming of how our world would be once we had our own baby. 'Would you really change your life for my child?' he had asked, and I had said, 'Yes, Chiefal. Only for your baby. I will give up my dance and every other desire for that child.' He had been awed by my decision. We had gone to the doctors to check on my pregnancy and perhaps reverse the operation. It would be a major operation, the doctor had said. 'We will have to join new tubes and even after that the chances are fifty-fifty. There's also a risk to your health.' Mario had dismissed the whole thing there and then. The wretched periods had come the next night. Our dreams had collapsed. And now he had gone away to be with his wife, the mother of his children.

Mario called from Switzerland. He sounded very serious, almost gruff. 'I've been relegated to the guest room,' he said.

'Why? Did you tell her?'

'Yes. I'm not a good pretender.'

'How's the scene?'

'Bad. It's natural, she's very angry and upset.'

'I want to reach out and give you warmth,' I said. 'I want to stroke your hair, to kiss you, to comfort you.'

'Thank you, I needed to hear that.'

'And the children? Do they know?'

'Not yet. When they do, I'll be the bad guy . . . I want to spend some time with the children. Who knows, it may be the last time I'm allowed to see them.'

'Oh no, Chiefal. That's awful. Isn't there a way we can all live together? Can't you have both of us? I don't mind sharing, you know that. There's enough unhappiness in the world. I hope she will understand.'

That night I dreamt I was being crunched under giant wheels. I woke up to the grinding of my own teeth. Mario had told me that I made an awful sound grinding my teeth at night when I was disturbed. My heart was palpitating. Oh no! I thought, as I turned to my side and an excruciating pain ran through my left side. What if I had a heart attack? Not me. Three of my men had already had it. It would be quite ridiculous for me to have one too. Poor Mario. Such a storm in his life! Was it worth it? Would I be able to compensate for such a loss?

A week later Mario called from a ski resort. There was pain and desperation in his voice.

'I've been asked to leave the house when we get back home—and legal separation within two weeks!'

'What? So quickly?'

'It's not divorce, just legal separation. I wish I had a friend I could talk to. It's terrible to be alone.'

'Wish I could be with you in such a difficult time!' I said. We humans will never learn, I thought, the same guilt, hurts, hates, and lack of understanding.

'Our joint bank accounts have been frozen and she wants to work the accounts by herself,' he said.

'Give her everything you have, Chiefal. It is a time of insecurity for her. It's natural. We don't need anything. I want you to know that you have a home. In fact, the carpenter's just been told to come and fit another cupboard for you. I thought you'd like to know that it will be ready by the time you return.'

He laughed. 'Thanks, I'd rather have you than a cupboard to

return to. That's only for putting your things into. And I'd like to put myself into you. Just you wait till I come home. You're going to get it.'

He sounded more together when he was able to joke, however feebly. I thought of Kabir, and how he must have felt when he left. He had left with guilt, a terrible guilt. He hadn't been honest enough to do it as a man. He had used devious, hurtful tactics. But even for him, no matter what methods he adopted, the parting was terrible. Though I had accepted it all like a lamb ready for slaughter, wanting to hurt him more by being understanding.

Would I be able to give Mario happiness and take the same from him? If two people are always alert to the needs of one another, then it is possible, I told myself. Where does it start going wrong, in so many small ways? I would have to caution Mario when I saw it starting. This time I was going to see it through. This time I was going to win.

'I'm the bad guy, you know,' Mario said when he called next. 'All her friends, the children treat me like the villain. It's too depressing, I wish you were here, then all this wouldn't matter.'

'Okay, I'll be there tomorrow,' I said impulsively.

'You mean it? I don't want you to sacrifice your time with the children. And they're going to school in a week!'

'All I'm asking is, do you want me there? If so, I take the Swissair tomorrow night, pick me up in Zurich.'

'Okay! What about your visa?'

'Don't worry, I'll organize all that in the morning.'

'Oh Kish! Now I'm happy. Nothing matters now!'

I put the phone down and saw Pooja looking aghast and upset.

'Are you going?' she asked.

'Yes. I'm sorry, but I have to. He needs me.'

'You're going to Switzerland!' Pooja said, face set, eyes accusing.

'Yes, I'll have to go. I'm sorry.'

She burst into tears and slammed the door and sat at my typewriter, writing to Susan.

I explained to Siddharth meanwhile—'Mario needs me. At this moment, he needs me desperately. For you, it's another one week of fun. You'll go to Panchgani! I'll take care of everything and make sure I'm back to put you on the train for school.' He nodded silently.

Pooja stormed in and burst out, 'You keep changing boyfriends all the time! In the beginning I thought that Mario was just like all the others, but you started loving him more and more, so much that you want to be with him more than with us. I hate him!'

Of course Pooja tore up the letter to Susan soon afterwards, when she felt loving towards me. When she knew that I was not going to relent, she accepted things.

And now what was I to do? What *could* I do? When Pooja was angry and rude and so unreasonable, I felt hopeless. There was frustration, humiliation and a feeling of failure. Why should this situation have arisen in the first place? Even though in my heart I knew that I had done my best and there was no reason to feel that I had failed, I could not free myself of the guilt.

I knew it would have been best for the children and for me if I left them in Kabir's care, now that they weren't babies, and wandered around looking for something to fulfil me. If Kabir agreed to keep the kids, I could fly with Mario anywhere and everywhere. It was not that I could give up the kids for Mario, it was not a barter. It just worked out like that.

Yet . . . I did not want them to think that I had deserted them. I did not want them to stop loving me. I did not want to gift them insecurity in their life.

But I had done as much as I could. Was their gratitude for my having been a wonderful mother so important after all? Did it get anyone anywhere? Would it stop them from being rude or undependable later on? Though, why did I want to send them away in the first place? Was what I wanted to do for myself really so important to me? Why was it so hard to be a mother!

It was not that Mario needed me desperately, or that I missed him so terribly that I had to leave my children behind and fly to him! Then why was I doing it? It broke my heart to see the children wither and become unhappy. Yet, all the time there was a voice in my head saying that it was time I did something just for myself. I was fed up of making sacrifices for everybody else. The kids would have to learn that I had a life of my own. They would grow up and fly away, and I didn't want to tell them at some point that I had sacrificed my future for them.

Mario said that it would be best if Caroline agreed to meet me, but she did not want to. 'Whatever happens, don't bring her to live in Switzerland,' she had said. She did not want to feel that she was being condescended to. So that was what she thought—that I would act superior because I had wrested from her what she once had? I thought of Susan, and how she must have felt coming home to me and the children. She was more concerned and worried about how to present herself to us. There were fears on both sides. I remembered how both of us had held hands at Raj Khosla's party to give strength to one another against the world. I would have liked Caroline to meet me. I would be putting myself out more than her. I was the one who needed to please, to be accepted by them. All she had to be was herself.

I felt numb throughout the flight. At the airport in Zurich I saw Mario standing behind the glass doors, looking very handsome, his body hard and lean in baggy trousers, and then everything seemed right. I loved this man. I had travelled twelve hours across a continent to be with him. I would always hold his hand.

On the way to the ski resort where he was staying with his two daughters, he told me all that had happened in his family. I was apprehensive of meeting his two daughters. 'How shall I be, Mario?' I asked, and he said, 'Just be yourself.'

A young girl skied up to the car. It was Vivienne, the younger one. I watched as Mario got off and helped her put the skis on top of the car. She got into the back seat.

'This is Protima, Vivienne,' Mario introduced me.

'Hello,' she said.

'Hi! You can call me Kish if Protima is difficult.'

She looked at me questioningly, then smiled. 'Kish? Okay.'

Silence.

'Have you ever seen snow before?' Vivienne asked.

'No, never. I'm so excited to see it. I want to get off and touch it, stamp on it, eat it!'

She laughed. 'Will you ski?'

'Oh! I'm afraid of breaking my leg. You see, I'm a dancer, and I can't afford to get hurt. Also, it looks so difficult, I'm terrified.'

'No, it's easy, you must ski.'

'Promise I won't fall?'

'I can't promise that, but you won't get hurt.'

'I won't break my leg?'

'Yes, I can promise that'.

'Then I'll try,' I said, 'but you must teach me.'

We both laughed, and I was relieved—it is so easy with children.

The older daughter skied up. Tension. She was fourteen. Cool and aloof. I tried my best to be charming. It took longer with her, but slowly it worked. Harriet didn't like cuddles or kisses, so I had to be careful. But Vivienne sat in my lap and chattered all the time. I danced for them in the evenings. They teased me about Franco, my handsome, blue-eyed ski instructor. I told them stories from the *Ramayana*. Then Harriet phoned Caroline. 'Ssshh. Don't speak too loud, she will hear you,' they said. I asked if I could say hello. 'No, no,' they all said, 'she'll get very upset if she knows you are here.' That made me sad.

'It's not you,' said Harriet, 'it's Mario. It's all his fault.'

'Goodnight, I want to go to bed,' I said in a broken voice, and Harriet turned to Mario and said, 'Now you've upset another woman!'

Caroline and four kids. Fifteen years of marriage. What was it that had made Mario give up all this for me? Good sex? A better love? A sense of belonging? Was any of that a good enough reason to put to distress five human beings? And if he could do this today because he had experienced a new feeling, what was to say he couldn't do it to me tomorrow for another feeling? Was self-fulfilment everything? And me, what sort of callous woman was I to permit all this?

Mario had to take the girls back. I stayed at the resort to continue my skiing lessons. Mario phoned every evening. He said the girls must have sung my praises because Caroline had said that I must be a remarkable woman. It felt good to hear that.

Some days later Mario and I drove to Germany, to the Goldhofer factory for his meeting and I made a round of the site. It was odd imagining Mario working there a long time ago when he first started. In India, someone who did all that was just a labourer. His early life had been difficult, like Kabir's.

I told Mario about the peculiar relationship I had with Kabir in the later years of our marriage—I wanted him to want me madly, but had no desire for sex with him. 'I need to feel that I'm wanted,' I said, 'then I don't need sex. It's enough for me.'

'That's not how I know you,' Mario said. 'You're so sexy with me.'

'But Chiefal, you're different. You are my idea of what a man should be for me. Someone rough and tough and good old-fashioned steady.' Despite the image I liked to project and the desire to have men in awe of me, all I really wanted was to feel emotionally secure. I was just an ordinary, vulnerable woman who wanted the ordinary things of life.

'I would not hold you to me if I had to live in Switzerland

for a job,' Mario said.

'Why?'

'It's not right for you. Could you live here, in this weather, not speaking the language, missing your culture, friends, relatives, work? And for what? To keep house, to cook and clean for four kids and me? If Caroline decided to walk out on her own, I'd be stuck! I'll have to live here and work and look after house and home. The only fortunate thing is that she is so attached to the children . . . It's quite funny when you think about it—how easy it is to screw men.'

'But Chiefal, you're such a good mother, I've seen you cooking, cleaning and keeping house. You do a wonderful job.'

'I like to do those things,' he said, 'but if I have to work as well, where will I find the time? And the burden of all this will naturally fall on you. I can see *you* being happy in such a situation,' he said sardonically.

'Are you sure I'm worth all that you've given up?' I asked.

'Yes! And I want you to know that it is not for you that I give up everything, it is for myself.'

'What does it amount to, Chiefal?'

'Well, by Swiss laws, after I've paid for the kids and for Caroline, I'm left with merely a fourth of my salary every month.'

'You haven't done yourself much good,' I said and we laughed. I hugged him tight. 'We'll manage on whatever we can get,' I said. 'We don't need much.'

I thought about my own situation. I had got almost nothing after my divorce. Kabir had had it too easy, but now I wanted him to take the responsibility of the children. He would have to spend four months every year with them. Their tickets alone (to fly them to the States) would cost him 48,000 rupees. The maintenance of the house and the bills could be another 25,000 at least. But I felt that he had to do it now.

Back in India, Mario continued his engineering work and I

started dancing again. We were always seen together, so people assumed that we were husband and wife. We hadn't got married formally, but how did it matter if people thought that we were?

'Are you married?' Kabir asked when we met next.

'No!' I answered.

'I don't understand this,' he said. 'You tell Jayant five minutes ago that you're married, and now you deny it. Why are you always lying?'

'Don't make lying sound like a heinous crime. Do you know how creative you have to be to lie?'

'Stop hedging. Or do you want me to be the last to know?'

'The husband is always the last to know,' I said smilingly, 'I cannot give everyone that privilege.'

o

In March 1984 I started training in kuchipudi dance with Guru Vempatti Chinna Satyam in Madras. Mario and I spent a weekend by the sea before I started my training. The sea was so blue, the beach so clean, and we decided we would buy a plot of land close to the sea where we would build our house ten years later.

After Mario left for Bombay, the dance kept me busy—I danced eight hours every day—but when I came back at night to the house I was staying in, I missed him badly. When he phoned, he sounded lonely and miserable. 'I love you, Kish,' he would say in a heart-rending tone and each time I would almost cry. Why did he love me so much?

I had asked Mario to look in my cupboard in Beach House for some files I needed. When he called to say that he had found the files, he said, 'There are so many papers! Loose pages with your writings. I was very tempted to go through some. You leave them all open. Very trusting you are!'

'You may read them if you like,' I said. 'In fact, it would be a good idea, you'll know me better. Of course, there will be an awful lot of things that you won't like, but I'm willing to take the risk!'

After I had put the phone down, I wondered about having one's man know everything. It wasn't right, some things had to be kept private. I wanted someone so understanding that I could talk to him about my emotions involving other men too, but I remembered how troubled Mario was when recently Kabir had come to dinner with us. After Kabir left, I had talked about various things, and Mario had remarked, 'Have you noticed how in your conversations you always end up talking about Kabir?'

I was stunned. Of course he was right. 'Mario,' I said, looking squarely at him, ready for battle, 'we've talked a great deal about many things, but it seems to me that you are picking out only Kabir Bedi!'

'No, I think you're quite hung up on Kabir. If he's in town, you become restless and want to see him every day. It's not normal! He's your ex-husband!'

I was quite exasperated by now. He was right, but that was how I felt, damn it, that was what I wanted. Why should he feel jealous or upset? 'I'm not jealous of him,' he said quietly, 'but I resent you going on and on. It's not easy for me. The way I see it, if you want to be with him, if he wants impulsively to pick up the phone and speak to you, it means that there's something you can't or don't want to share with me. And that hurts. It makes me feel inadequate too. It must make Susan feel inadequate! Just try and understand that!'

'If I'm hung up on Kabir, then you'll just have to accept that. Or would you like to change me? Will that make you love me more?'

'Of course not! But all of us need emotional security, and if you say you still love him, then I wonder what you mean by love. You see, our situations are opposite. Your marriage to Kabir didn't work—you didn't like being a wife, he was a lousy husband. But I had a good marriage. I was a good husband and

Caroline a good wife. Everything worked well, only thing was that I didn't love her!'

His words had a shattering effect on me. He was an engineer, after all. He could dissect and see things clearer. 'Perhaps I use the wrong word,' I said. 'Maybe love is not the word. You know that I don't need him, don't desire in a physical way, but he's just such a likeable, wonderful guy that I like his company.'

Mario smiled resignedly. 'Yes, I understand . . . the word love is very confusing and you use it in so many different ways. How am I to understand how you mean it?'

There were tears in my eyes by now. I hugged him tight. 'Chiefal, I love you, and I want only to live with you.'

That had solved the misunderstandings of that day, but I had wondered how many more times I would have to explain different things to him.

And now I had allowed him to read my writings! Would he think of me as a hard-hearted bitch, an opportunist, a fraud? A few days later, when he flew down to Madras, I waited for him to say something, but he said nothing.

'Do you think I'm hard-hearted?' I asked. He looked surprised. 'No. Why? Do you think that about yourself? In fact, you are a very lovable person. Honest, and innocent in many ways.' I almost fainted with relief. I needn't keep a part of me hidden from the man I loved. I could show him the crumbling walls, the cobwebs, the dust. It was really like bringing your man home, afraid of what he might think of your untidy house. Once he was in, and once you saw that he didn't really care, that he loved you more than to judge you by the way you kept home, you knew that you could count on him to help you tidy up the place and make it comfortable.

But a month later, things were different. I returned from a dinner at about 11.30 p.m. to find Mario in my room. He had flown in unexpectedly from Bombay.

'The one night I go out in Madras, you arrive! Had I known,

I wouldn't have eaten so much garlic chutney,' I laughed happily. But I could sense that something was not quite right. Perhaps he suspected that I had been out with a man! I started feeling guilty for no reason at all. And then of course the resentment built up. Stop, I told myself.

'I came upon some wild things you've written in your book, some things you forgot to tell me,' he said with a strange laugh.

'Which ones?'

'The bit about Robertino in Italy.'

Oh no! He had picked on the one I was most afraid of.

'I was very upset. What a fool I've been! And you told me that you could not bear for any man to touch you! I was going mad in Switzerland, calling you from everywhere, and in between two phone calls, when you were saying how much you loved me, you fucked Robertino in Rome! How could you!'

I felt nauseous. Was there going to be another scene? He was pacing up and down, hurt, wanting to fight. I wanted to hold him to my heart. But it might inflame him further, I said to myself, let him burn himself out.

'How can I trust you? I know you mean what you say, but that's just for the moment. Oh God! What a fool I've been! I left my family and home for you, and what do you do—a stupid Indian chick gets high and it's so easy to lay her!' I could see the pain in his eyes, and the anger, for he didn't like to use the kind of words he was using.

'Mario, there's nothing I can say that's going to make you trust me, so I won't,' I said. 'But what happened in Italy was not in the least important. Also, I didn't have you one hundred per cent. You were with your wife in Zurich. Yes, you said you loved me, but so have many others. They did not give up their wives for me. They gave nothing up. Only took. But now that you've given me all of yourself, you'll have one hundred per cent of me.'

He quietened down for a while, then said, 'I'm going back to

Bombay by the morning flight.' He got up and went out of the room. I was angry. So what if I had slept with Robertino? I hadn't planned it, the thing had just happened, it didn't mean I would go searching for that experience again. And how dare he talk of what a fool he had been to leave his home! If this was any sampling of what life was going to be with him, I didn't want it. Damn it, it was I who was looking after him. He was staying, eating, washing at my place. I owed him nothing and he owed me nothing. If he wanted to walk out he was welcome to do so, but not by throwing shit on my face. I was not responsible for his broken family. I had never asked for it.

In the morning I woke up in a panic. 'Get up, you bitch,' I screamed at myself. 'This time you're going to make it work.' I had to put an end to the vicious circle I always created for myself. I was not going to fool around with this man. I scrambled out of bed and sat by his side on the sofa outside. Unfortunately Meera and Alexander (who were staying in the house) were also up, and so were the servants. We all drank tea. I made light conversation with everybody. Mario made a few nasty remarks. I told Meera and Alexander that Mario was going back to Bombay the same day. I said it again and again, so that he would know that I had accepted it.

'It doesn't seem to make any difference to you,' he said after tea. 'That's what hurts. You just accept it so calmly.' And I understood—he didn't want to go; he was appealing to me for something to end his misery.

'Mario, please don't leave me. You said you would never leave me, didn't you?' He was standing before me, and I hugged him and cried into his stomach. He stroked my hair. We went to bed. He tried to make love, but images of Robertino kept plaguing him.

'Let's go to Fisherman's Cove and drown the demon,' I said.

'Yes, it's a big one.'

We walked hand in hand to Fisherman's Cove, our private spot on the beach.

'I need you to have faith in me, Chiefal, because I'm worthy of it. Promise me that whenever we have a fight, we'll just pack our bags and come to Fisherman's Cove.'

We stood in the dark, embracing. I hated to say how much I loved him, for I had said that to too many people. Standing there in Mario's arms, I didn't want to repeat those tired words. This was special. I was convinced that I hadn't loved anyone as well, as completely and as deeply as I loved Mario.

I missed Mario all the time. Once he phoned from Delhi to say that he was taking the morning flight to Bombay. I said I'd take the morning flight from Madras to Bombay too, so that we'd reach Bombay at the same time. We laughed wildly. I wanted him, I needed to be with him, I had to touch him, feel him. My relationships had never been so sexual. Sometimes it worried me. What when this blatant sexual urge started diminishing?

Mario and me, together, everywhere—on the bed, on the floor, on the chair, on the toilet seat, under the shower, on the beach, everywhere, everywhere. It was not possible, I kept telling him, that I should feel such an urge for sex, should want him all the time. We were exhausted every single morning. We smoked grass often—it used to add to the excitement.

One night there was a phone call from Manu. We were in bed. I was conscious of Mario listening carefully. I tried to talk casually. I didn't want him to think that I talked one way in front of him and another behind his back.

'Will you come over and have lunch with me at Reggie's house?' Manu asked.

'Fine, I'll see you at Reggie's then.' I said it purposely in front of Mario, knowing that there was so much history attached to lunch at Reggie's with Manu. After I'd put the phone down, I said to Mario, 'Are you upset that Manu called?'

He turned around and looked straight at me. 'It's not easy to sit here and listen to your own woman making a date with her ex-lover.'

I remained silent, hoping fervently that there wouldn't be another one of those wretched scenes of hurt and bitterness.

'I agree, it was wrong of him to have called at this hour. But he didn't want me to misunderstand, about his having been here and not met us.'

'Kish, I don't like him. He's a fraud. Anyone who occupies the ministerial position must be corrupt. And the way he phones you is very sneaky and corrupt.'

My heart sank. I knew that he was wrong. Manu was a good man, I could not imagine him phoning me with ulterior motives. I knew that Manu had understood and accepted the way our relationship was going to be—Mario's and mine, Manu's and mine. I knew that he would never want a quick encounter behind Mario's back.

I hated my situation. Why did Mario have to feel bitter and resentful? But how could I leave him alone to carry this unnecessary burden? Wasn't I his woman? If he was unreasonable, I would let him be. And anyway, Manu was not so important in my life that I had to quarrel with my man because of him. Part of me told me otherwise. Manu was my friend and I wanted his friendship. He was a good man. Why should I give up the friendship only because my man was so narrow-minded? This was the first step towards subservience! But I relented.

'You're right,' I said, putting my head in his lap, 'he shouldn't have called, not this late. In fact I should have told him that if he ever wants to see me he should come home and be with us. If he can't do that, why should I see him in someone else's house? I won't see him in Delhi.' Having said this, I felt better for Mario and for myself. I saw him relax visibly. He hugged me and he was once more the Mario I loved.

'I don't mean to be petty,' he said. 'I don't want you to break your friendship, please. Do you understand me?'

'Yes, Chiefal, I understand,' I said, not really understanding. He smiled, hugged me tighter. His balance was more important to me than my idea of right and wrong. We made love. It always seemed the 'rightest' thing to do.

In Bombay many of my friends dropped in to complain about their husbands and marriages. Mario listened quietly for hours. He looked really sad. When I asked him, he said, 'You know, I've never really been with Pietro (his son), he's only two, and when I hear your friends talking about how neglectful their husbands have been towards their children, I long to be with Pietro.'

'Why don't we invite the young ones here?' I said. Caroline was finally moving to London, trying to start a new life for herself, and I thought she'd be relieved to have the children off her hands for a while. He said he'd try.

And again we made plans for the future. He did not want to stay in India, as the job prospects were not so good. He would have to find projects elsewhere—in Nigeria, or Indonesia, perhaps. I tried to visualize how it would be for us, for me, in a foreign land. What about my dance? My friends, my family, my culture? As long as I knew that I would return to India soon, it didn't matter. Of course my dance career would suffer, but so long as I could continue the dance in some way or another, it would be okay. I could see myself keeping house, dusting, washing, cooking, and it didn't seem so bad, but I knew that if I had to do that for longer than a short while, I would start resenting it.

Mario could not think of settling down in India when he retired. He could only live in the south of Switzerland. It seemed ridiculous to be thinking so much about where one wanted to be fifteen years later, but I too couldn't think of my retiring anywhere outside India. I was absolutely determined now to buy the land near Madras.

I had lunch with a friend, Mrs Diwan, before returning to Madras. She said, 'You've taught me a lot, Protima. I'm really so relaxed in my mind these days. How can anyone get everything from one man? And really, it's not important to find it all there.'

'Yes,' I said, 'it's almost impossible to find everything in one man, but miracles do happen sometimes. I have found everything in my Mario, and I want to be his for the rest of my life.'

She looked aghast and incredulous. 'How can *you* say a thing like that?'

I smiled. 'One changes all the time. There was a time when you thought like this but you weren't happy, and you couldn't understand my relationship with so many men at the same time. Now you're experiencing what I had, and you enjoy it. It was right for me, too, but I've found my miracle in Mario and I'm content. I want to marry him, to be his wife and live with him for the rest of my life.'

I told her all about how wonderfully we were tuned to each other sexually. It had been one full year and it was still new, exciting and intense.

'How's it possible, Protima?' said Mrs Diwan. 'I don't believe you. It's a miracle, I tell you!'

o

Mario and I went on a holiday to Kashmir, just the two of us. We lived in a houseboat on Nageen Lake. It was like being in Paradise. Vendors on shikaras glided past our houseboat—fruits, vegetables, flowers, the dhobi, wooden and silverware were all available on water. It was idyllic. Just the two of us in the snow, singing, dancing and joking by camp fires with the horsemen.

When we returned to Srinagar, to news and politics and people, it was like a rude awakening. Bhindranwale, the militant Sikh leader, had finally been shot dead (something that should have been done at least a year ago) and the Army had stormed into the Golden Temple to capture the terrorists. We decided to go to Kasauli to pick up Pooja and Siddharth from their boarding school. Their vacations had started, and in view of the Punjab situation, it was wiser and safer to accompany them to Bombay.

The first day at home and the fireworks started.

'Kish, where are my diamond and emerald earrings that I gave you to keep safely?' Pooja asked me.

'I don't know,' I replied, 'they must be in your box.'

'No, they're not there.'

'Well, then I don't know.'

She yelled, 'I can't trust you at all! I leave you in charge of the whole house. You are responsible for everything here. So if they are lost, you are to blame.'

'Shut up! Don't you talk to me like that, understand? I will not have idiotic sentiments here.'

'You're the one who is a fucking idiot!'

'Pooja! How dare you call me an idiot!'

'You called me one, so I can call you one too.'

I was furious, but, as always, didn't know what to do with my rage. I cannot direct it at my loved ones. Mario walked in. He had been standing at the door.

'Pooja, listen,' he said firmly, 'you are not the daughter of a labourer to talk like that. I don't care what the argument is about, but if you call Kish a fucking idiot again or abuse her ever, I swear I will slap you till kingdom come.' His voice was choked with emotion. Pooja glowered at him with big angry eyes, tears welling up in them, her fists clenched, trembling with rage. I walked out. It was utterly relieving to know that there was a man who would stand by me, side with me. Pooja kept quiet.

I lay down in my bedroom, thinking, smoking. Why did all this have to happen? Why had Kabir created tensions between mother and daughter by constantly reminding Pooja that it was she who owned Beach House, not I?

Mario was in the kitchen. Pooja went to him and said, 'If you ever slap me, I will tell my father.' Mario came in laughing and told me about it. 'It's all a sham, Kish. I told you so. Why don't you get angry with her? Why don't you let it all come out? If I was you, I would have slapped her.'

'Chiefie, I don't know how to get angry anymore.'

I went into Pooja's room. She was lying on the bed.

'Okay, what's bothering you?' I asked.

'You won't understand, so forget it.'

'Why should you decide what I will understand and what I won't? I must know. Now, enough is enough. I will not stand for any more nonsense.'

'Then don't!'

Exasperated, I said, 'All right . . . since being with me is such a pain for you . . . '

'Why can't you understand?' she burst out. 'I want you so much to love me, but you just don't care. You have no feelings at all. All you can think of is Mario, Mario, Mario.'

'Well! Is that it? Is that what upsets you? Why are you so angry with Mario? Because he's my man? It has nothing to do with you! You're my daughter, not my lover. You cannot take his place and he can't take yours.'

'But we used to be so happy before, and you had so much time for us, and now . . .'

'Wait a minute, Pooja. Mario has come into my life only a year ago. You have been fighting with me for seven years now, and always unreasonably.'

'Why always me?' She started crying. 'Papa left us when I was five years old and then we had only you, and now even that I don't have.'

'Don't be dramatic! Papa left home, but he never left you. And he makes it a point to be with you every year. And how is it that you take it all out on me alone? Have you ever accused him of not loving you?'

'Because we hardly have enough time with him, and also because he is not going off and marrying someone silly like you are.'

'But he's already married to Susan. How is it that you don't grudge him that?'

'Because I like Susan and I hate Mario!'

'That's okay. You don't have to like him. You're not marrying him, I am. I have gone out of my way to compensate for your father's absence. My fault, I should never have done that. I compromised on my profession, my personal life, just so that you could be happy and secure. I was wrong. And the thing is that you don't seem to mind if men came into your mother's life just to have a bit of fun with her. Now when I have finally found someone to truly care for me, to love me, you resent it. What would you have me do? Play housekeeper and matron till you two find your own partners and then leave me to end my life? No way! I love Mario, he's my man and I want to live with him. I would be very happy, we both would be very happy, if you two came to live with us and be part of the family. But if you don't want it, then you have a choice—you can go to your father . . . if he will have you. Or you can go to your various uncles and aunts.'

'See!' she cried, 'You want to push us out of the house and out of your life. How do you think I feel, that nobody wants us? You don't want me, and Papa may not want me and we are being pushed to stay with Ranga and all the others!' Then she cried big tears.

'You *want* to be unhappy, Pooja, you *want* to hit yourself on the head all the time and keep crying. Nobody can stop you. And there's Siddharth! He's in the same situation as you. He has the same things and people as you. He's not miserable. Then why you?'

'Of course he's miserable. He's terribly unhappy.'

I called Siddharth in and hugged him. I asked him. 'I only want to be with you,' he said. 'If you are with Mario, then I'll join you. I want you.' My heart went out to the little boy; his love was so clear and simple. Pooja was quiet for a long time, as I continued talking, telling her where and how she was wrong. She listened. Finally she said, 'All right. It's up to me to decide whether I want to be happy or not. I'll try my best.'

'Just be happy, my baby, just be happy,' I said and we both wept and hugged each other. 'Please don't be so jealous of Mario. I love you as my daughter and he is my man. Please don't be jealous of him.'

I had gone wrong. It was easy to go wrong. It all stemmed from the fact that I loved my children dearly and wanted to protect them and keep them feeling secure. I was always trying to compensate for the loss of the father, giving too much of myself. It was a mistake, I felt. Children had to be dealt with firmly. What I did with my life was none of their business. Once that was established, they would look up to me and respect me. 'I don't respect you!' Pooja had said to me once and that had been quite a blow. Why didn't children feel the anguish of their mothers? How cruel they could be! Many nights I had cried into my pillow because my daughter did not understand or care. She did not respect me. And yet my heart went out to Pooja at that very moment. Poor darling, suffering like that. My heart was heavy with her pain. How unfair that she did not have a broader perspective. It was not her fault. It was her age.

Well, if worse came to worst, Pooja would not forgive me and hate me for the rest of her life. But it wouldn't stop her from living her life the way she wanted. It wouldn't stop her from loving someone, from being happy in other ways. She just wouldn't love me, but did that really matter? Wasn't it more important that I should love her? If I truly loved her, I would do only that which was right for her, no matter what the result would be for me personally. What was I like at fifteen? Terribly mixed-up, full of self-pity, ignored—but was there any trace left of all those things? My relationship with my mother was still not easy, but as a person, as an individual, I was all right. My daughter would also learn, she would come to terms with herself. She had the capacity to laugh at herself, and she had a good heart. She would be okay.

If I sent Pooja and Siddharth to their father, perhaps they would realize my worth and value me more. But that seemed highly motivated and selfish. The choice was quite clear—keep them and be hated by them or send them away and see them disintegrate but with their love for me assured. No, I would keep my children, no matter how difficult.

o

[*Protima and Mario spent part of every year in Birrwil, Switzerland in the mid-eighties. Caroline had moved with the children to England.*] In 1985, I was in Birrwil, and the kids were in Bombay with Mario. The night before the children were to return to their school in Sanawar, Mario tried to act funny with Pooja. She told me about it the next morning when I called from Birrwil. I had difficulty believing her at first, but she was my daughter. The incident pretty much ended my relationship with Mario—though the association continued for another six years or so, the end had begun.

I wrote to Pooja some months later, telling her how much I admired her great generosity. She had forgiven Mario over a cup of coffee, just like that. She had been wronged more than me—especially since I too had let her down by refusing to believe her in the beginning—and she had every right to be mean and nasty and unforgiving, but she wasn't. I tried to follow her example but my heart could not forgive. I thought a great deal about the situation. Mario couldn't be special to me anymore. He was just another boyfriend. That was all that his status could be in my life. I made it clear to him that I could promise him nothing anymore. I couldn't even let him stay in my house.

But my heart was not in other men. I just couldn't bring myself to share my whole self with another man. I packed all the stuff I had in Birrwil. I had decided to leave. But again, I couldn't bring myself to leave the garden I had worked so hard to put together, the house I had worked so hard to restore. My heart was heavy.

Mario arrived and pleaded with me to let things be. Did half-an-hour of foolish behaviour negate two-and-a-half years of happiness, he asked me. 'How can I ever trust you again?' I answered.

'I ask you to give me a chance to prove that it was a mistake,' he pleaded.

'I don't believe you'll change,' I said. 'I don't believe you really love me.'

'If that be the case, then why am I pleading with you? What do I gain from being with you if I don't love you? Am I after your money, your property, your body? I admit I made a drastic mistake. Sometimes—I don't know why I do the things I do. If I had thought of you at that time, if I had known how much you'd be hurt, I wouldn't have done it. But I never even thought about what I was doing. I was like a bloody animal. Please, please don't leave me,' he begged.

I couldn't give him another chance. I wondered how Pooja had had the generosity and the magnanimity to forgive and forget. How could it have been so easy for her? How could she carry on as though it were a small thing, over and done with now? I wished I had that capacity. My mind was narrow and my heart too small. I wished I could wipe out the incident from my mind because I had been happy with the man as I had never been with any other. He was the perfect companion for me, active, outgoing, quick-witted, funny, ready to do anything, anytime. I had admired him because he was hardworking, honest and loyal. What could have changed him? I knew I would never again find someone who matched me so well, and I knew that he could never again be what he used to be for me.

But I was grateful to him for one thing, though—because of him I had come closer to Pooja and Siddharth. Had it not been for that incident, my children and I would have drifted further and further apart.

I gave up on Mario. Perhaps I would find someone else to fall in love with all over again, I thought, and felt stupid thinking that. I was nearing forty! Maybe love just did not exist.

a dream come true

When I was in Birrwil, I spent a lot of time in the garden. I pulled out basketsful of stones from the flower beds, watered all the plants and spoke to a few flowers. And I started daydreaming.

I had a clear vision of what I had long desired—my own farmhouse-cum-dance school. When I was very young and ugly and unloved, I wanted a small farmhouse, unpretentious, unfashionable, but strong and warm and homely. I always imagined a huge, rough wooden table with benches on either side to seat my ten children, and a big pot with the evening meal steaming away in it. When dance came into my life, the desired farmhouse became bigger, with additional rooms to accommodate the dance school. The students would work on the farm for two hours in the morning, then dance till lunchtime, then dance again for three hours after which they would prepare the dinner and work in the farm for another hour. After dinner, there would be baths, washing up, and then the theory of dance, the explanation of mythologies and religious philosophies, and meditation before going to sleep. The farm-school would have to be self-sufficient.

My longing for a large family that I would be the head of, surrounded by people who admired and respected me, my longing to till my own land and live quietly with nature and to dance for ever—all these things could be possible with the creation of the farm-school. When two students arrived from Munich to spend some days with me, learning odissi, my dream seemed more valid than ever.

I wanted to leave something behind for posterity, besides my children. As far back as 1982, I had thought of setting up an Indian dance centre like Kalakshetra in Madras. I had had a very difficult time when I started learning odissi. There was no place where I could practice and train in Bombay. I had to travel frequently to Orissa. Then there was the problem of finances, especially after Kabir and I split. I could only imagine how difficult it would be for girls who did not have the resources or opportunities that I had. I wanted to set up a place where anyone with a passion for dance could come and stay and train, not having to worry about finances or anything else, and devote themselves one hundred per cent to dance. The students would live on the campus learning all the major classical dance styles from the best gurus. I had hoped that if Antulay remained in power I would get a grant of five acres of land on the outskirts of Bombay.

In 1987 I was in Bangalore, looking for land for my dance centre. The maharaja of Dharampur took me in his blue Matador to his 150 acres, twenty-five kilometres from the city. He showed me his property from a distance of two kilometres, through foggy, twenty-six-year-old binoculars. I could have ten acres for one lakh rupees, he said, but only after he had found some one to buy the rest of the land. I kept telling him that a bird in hand was worth twenty in the bush and that he should give me the property immediately. There were deliberations, but each time we seemed to be getting nowhere. He ranted about the Indian government and privy purses and the unfairness of it all.

'I call it highway robbery . . . If it wasn't for us, there would be no Union of India . . . How can we manage? Any businessman won't think twice if he has to go to Mysore. I have to think fifty times before I can go to a petrol pump and ask them to fill her up—Rs 400 to Rs 500 gone just like that! And the villagers have encroached on fifty acres of my land. I don't have the money to fence off my property and so I keep losing more and more acres every year. I have court cases pending everywhere and no money to look after my property.'

'If I get you back your fifty acres which have been encroached on by the villagers, will you give me some land free?' I asked him.

'If you can do that, I'll give you half of whatever you can get for me,' he said. I thought of telling Mr Hegde about the offer when I went to meet him the next day. [*Protima had already met Ramakrishna Hegde, then Chief Minister of Karnataka, a few times and he had promised her some land for her dance centre.*]

I phoned the Chief Minister from my hotel the next day. He picked up the phone himself, and when I told him who I was and that I had returned to haunt him for my land, he agreed to meet me.

A car from the CM's office came to pick me up the following morning at a quarter to nine the following morning and I was taken to his guest house. Mr Hegde was being photographed. His right hand gripped his left wrist tightly and the fingers of the left hand moved about nervously. He was clearly camera-shy. I watched him, amused. When he saw me, he strode up and asked, 'What is the matter?'

'You know very well what it is. I have a dream about my institution and it has to be perfect. You give me land in Manipal which is rock-hard and in an environment not conducive to my idea of the centre. Just because it is free does not mean that I will take it. It has to be right. I want land outside Bangalore city.'

'How much land do you need?'

'I must have a minimum of ten acres. It must be agricultural land. I want the centre to be self-sufficient. I want to keep cows there.'

'Do you mind if it is twenty-five to thirty kilometres away?'

'That is ideal for me. But all this talk is nothing if there is no immediate action. I know you're going to America soon. I want to finish everything before that. How long will you be gone?'

He smiled. 'About six weeks or so. But you can't expect things overnight. Whenever you remember about your centre, you suddenly write to me.'

'That's not fair. I have chased you all over India. You were to have dinner with Reggie in Delhi. I flew down just to meet you and you cancelled the dinner at the last moment . . .'

'Last-minute things happen, you know, and I have to change my plans. I can't help that.'

'I'm not attacking you. Just defending myself. Do you know how much time and energy and money I have spent just trying to get hold of you? Don't make me run around. I have a good thirty years ahead of me for real work and I'll give up my dance career to put all my efforts into this academy. There's no time to waste. I have already lined up teachers of kalaripayatt and chhau dance forms and we're going to create a new language of dance. I can't even start collecting the funds until I have the land for the centre.'

'You'll have to pay something for the land. It can't be totally free. Your trust will have to buy it,' the Chief Minister said, and I immediately produced the trust papers—'Here are my trust papers. It's a registered trust and it has 80 G tax exemption,' I declared triumphantly.

'You write to me again,' he said, 'with a proposal as soon as you can and . . .'

I opened the big envelope I was carrying and pulled out the

letterheads of the Odissi Dance Centre. 'Right now, here! Have the proposal typed and I will sign right here and now.'

He took the paper, looked at it, and called his PA. 'Type out this letter and deliver it to Mrs Bedi at her hotel. She will sign it, and give her a copy.' Then he turned to me: 'You know, we are planning to have an artistes' centre—painters, actors, musicians, dancers, all in one area. Would you like to have part of that land? It's on the Bombay-Pune Road.'

'Is it high, with trees and the wind blowing all the time? Is there water on it?'

'There's a lake there and it gets full when it rains. But we haven't had rains for the past two years. There is a water belt which will have to be tapped with a bore well.'

'Can I have ten acres?'

'Yes.'

'All right then. Give me the directions to the place and I will go there now.'

He called his PA and secretary and talked to them in Kannada.

'They will take you to the land. Look at it and let me know before I leave for Delhi, this evening.'

'Thank you. I hope all goes well with you,' I said, and added, 'and incidentally, I'm offended that you don't send me your paper. Only Kamala Das gets it. I too am part of the intellectual circuit, you know. I write my political views in the *Times*!'

He laughed uproariously. 'Oh, that!' he said, did a sweet namaste and left.

I got the land from the government of Karnataka on a thirty-year lease. The land was in Hessaraghatta, just outside Bangalore. Everything on it belonged to the government—I didn't own the land, I couldn't sell it or do any business on it. It was meant purely for charity, for my dance village. And it was made quite clear to me that I would get no money from the state government.

But I was determined to make my project [*Nrityagram*] a

success. There was a great deal of work to be done, and I had decided to stop dancing actively after April 1988 till I had completed the project. I had to put all my energies into it. So I gave up on the house in Birrwil, set up permanent base in India, and went back to the sari and the tikka and my Hindi. I had to beg all over the country for the first ten to fifteen lakh rupees that I needed to start work on the building for the institution. Thereafter I would need a steady six to seven lakhs every year to keep it running. I also started learning to read and write Kannada, which I knew would be of tremendous help when I moved to Hessaraghatta.

Kabir was back in India and would come over for dinner from time to time. [*Both Pooja and Siddharth were studying in USA. Mario had set up his own company and was busy with a project in Jagdishpur.*] We would sit and laugh at all the games of life. It seemed a pity that we had become so much more tolerant, understanding and wise when we didn't have all that much to attend to and nurture in terms of our interactions with other people. If only we hadn't been so self-centred in our youth, our lives would have been so much more wonderful, I thought. Kabir was looking splendid—slim and youthful. It suited him to be by himself. He had been jumping from one relationship to another. This was the first time he was really on his own, and it was good for him.

My mother was undergoing treatment for cancer, and before the deluge of work on Nrityagram started, I went and spent some time with her in her flat. I often felt guilty about all the embarrassment and unhappiness I had caused her. We had very little in common except mutual affection. We spent time cooking delicacies and watching video movies—doing the simplest things of life that give one the greatest joys.

○

One day in March 1989 I put my suitcases, my white marble

Nandi bull (a gift from the Maharana of Udaipur) and a cheque for Rs 2,00,000 into my red Maruti car and drove from Bombay to Hessaraghatta. The land was dry and barren, infested with snakes and scorpions. I remember standing in the middle of nowhere and wondering how and where to start. I realize now, of course, that I need not have worried. Nrityagram had its own longings, its own dictates and its own desires. I was a mere tool, a slave, ready and able to do its bidding.

How does one start when one arrives in the middle of a wilderness armed only with dreams? Well, first, having acquired a tent, you go shopping and buy yourself some cooking utensils and a camp bed and mattresses and what have you. Then you dig and slope the ground where the tent has to be pitched, and make a snake pit around it. Then you find some farmer as close to your place as is possible and request him to supply you with some water. All this takes you about four days. Next you need cooking gas because you realize that you cannot keep cutting down the casuarina for tea and coffee. So the sadness begins. The gas company will not service the rural districts because there is not enough demand. They will not allow you to cash and carry either, as it is against their policy on safety. Use kerosene, they say. I *had* tried that first, but it was in short supply!

It took me twelve days of running from one company to the other, pleading, threatening, charming, begging, until the ex-chief minister happened to be in town and I insisted on having breakfast in his house because I could not cook my own. I got my gas connection the next day.

I was everywhere, doing everything. I was telephone operator, typist, planner, fund-raiser, office-bearer, peon, postman, driver, labourer! I also found out various rates for granite, sand, cement, Mangalore tiles and wooden rafters, opened a bank account, made friends with all the farmers near me, and tried to clear the one acre of land which would house the first gurukul. Two snakes had to be killed as they were cobras and we had surprised them. I wasn't sure I had done the right thing.

Then, one fine afternoon a forest fire broke out in the next farm and the wind helped it along to our side, where we had collected all the nice high grass for thatching roofs. Daksha Sheth, the chhau martial arts dancer, and her husband, Devissaro, who were with me, suffered a few burns on their hands trying to put the fire out. A young odissi dancer burnt her left leg. That very night, a neighbour yelled at 1.30 a.m. and there was such a moaning and screaming that we all rushed to his place. Dacoits had struck. They weren't able to get anything, of course, because the people in Hessaraghatta always slept with long, pointed steel rods and sickles by their pillows. But we weren't armed, and it was frightening.

Three days after the attempted dacoity, I went trying to find out how one could procure a gun. Wasn't easy. While I was still trying, the government fell. When the state is run by administrators and not by any political party, miracles happen. I floated into the chief secretary's office in my sparkling white mundu, and came out with the gun licence application duly filled in and processed. The police station was informed that two police constables had to be posted at Nrityagram at nights.

The next day, our bore well equipment arrived and after shooshing up the red earth for two days and three nights, they struck water at 210 feet.

We soon had five volunteers, students from the fine arts college, Trivandrum, and they were put in charge of producing bricks from our brick-making machine. Six dogs arrived uninvited to stay near us, and they would watch us imploringly as we ate our rice and sambar in the evenings. We also had a goat donated to us, and some geese. The latter were a noisy lot—cackle, cackle, cackle all night long. (I'm told that the Germans had used geese to patrol the Berlin wall, as they made better watchdogs and cost much less.) At night packs of wolves or hyenas came whooping in. We waited in the dark until we heard a terrible squawking—

some chicken or hen being carried off—and then the whooping receded and we went back to sleep.

One acre of land was cleared first and the foundations dug. One temporary thatched shed was made first so we could store our construction material like sand and cement in it. We planted quite a few mango trees and casuarina and silver oak in June. And with two little students to dance with me in the evenings under a large tree, I waited for the first gurukul to be completed.

Then came Usha R.K. and her husband Radhakrishna, offering all their time and energies to help me. We organized festivals of music and dance to raise funds to continue the construction. Renowned and revered musicians and gurus of dance and music contributed with free performances to see a dream materialize. Vimla Gujral gave the first cheque for sponsorship of the Yoga and Meditation Centre. At the most difficult time, when there were no more funds left to put up the roof of the odissi gurukul, Vijaypat Singhania came forward to sponsor the construction, and when the gurukul was completed in September 1989, he became its patron and it was named the Raymonds Odissi Gurukul. Vijaypat was to become Nrityagram's most consistent and generous sponsor. For five years I continued to turn to him for assistance, and though he was exasperated sometimes, he never gave up on Nrityagram.

Sometime in January 1990, as I drove past Hessaraghatta village, a group of very young boys shouted 'daynse', 'disco daynse, braike daynse'. Initially I was amused that these words had reached remote villages. As the days passed I realized that for the local people, anything to do with the cities was necessarily Western. A woman driving a car was decidedly Western, and if she was building a dance school, it had to be for disco or break-dance. The next time I heard the boys shout 'daynse, disco daynse', I stopped and asked them whether they knew what bharatanatyam was. Some said yes, most didn't know. The ones who said yes had seen it in Kannada films. They knew that

Kamalahasan did bharatanatyam. They had never heard of Yamini Krishnamurti or Birju Maharaj. Clearly, our country's heritage was anything but alive and well in the villages.

So I organized an odissi dance recital in the village square. Unsure of the reactions, I invited the Kannada film star Shankar Nag to be the chief guest. Thousands came! Even the mandal pradhan was there with his family. Shankar held them spellbound. He told them about my popularity as a dancer, about my achievements and my travels to far-off lands. He said, 'You people must have done some great deeds to deserve such a person and such an institution. People pay thousands to watch her performance, and today you see it free! She does not ask you for money. You can help in so many ways. If each one of you goes and makes one brick, it's enough for a full gurukul. Send your children to Nrityagram for free dance training and be proud of your own culture and heritage.' Then I started dancing and there was pin-drop silence. I danced for two hours. After the recital, we announced that February third was the day for registration and thirty students would be selected for dance training. Those interested should come to Nrityagram at one that afternoon. Classes would be held every Saturday and Sunday from 3 p.m. to 5 p.m. The only condition was one hundred per cent attendance.

The response was amazing. On the morning of 3 February, a dozen children accompanied by their parents arrived. They were told to wait or to come back at 1 p.m. since we were busy trying to finish the flooring of the odissi gurukul. By noon, there were close to 400 people, and by 1 p.m. there were 600 children with their parents. Even the mandal pradhan arrived with ten children from his village. There was pandemonium. I was overjoyed, awed, panic-stricken and utterly helpless.

I managed to pick 140 students. Then came the devoted ones, clutching their shiny one-rupee coins in their hands, because I had asked for contributions of a rupee each for the registration.

It was straight out of some old story. One stubborn girl lurked outside my tent till sunset, her black, luminous eyes anxious and hopeful. 'Illa admission,' I kept telling her, 'hogi (go away).' But she only moved back a couple of steps and stood there, waiting. By 6.30 p.m. I had tears in my eyes. I asked her why she was standing there. In a broken voice, she said, 'Daynse.' I called her in, put her name down and she dropped her coin into the contribution matka. From 3 to 6 February, I had to accept another fifteen students.

Guru Kelucharan Mahapatra, who was in charge of the odissi gurukul, had sent his son, Ratikant (Shibu), as his representative, and he took the best thirty students. Usha R.K. said she would teach the others bharatanatyam. And so began bharatanatyam too! It was a wonderful beginning.

Soon we had our first full-time residential student—Uday Kumar Shetty, a twenty-six-year-old from the Shimoga district of Karnataka. He came with his brother-in-law, a security officer. He spoke no English or Hindi. He had apparently seen me dance for the Janata Dal party at his home-town and had heard the accompanying message of Nrityagram waiting to receive dedicated students. His family sold milk and earned Rs 200 a day, he said. He could afford to pay. I admitted him, but refused to take any money.

Shortly afterwards came Yumiko, a Japanese girl from Osaka!

When some of the buildings had already come up, the local mandal panchayat created problems. I hadn't got a No Objection Certificate before I started building. I had sent the blueprints, duly signed. I had written off letters and applications. But all this was taking so long that I started construction anyway. Besides, since the government itself had leased the land to me for Nrityagram, wasn't it logical to presume that it would have no objection to its construction? But clearly such simple logic was no defence.

The eight men and two women who had arrived from the

panchayat looked quite sombre, sitting stiffly in their chairs, their arms folded. I took my neighbour Raj Gopal with me to act as the interpreter. I was to pay Rs 12,000 or more as taxes for having kept the land empty for two years. And I would have to pay every year. I put out my sari pallu in front of the pradhan and said that I had come to them for a donation. I was teaching 150 rural children for free. I needed support. Everything at Nrityagram came from goodwill. I had no money, how could I pay the tax? They whispered, discussed amongst themselves, chopped and changed the taxes around and slashed them down to Rs 8,000. But I wasn't going to pay. So they looked at it once again, made more concessions and I was asked to pay Rs 6,000. That was the limit, they said, as the rest was to be given to the state government.

They knew better, I said, but what a shame that the poor students would now have to pay fees, because how else could I manage? So many students would drop out. So they looked at the amount again, and after much discussion, they finally brought it down to Rs 3,000. Then I was happy, but the thought of paying every year was awesome. They suggested I write to the minister and ask the government to waive the taxes from the following year. If this was done, the mandal panchayat would refund the present amount too! They then offered two smokeless chulahs as a present for Nrityagram! And all this while I had the cash in my bag to pay the original tax bill. Obviously, I had become street smart.

When I first arrived to start Nrityagram, I had no corporate or government support. Grants and assistance from the Sangeet Natak Akademi and the Department of Culture came much later, when the institution had proved itself. I remember friends saying that I was mad to jump into such a huge project—I wasn't rich, I wasn't married to a rich man. Yes, I had some rich friends, but how much could they give, and how often? I was lucky that in Raymonds and then in the ITC group I found consistent supporters. Help also came from unexpected quarters—Hotline, for instance (yes, the company belonging to Rekha's late husband, Mukesh Aggarwal), donated a TV set, cooking ranges, mixers and grinders; and Prasad Bidappa gave me space in his large office gratis, with permission to use all the equipment when I was in Bangalore to organize a three-day dance festival. But there were times when I almost gave up, and this anxiety about money was to continue through the next five years.

And I had to fight for everything, from electricity connection to security. The money was never enough. In less than a year there were over 200 students to be trained and fed. Many came from the surrounding villages, so there was money needed for transport as well. There were times when I went begging for fifty kilos of rice or flour just to feed the students and the staff.

I wanted Nrityagram to be India's first and only dance village for all the classical dances. There would be nine gurukuls, the navagrahas or the nine celestial planets, making our universe complete. There would be seven gurukuls for the seven classical dance styles and one each for chhau and kalaripayatt. Each gurukul would be named after whoever sponsored it.

But not many in India, I discovered, would part with their money for culture. When funds were running low, I went berserk with worry. I couldn't afford to put the brakes on the construction once the momentum had built up. I remember weeping in sheer frustration and anger one day. This was after a big industrialist from Ahmedabad arrived to take me out to dinner. He spent Rs 1,089 on my wine and Chinese food, but wouldn't give me a donation of even Rs 100. I took him to the village and he couldn't believe that Protima Bedi was staying in that tent and roughing it out. He said, 'Why are you doing this crazy thing? It's too big for you, you'll destroy yourself and your future. Let someone else do it. It doesn't suit you.'

It was hopeless. Even Rajiv Gandhi, when I met him at the Raj Bhavan in Bangalore, said, 'I think your project is too expensive, we can't afford it.' Mani Shankar Aiyar pitched in and said that I could have 'the two lakhs for construction which we give' from the Department of Culture, and Rajiv Gandhi nodded, but the grant took a very long time coming my way.

I often felt tired, depressed, dejected and quite miserable. And then I would ask myself why I had to do it at all. Why had I left my family, my friends, my social life, my city, my profession to rough it out in the wilderness? Would I ever achieve what I had dreamt of? I could simply drop the whole project and fly back home. I tried . . . I failed. Happened all the time.

But the dejection never stayed with me for too long. There was encouragement and support from many who mattered. Guru Vempatti Chinna Satyam came unannounced to Nrityagram and went away terribly pleased. He said it was going to be an international centre for dance and he had great faith in my abilities to see such a big project through. Then Kalanidhi Narayanan, the great abhinaya guru from Madras, came visiting at 6.30 one morning and was also impressed. She gave many positive suggestions for running the place once it got going, cautioning me about the possible problems in dealing with gurus and senior artistes.

Besides, I believed in miracles. The dark clouds would pass. Meanwhile, one acre of land was ploughed for mulberry saplings, and a sericulture unit was set up, which, hopefully, would bring in basic survival funds. Behind my camper, six vegetable beds were also made. We planted nine hundred trees, and waited for the fruits. I had struck roots in Hessaraghatta.

o

During the election campaign in November 1989, I had danced in the smallest villages and towns of Karnataka—giving two performances every night—canvassing for the Janata Dal and their prime ministerial candidate, V.P. Singh. Quite apolitical temperamentally and also knowledge-wise, the only reason I had agreed to do this was Ramakrishna Hegde. Not because he was responsible for the ten acres of Nrityagram, but because I found him extremely cultured, dignified, able, relatively honest and exceedingly attractive.

Six months after the elections was the inauguration of Nrityagram, and I was thrilled when V.P. Singh agreed to inaugurate it. The inauguration was fixed for 11 May, and on 3 May I received the PM's tour programme. He would arrive by helicopter at 1.05 p.m., inaugurate Nrityagram, have lunch with us, rest at our gurukul for an hour, and then depart at 3.10 p.m. It was final. People were awed by my 'magic' and wondered how I had done it. In Karnataka, they spoke in hushed whispers about how 'powerful' I was. It was a heady feeling.

The inauguration went off well. I liked V.P. Singh. He came across as a sincere man, very down to earth. No aura of power and glory about him. He seemed like someone you could spend a quiet evening with, watching a gorgeous sunset. After the inauguration was over and the PM had left, I was incredulous—had it really happened? For that matter, had anything ever really happened? So many dramas, undercurrents, worries, expectations and frustrations had filled the past. It was just timepass. And we all got so involved with things!

Actually, it was a wonder that the inauguration had gone off smoothly. A week before the inauguration, a group of artists had got together to protest against the success of Nrityagram. The excuse was a stupid complaint—that local Karnataka artistes were not being promoted by the government. It was the 'outsiders' who were being given land. 'Outsiders' like Protima Bedi. Their true problem, of course, was my success. They had many meetings at the Ravindra Kalakshetra lounge in Bangalore and they also called for a press conference. Fools, they simply exposed themselves to ridicule. My dear friend, Dr Sunil Kothari, who had come for the inauguration, went to attend the press conference. They refused him entry. It made news. The whole thing backfired on them.

I was told that Jeevraj Alva was behind the protest. Perhaps that is true. How else could lightweights like P.C. Subramanya, someone called Kapanna from the theatre scene and Keshavamurthy from some dance academy have managed to come together in an anti-Nrityagram campaign? They threatened to bring out a black-flag demonstration against Nrityagram for the benefit of the Prime Minister. When we heard about it, we were thrilled! A great theatrical scene was being rehearsed and we wanted to participate in it. We decided to make our own black flags and join them against ourselves. What fun. I was looking forward to it. Theatre! Real theatre!

Others scoffed and said those local artistes were showing their pettiness by protesting. They were frustrated and bitter. They were jealous. One should simply let them be, I was told.

I thought about their calling me an 'outsider'. If I was an outsider there, then where was I an insider? My father was from Haryana, but I had never lived there. My mother was from Bengal and I hadn't lived there either. I didn't speak either language. I'd lived in Maharashtra all my life, but I didn't feel Maharashtrian, didn't even speak the language (nor did I want to!). I was steeped in the odissi culture, but I was not Oriya. I was now living in Karnataka, and as far as I could tell then, I was there for good. I was even trying to learn the language. And now if I was considered a non-Kannadiga, where did I belong?

It should have been interesting for those protesters to consider a few obvious facts. I had ten acres of land on lease from the government. I did not own it. But I paid taxes and rent for it. The cost of that once-barren land couldn't have been anything more than a lakh, and I was putting up a three-crore-rupee project on it! I was bringing money from other outsiders into Karnataka, all for the benefit of the Kannadigas. Only the Kannadigas were profiting from my work!

Besides, the handful of people who kept culture alive didn't do that only for themselves. What they did was for the good of society as a whole. Song and dance and art can change the moral fibre of our society.

Well, coming back to the agitation, I was informed by friends as to who all had participated in the protest. On the day of the inauguration itself, many artistes phoned one by one, assuring me that they were not part of the anti-Nrityagram group. Some even came to the office in person to clear their names!

Eventually, nothing happened. Just like the time when we had had our festival at Ravindra Kalakshetra, Bangalore in June the previous year. Much noise and no action.

There were ridiculous reports in the press after the inauguration. It had been possible, they said, because Hegde and I were having an affair. I wish it was true. The man has such a sensuous quality about him. The glint in his eye makes everyone feel that they are special. It's a great quality. And I was single, I was free to interact, to relate with another human being. It should have been interesting.

Soon afterwards, people from the Sangeet Natak Akademi, led by Keshav Kothari and Girish Karnad, came for dinner. Now we had the cream of the cultural world at Nrityagram. We were hardly a year old, and everyone knew about us. Now we had only to produce the students. That was a job for the gurus to do. I had to go out there and get more donors and sponsors for the next phase of constructions.

O

We had chosen Gauri—the goddess Parvati—as the presiding deity for Nrityagram and installed her idol on a granite slab in the yoga centre, with our neighbour Raj Gopal officiating as the priest. I also changed my name to Protima Gauri. There was a very good reason for this. When I arrived in Hessaraghatta, the local people would snigger and smile each time I introduced myself. It was a while before I discovered the reason. 'In Kannada,' I was told, 'Bedi means loose motions.' I dropped the Bedi immediately; I had no desire to be known as Miss Diarrhoea. To the students and local residents, I became Gauri Amma.

I did wonder at what I was trying to do—reviving something as old and forgotten as the 'guru-shishya parampara'. But it seemed feasible. I was surrounded by the most lovely and lovable characters at Nrityagram, all of them extremely supportive. There was Nayar, the cook, with his wife and three daughters. The eldest, Jaya, a very sweet, innocent girl, had just completed her tenth and I had decided to give her training in sericulture and let her look after that unit. Saraswati was the major-general. She was a big, tough girl with a soft heart. She was in charge of supervising the labour and bringing milk in the morning and other odd jobs.

The youngest, Anita, was a full-time odissi student. She was a beauty, quiet, shy and dedicated. Her body was an extension of the fear that she had lived with for sixteen years—fear of her father's wrath. Nayar had a hot head. It took me two months to get Anita's body to relax. I was beginning to see dance movements and body exercises as therapy for the mind.

Then there was my favourite student, Uday Kumar Shetty, dedicated to dance and ready to do any job, and Shilpa, of the lovely face and long limbs, who came from a family of theatre people.

And Gerard da Cunha, the architect. What would my one year in the tent in such harsh circumstances have been without his energies? He was as driven as I was. Life was doing to him what it was doing to me. He too was restless, on the move at all times, feverishly working, working. Out there in the sun, with his straw hat, short pants and white shoes without socks, intense and passionate about his job, he looked like a Latin bandit at most times. 'I will not allow architecture to be second to dance,' he would say. The odissi gurukul was his statement. In the wilderness of Hessaraghatta, he had created a small paradise for me.

They were my big family. Sometimes I wondered whether I should perfect my new role by wearing a sari and tikka at all times and behaving like Rukmini Devi Arundale, being a sage and living an austere life. Would I be more successful if I did that? It was very tempting. Perhaps it might also add to the success of Nrityagram.

I had told Mario that once I began the project, I would change. I knew I could not remain the same, wanting the things I once wanted. I had known that my involvement would be absolute. Once I accepted the responsibility, I would not let go. I was free of Mario. My mind, body and soul did not belong to anyone. My need to love someone was taken care of by Dulo, my dog, and I spoiled him silly. He even slept with me and was fiercely possessive about my company, especially in bed.

At night, when the gurukul was quiet, with lightning flashing in every corner of the sky sometimes and strong cool breezes blowing, it was beautiful in my tent. It seemed insane that people should live in pucca structures. And people thought that I was making a great sacrifice by not building myself a house and roughing it out in a tent. I'd let them think that. I'd play the martyr. It was impressive.

There was a makeshift mosquito net hanging from the ceiling-frames of the tent, tied with my coloured hair ribbons with beads and pompoms. In the middle of the tent hung a large bedcover like a curtain, behind which I would change my clothes hurriedly. A broken mirror leant against a makeshift table of ceramic pots and leftover strips of polished granite. Four suitcases were lined up at one end. On a long horizontal rod hung my work clothes—three pairs of jeans, six T-shirts, two pajamas. On the dozen hooks dangling from the ceiling frames hung plastic bags full of socks, underwear, my bathrobe, and a myriad other things like working gloves, an orange hat with a flower and a shopping bag. Apart from these there were a collapsible table in a corner and two wooden chairs, one cassette player, one yellow bedside lamp and two light bulbs suspended with stiff plastic wires from the ceiling. That was all I had. It was a lot.

Alone, but for Dulo curled up beside me, I'd lie in my tent listening to Santana, smoking my cigarettes, enjoying the weather and being by myself.

A month after the inauguration I went to Bhubaneshwar to find an odissi teacher. My eyes were set on Kandori. I had already spoken to him when he had come to Nrityagram with Guruji's Odissi Research Centre troupe for the inauguration. He had been afraid to talk to me. What would Guruji say? They were all the same, the Oriya boys—no great ambitions, afraid to initiate anything, no confidence, no innovation. There was tremendous politics at ORC and everyone was wallowing in it. Kandori told me, most apologetically, that he couldn't come. He was due to get married in two months' time. He couldn't postpone it, it was a promise he had made his ailing mother. Of course I had to laugh when he said, 'I'm really feeling very bad for you!' Bad for me! The fool was kicking his destiny; *he* would be the loser.

Guruji had his own politics. He had always maintained that he could not trust anyone to teach odissi according to his discipline. Therefore, no one was good enough to be recommended. A year ago, he had insisted that between him and his son, Shibu, the odissi gurukul would be looked after. So Shibu came for three workshops of ten, seven and fifteen days each. I had to pay over Rs 3,000 for his accommodation and food. In the bargain, I had my car damaged and got hefty telephone bills. I told Guruji that I would have his son at Nrityagram only if he was prepared to stay full-time.

Guruji insisted that no one else was good enough to be sent.

He couldn't come personally and he would not allow any other guru to be invited! I said that in that case I would close down the odissi gurukul and start the kuchipudi gurukul, which was ready.

'No! That shouldn't happen,' he said.

'Then what am I supposed to do? I can't close it. You can't send someone. You won't come yourself and you won't allow others to come either!'

Finally, he said, 'Okay, go ask Ramani. See if he is willing to go, but tell him that he must teach according to my discipline. I will visit twice a month.'

That was smart of him. He knew that Ramani was a guru in his own right. Ramani would never agree to interference from Guruji. It was either Ramani's gurukul or Guruji's. Anyway, I went and spoke to Ramani. He was open to the idea, but we didn't fix anything definite. I went back to Guruji to tell him that Ramani had agreed. Guruji was furious!

'In which case, I have nothing to do with your institution. It's either him or me,' he fumed.

'But Guruji, you said you could not come.'

'Wait, I will see if any of my boys will go.'

And so, I met Vichitranand Swami at the house of Gangadhar Pradhan. He was teaching there. He was not as good as Kandori, but he didn't have a family, he'd been thrown out of ORC for indiscipline, was earning only Rs 300 and was dying to get on to bigger things. 'Please take me,' he said. I asked him to show me his dance. It wasn't very nice, but he said he was out of practice and breathless. His form was good, and he had studied under great gurus, so I said okay and went off to book his train ticket.

I arrived at Nrityagram, driving my red Maruti. As I approached, my mind cleared, my spirits soared, my heart sang and my face smiled. It was wonderful to be going back home. On the newly-tarred road, the girls were cycling off after their Saturday classes. 'Aunty, we missed you so much,' they said.

There were many cars coming out of Nrityagram. The entrance was full of people, some going in, some coming out, and the boys and the girls, from the poultry farm were doing hectic business with the brochures and the entrance fees.

I honked. They saw. They dropped everything and came running towards the car. 'Aunty, aunty, you're back. Look! We made 1,300 rupees! So many tourists are coming. We got 195 rupees from tea and coffee alone.' I laughed, happy just to be in their midst. My heart was full of joy. What else did one live for? So much love, so much affection. My own children were never as thrilled to see me. These were *my* people.

The previous week, we had been in the front pages of local newspapers. Some ministers had raised questions in the legislative assembly as to how and why the Karnataka government had given land to a dancer. Imagine! We were being discussed in the legislative assembly! But the euphoria had been shortlived. As the seriousness of the situation sank in, I began to worry. What if they made trouble? What if, after all the work, they made it impossible for me to continue on that land? Already so many buildings had been constructed! But was it worthwhile fighting with the government? The local people would have to fight for Nrityagram. I was not going to do it.

Suppose I had to leave for some reason—why should I be so upset? I had come here for a specific purpose. I had worked towards it. I had greened the land and put beautiful structures on it. I had brought in the students and teachers. The joy of the doing was all. I had to learn to let go.

'Uday, suppose things get bad, I will move over to my property nearby and pitch my tent under a tree and start all over again,' I had said. 'You people will have to go home. Or would you prefer to stay back at Nrityagram?'

'No, ma, we will go wherever you go,' Uday had said. 'If you go under the tree, I will go also. You teach me dance, under the tree. I will help to build another Nrityagram with my own hands.'

'Shilpa? Anita?' I had asked

'We will also come with you, aunty. We won't stay here.'

My heart soared. They were my people. In the face of such integrity, what was Nrityagram? A few buildings, some trees. We'd do it again.

Vichitra, the new odissi teacher, arrived. But I worried about him. He used to brood a lot and would repeatedly ask me if he could go back to Orissa for just a few days. He was homesick. I consoled him, scolded him, and instructed the students to draw him out of his shell.

And Nrityagram slowly took on another character. In our strife-ridden country, where language and state-borders had become such big issues, where Punjab and Kashmir were burning, Nrityagram had a small community of students from all parts of India, each speaking a different language but together for a common aim—dance. They understood body movement and rhythm, which was far bigger than the pettiness of chauvanistic people. There was Uday from the interiors of Karnataka, Yumiko from Japan, Anita Nayar from Kerala, Shilpa from Punjab, Surupa Sen from Bengal and Vichitra from Orissa. A new boy was due from Tamil Nadu, and a girl from Andhra who only spoke Telugu. But we all got along and enjoyed ourselves.

Uday was at that time the bright spark of the community. Nothing daunted him. He was always ready with his jokes and his silly remarks, full of good humour and sincere effort. He reminded me in those early days of myself. I wanted to help him become a name in the dance world.

I felt complete when I sat in my tent writing and thinking and heard in the background the sound of the stick on wood, beating out the basic exercise rhythms of the dance. This was what I had dreamt of. It had come to pass. I was happy. It was the blessing of the gods, their design.

The students had their first performance on 24 August 1990. It was Gauri and Ganesh puja day. We danced for the inauguration of Shankar Nag's country club. All the girls had beautiful odissi costumes. Everyone praised their performance. Vichitra and I did a duet, in which I allowed him to take centre-stage. I didn't want to do full programmes by myself. I found it very boring. I'd been centre-stage for too long, I wanted to see others there.

In the evening, we immersed the idol of Ganpati in the water tank. It was a subdued group of five students, and Usha, Radhakrishna, Vichitra, Gerard and me. We were all tired. Somehow we did the puja, lifted the idols and sang 'Ganpati Bappa Morya'.

Suddenly, at the tank, an electric charge passed through the group. The bell pealed louder and the pakhawaj got a better, louder beat. Radhakrishna and I broke into a dance, lifted the statues over the steps and circled the tank. Uday took his shirt off and got into the tank. We sang and chanted while he went round the tank seven times with Ganpati on his head and then immersed the idol. In a prankish mood, he threw handfuls of water at me. I jumped into the tank in my white sari, white blouse and petticoat. Once I had jumped in, the others followed. Soon all of us were in. We held hands and danced, chanting and laughing. Vichitra was in his element, diving, doing head stands, letting the students dunk him seven times in the water. We were amazed at his playfulness. He had opened up suddenly. Yumiko was amazed and kept saying, 'But this is most unexpected and surprising. I could not imagine such a situation! This is most unexpected!'

Ganesha, the remover of obstacles, had removed one more obstacle. Vichitra had bloomed. These were all my children. I was responsible for them.

That night the moon was full. Close to midnight, I took the cassette player to the amphitheatre. I had my ghungroos on. Dulo followed me all over the stage. He was my only live audience. The mud felt good under my feet. I danced the arabhi and the Shankara pallavi. The stars, the clouds, the moon and the trees watched. Perhaps a few ghosts were watching too. The sound of ghungroos jingling in the night must have sounded eerie to those who could hear. Perhaps someone walking home late would see me and tell the villagers. They would think me crazy.

On my way back I picked up the empty breakfast bowl that had been lying on my work table since morning and put it away in the kitchen. I noticed a dead frog on the seating area, stuck to the seat. I scraped him off. He must have been lying there, dead, for days! What did all those people do all day long? Careless! Near the office, a young sapling was drooping. It needed support. I'd have that done in the morning. On Monday I had to look into the accounts for the week. I should send word to Chetan to pick up groceries and provisions from the city. Had I left a note for Usha to get a photocopy of the letter to Sweden? And the mandal pradhan had to be told about the man who had promised to send two tractor-loads of gobar—it had not arrived. Nor had the material for the fence.

And the money—where would it come from? How would I manage? Dear God, help me!

By September 1990, most of the students were dancing magnificently. I was very attached to the kids. If they went out of Nrityagram and stayed away too long without informing me, I became anxious and sick with worry. I had become a fussy old mother. When we were preparing for our performance at the Mysore Dassera festival celebrations, I was on edge. I was giving them a chance to dance with me in front of 3000 people! They were practicing day and night for it, and I was also terribly involved. Perhaps my tensions were proving bad for them. I would get impatient and shout at them, especially at Uday, who seemed to have lost his dedication to dance. He was not the eager, sweet-natured and hardworking boy anymore that he once was. My favourite student was fast becoming my biggest disappointment.

After lunch one afternoon, as I sat on my soft bed in the tent, Uday came, crestfallen, hesitant and awkward. He fell at my feet, held on to them with both his hands and wept copious tears, his body shaking and trembling.

'Ma, you have been so angry with me, shouting at me, in class, outside class. What is my fault? Why cannot I do anything right?' he sobbed.

It was just as well that he didn't look up then, as my eyes were filled with tears and my soft, weak chin was trembling with emotion. When I had composed myself, I spoke with great concern for him. 'What's troubling your mind? Are you tired? Are you unhappy? Do you want to get married?'

He just shook his head and kept clutching my feet. We sat there like that for a long time, till his heart-breaking sobs died down. 'So this is how it feels to be a guru!' I thought. 'The shishya at my feet. Shit! I've placed myself so perfectly in this role. I actually fit beautifully!' I stroked Uday's head maternally (another deviation from normal feelings!), lifted him up gently by the shoulders and spoke with great warmth and brought back resolve into his life. Later I marvelled at how well I had played the part. It was very easy to take oneself seriously in that place.

A few days later, a wonderful discovery! The expert from the horticultural institute came to check out his banana saplings at Nrityagram. I insisted that he inspect the roses behind my tent. He did. He also saw a plant which startled him. Where had I got that, he asked. I said it had always been there. He suspected it was cannabis. I was thrilled to hear that. He took a sample and went away. I stripped the top leaves, dried them in the sun for a few days and hoped like mad that the doctor was right. When I met him again, he broke my heart. 'It's not cannabis. But it is a distant cousin. It's not potent, quite harmless,' he said. He seemed relieved. I stared long and hard at the pretty leaves in the golden sunset, willing them to be a closer relation of the 'real thing'. Undaunted, I decided to roll the dried leaves and have a smoke anyway. It was such an exciting thing to do. And I thought, here I am, The Guru, gleefully rolling my joint and having a smoke. What a pity the students wouldn't enjoy the sight. They were bound to one image of me.

Things were getting too serious. I refurbished my tent to bring some fantasy into my life. My tent became something straight out of Arabian Nights. It was not my taste but I had decided to be playful. I enjoyed playing the princess. I only needed a eunuch at my door, a big, black, flabby beauty.

O

Despite my disappointment with Uday, I continued to harbour my vision of Nrityagram as an idyllic dance village peopled with idealistic, hardworking, extremely talented and dedicated young dancers. I wanted girls with a dream in their hearts and the courage to go through fire to achieve their objective of being great dancers. I found the ideal dancer in Surupa Sen. She had come to Nrityagram in 1990, a petite, frightened, intense, nondescript twenty-year-old. But soon it was clear that she was a born leader. She was brutally honest, worked herself to exhaustion and insisted that the others in the group follow her example. She simply took charge, like the army officer's daughter that she is. Her integrity and diligence had a very positive effect on the other girls. Their skill and commitment made me forget every problem.

I took the students to a prestigious dance festival in Trivandrum. They danced magnificently, even though it was hot enough to make one swoon and on stage they had 10,000-watt lights focused on them. The critics were ecstatic about their group performance. People oohed and aahed at their lecture demonstrations because their bodies were so fit and they were doing incredible things.

After the Trivandrum performance, we visited Kalamandalam,

the famous school of Kathakali. Its founder, Vallathol, was one of the greatest Kathakali artistes. He had built a small, beautiful house on the banks of a river. He started with two boys who lived with him as his students. By the time he died, his house had become an immortal institution. The government ran it now. They had shifted the school from its original place to a site next to a busy road. The construction was all concrete. There was no spirit there. I insisted on going to the original place. It was very neat and tidy. They'd converted it into a museum! No one stayed there. On one side was the samadhi of Vallathol—also in concrete.

I felt a great sadness descend on me. Was that the end of one's dream? I thought of my very own Nrityagram. I had to save it from such a fate! What would I like after my death? I would like to be burned in the amphitheatre and my ashes to be placed at the foot of the banyan tree facing the yoga centre and the main gate. No plaques, no memorials. And I would nominate one of the students to be in-charge of Nrityagram. It could never go to the government! They might convert it into a hotel! And probably have a disco where the present dance-hall was. Though that also sounded like fun, actually. What did it matter what happened to one's projects after one was gone? We are all busy with some thing or the other in life, passing time. Timepass, what else? You are here, you have to pass time. Up to you how you want to do it!

shaping nrityagram

Nrityagram won the 'best rural architecture' award. Gerard got Rs 25,000. We got fame worth more. But it did not change much: the mohiniattam gurukul had to be constructed, and I had no funds, no sponsors. I decided to start the construction anyway. Help arrived at almost the last moment, when BPL agreed to sponsor the gurukul.

On the whole, though, we were going through a very bad time financially. We were in debt to the banks. Every month I had to earn enough money to support both the gurukuls. Even the smallest of donations did not happen automatically. I always had to ask. It was a thankless and tough job. They would all say: 'What a wonderful job you have done. Keep it up.' But they didn't pull out their wallets and say, 'Here's a small contribution towards the great work you are doing.' I was now depending on the foreign students to pay something and keep the gurukuls going for a few more months. But Guruji, the star attraction, would often not show up for workshops. He would promise to come, and I would set up many meetings and organize all kinds of things to make good use of his presence at Nrityagram, but he would let me down.

I did pujas, hoping for miracles. Once it even worked. Two pundits did a puja for four hours, cleansing and purifying the atmosphere. They put all the negative energies into a huge pumpkin and broke it viciously at the entrance to Nrityagram. Within ten days I would see the difference, they said. All obstacles would melt away. The next day I collected a cheque for Rs 3,00,000 from ITC!

For the sake of Nrityagram, I was forced to start building a tourist resort, Kuteeram, directly opposite Nrityagram. It was to have ten cottages and a restaurant for high-profile foreign tourists. Work started in 1992 and I was in terror, thinking of the huge loan from the Karnataka Finance Corporation to the tune of one crore. Never in my life had I done business and I was mortified thinking of what I had undertaken. But then, I knew that I couldn't keep begging all my life for Nrityagram. Kuteeram was my effort to become self-sufficient.

All the tension of looking for donors and administering a place with so many different people was taking a toll on me. My health suffered. It was a strange feeling to have students sleeping in my bed every night. They took turns: Yumiko, Anita, Surupa, Sushama and Shilpa. They did not want to leave me alone, just in case I had a spasm or my heart stopped functioning. I was only forty-three and hardly a candidate for cardiac problems, yet something was certainly not all right. I had shooting pains in my chest sometimes, and sometimes a dull ache in the heart area. My left arm felt heavy and numb and there was a tremendous feeling of tiredness all day long. But it seemed ridiculous to me that I should have such problems. I was as strong as an ox. I had worked day and night to build Nrityagram in just a year's time. Hard work never killed anyone. It was the mind that did it.

It was age! The new lines on the face, the small aches and

pains, the inability to carry two twenty-five-kilo suitcases without it being a major effort. One could, perhaps, shrug it off. But when the emotions within changed, one couldn't close one's eyes to it. I used to love having sex. I used to enjoy looking and feeling sexy and getting attention. It used to occupy most of my time. But now it had been relegated to the 'no-time-for-it' section. For more than two years I'd had neither the time nor the inclination for a physical relationship. And it simply did not matter anymore. It was wonderfully liberating. I welcomed old age.

O

It was easier to do physical labour than to administer a campus full of young people. The problems they had just growing up!

Kalyani Kutty Amma (who taught at the mohiniattam gurukul) came into my tent early one morning (thank God there wasn't a man in my bed!) and said she was worried about Sushama, her granddaughter and a senior student at Nrityagram. She thought that Sushama's parents would get her married off to someone in Cochin and that would be the end of her dance. Besides, Sushama wanted to marry Uday. 'What shall I do?' she said and wept.

'Simple,' I said, 'let Sushama decide.'

'Sushama has decided. She will marry only Uday. After six years, when his training is over, he will be in charge of the odissi gurukul and Sushama in charge of mohiniattam. It will be very nice,' said Amma. I felt like shaking her by the shoulders and putting some sense into her head. Nothing was idyllic. Uday was a very promising dancer and I had been very fond of him in the beginning. But gradually all his faults were becoming apparent. I could not ignore the fact that he was, essentially, a small-minded village rooster. He would make an overbearing husband, I told Amma. He had already promised Shilpa that he would marry her, and the poor girl had had to pay an awful price for having trusted him. He definitely could become a wonderful dancer, but only if he worked very hard. Instead, he was wasting his time gossipping and playing dirty politics. 'It would be good for Nrityagram to have two senior students marry,' I told Amma. 'But personally, for Sushama, I didn't think she should marry Uday.'

Amma cried, 'But what will happen to her dance? Please tell me what I should do.'

'Do? Why should *you* do anything? Isn't it Sushama's decision? Let her decide. She will know in her heart the right thing to do. Allow her to make her own mistakes in life, please.'

Then she took off on Yumiko. 'Yumiko is doing some mantra, I know. She is doing very bad things. I saw her going early morning to the city one day to do mantras. See my neck, my back—look, so many boils. Even Sushama is having them. You please stop Yumiko from going to the city. And she is sleeping with boys there!'

I was truly exasperated. What could one say to all this? And Amma couldn't even hear properly! 'Please, Amma, stop all this talk. How can you believe such things? And if Yumiko is sleeping with boys, isn't that her business? I am not stopping anyone from doing what they want. They are grown up.'

It was Amma who had encouraged Sushama and Uday in the first place, putting ideas in their heads. But only a couple of months later she changed her mind about Uday, and he became a villain. It was all a messy affair.

Eventually the two did get married. But Uday, on whom I depended a lot to help me run Nrityagram, was beginning to lose his dedication to dance. Sushama's behaviour also changed. The atmosphere had been vitiated, and Amma, whom we had considered ourselves so fortunate to have, left Nrityagram. She wished me the best, she said, but she had lost the enthusiasm to create a great mohiniattam gurukul. We all respected her, but her attitude, I knew, was very bad for Nrityagram. It had to be a place free of narrow-mindedness, a place which was open and free and where there was no gossip and politicking.

Also, some teachers beat their students too much. How could these kids take their role as gurus so seriously? They didn't seem to know the difference between discipline and oppression. Uday's attitude was the worst in this respect. He was totally out of control after the marriage and played dirty politics. The students were in a state of revolt against Uday, and eventually I had to ask him to leave Nrityagram. Sushama chose to leave with him.

And I had thought that I could concentrate on getting money and let Shibu or Uday handle the day-to-day functioning of Nrityagram! Now there was little hope that I'd be free of the burden of Nrityagram. Perhaps the real artists, the gurus, should run the place, I thought. Each guru in charge of a gurukul. Could it work? Would the gurus understand this logic? I felt that my job would be more than done once funds for the gurukuls were ensured.

Collecting funds had to be my priority. The students had to be promoted. Their lodging and boarding for performances had to be covered by Nrityagram. The weekend students, who walked five to six kilometers to attend classes, needed dinner, breakfast, lunch and tea. I didn't have the heart to tell them that they couldn't stay because I couldn't afford to feed them. But each expense meant that the cost went up. The electricity bills were phenomenal. The office and transportation bills were killing. There was money needed for our annual Vasantahabba music and dance festivals, too. I had tried just about every corporate house, but I was still begging. Yet, when I saw the kids dance, and with so much dedication and joy, I felt I could work twice as hard for them.

I also looked abroad for money, and after much effort there was success. Even before I started work on the kathak gurukul, INLAKS agreed to sponsor it. There was magic in this gurukul, because soon we also found the ideal guru for it in Kumudini Lakhia.

o

Guru Kelucharan had told me that he considered Nrityagram to be his home. I had dedicated Nrityagram to my guru, and the odissi gurukul was built for him. He used to come there every three months and stay for a while. But that was all the time he had. He was a busy man, of course, and it was impossible to hold him to one place. It was also not fair to expect too much of him. He had commitments at the Odissi Research Centre for another year, in addition to a whole lot of foreign tours and workshops. That was the reason—he said—why he had sent his son Shibu to Nrityagram to look after his gurukul. I was impressed with Shibu's teaching in the beginning. He was a strict teacher—a little too strict, I felt—but he seemed to get results.

As it turned out, my experience with Shibu was an extremely unhappy one. Had it been a question of discomfort or unpleasantness only between the two of us, things would not have reached the state they did. But everybody at Nrityagram and many artistes outside had problems with him as well. I suppose no one trusted him—I certainly did not, and I had good reasons for it. Unfortunately, he also became the reason for misunderstanding and discord between Guruji and me.

The problem at Nrityagram was this: I had a wonderful dream of reviving the guru-shishya parampara in the right kind of environment. I worked extremely hard to make it all happen. However I forgot one very important aspect. These were modern times. The world had moved on. The students were educated, liberal-minded, and they expected things to be logical and wanted reason and respect. They would refuse to follow anyone blindly just because he or she was a guru and had the advantage of age and authority. They had come to Nrityagram on their own steam. Most of them were grown-up girls who made their own decisions—they wanted to learn classical dance and were prepared to spend six years of their young lives at a remote ashram learning and perfecting it. It would have been ideal if Guru Kelucharan Mahapatra had actually lived at Nrityagram full-time. I had built the odissi gurukul on his assurance that he would be responsible for it. However, he had chosen to send his son, as his heir to the odissi throne.

When one has worked tirelessly for ages to achieve respect and recognition, it is one thing. But it is an altogether different thing when a position of power comes to one easily, with no real effort on one's part. It makes one arrogant, oppressive and unreasonable—in short, a dictator. Students will take that from a 'real' guru whose genius and dedication to nurturing talent is obvious. But no one will take that kind of nonsense from a two-bit youngster whose only claim to anything is being the son of a great man.

This a disease in our country. Merit does not count. No one hears of any male students of Guruji. Most of them are gurus in their own right, but no one may make a name for himself in odissi. Yet no one dared to speak out. They all muttered under their breath and continued teaching. The sceptre was to be handed to the offspring. He would be groomed to take over. And he was totally undeserving.

The entire odissi student group and the mohiniattam girls complained en masse about the system. Two of my wonderful students had already left, disgusted with the guru-shishya parampara. I had to open my eyes to reality. It was not an easy decision for me to take this problem to the trustees and discuss the future of the guru-shishya parampara and whether the system ought to be thrust upon the students or discarded or modified. There were many valuable aspects of the guru-shishya parampara which if modified to suit the modern times could be more effective than the old tradition. I spoke to the gurus about the modifications. What if Nrityagram became a centre for workshops? We could open ourselves out to every single nuance and idea in odissi and other dance forms by inviting different gurus every month or two to conduct workshops and teach new compositions. They all had the same style, but each had coloured it with his or her own personality. Suppose the students, who had their basics firmly in place, were given a chance to see and assimilate everything which was aesthetic, which suited their individual personalities? Should there not be more awareness, openness and interaction between different 'gharanas'? Was it not ridiculous to expect a guru to give moral, spiritual and intellectual direction, when the student was perhaps more aware and educated than the guru?

Was this not the age of specialization? Wouldn't it be more meaningful if the student could learn dance from a dance guru, the theory and history of dance and mythology from a theoretician, poetry from a poet and yoga from a yoga expert? Everything had to grow and change. But it was not going to be easy to get Shibu to leave so that we could institute this system.

I would have been content if Kelubabu had lived at Nrityagram even for brief spells of time. But he was firm in his blind belief that if we did not have his son as guru, it would be a personal affront to him. He told me that if I brought in any other teacher to replace his son, he would have nothing to do with Nrityagram! So I was damned if I did, and damned if I didn't. I couldn't have the son, or rather wouldn't have him—the students were quite categorical that they would not live with him and his woman, Sujata Mohanty—and I couldn't ask another teacher, not even a student of Kelubabu, to take his place. This to me was sheer exploitation.

I was taking the odissi students to USA on a dance tour in 1993. I was without a male dancer, so I went personally to Bhubaneshwar to ask Guruji whether I could take any of his students with me. I have him on record saying that if any student of his went to USA with me in place of his son, he would not touch him in future. It was outright blackmail.

I spoke to senior artistes at the Odissi Research Centre and to Sanjukta Panigrahi about the situation. They sympathized, for they all had their own stories of having had a rough time because of Guruji's son. But we were all helpless, as Guruji was completely blind to the faults of his son. Where was the way out of this mess? Should I simply defy my guru and invite other odissi gurus to visit Nrityagram? My Guru hadn't left me much choice, had he? Also, since the guru-shishya parampara was not conducive to our times, how should the learning process take place? What were the alternatives? Nrityagram had its plans in place for the next year. We had fixed workshops in odissi, mohiniattam, theatre, music and the martial dance arts by Kalanidhi Narayan, Sanjukta Panigrahi, Bharat Shivaji and Mandakini Trivedi, among others. The students were all enthused about this. What was the way ahead now?

None of us at Nrityagram respected Shibu as a guru. We only put up with him because he had been foisted on us as a guru by Kelubabu. He began spreading the most malicious and filthy stories about me and the girls. Nrityagram was no place for decent people to send their children to, he said. Some of his malicious stories were even published by some magazines.

Guruji was hurt and angry by reports in the press accusing Shibu of financial irregularities at Nrityagram. He thought it was my doing. I wrote to him explaining that it was Shibu himself who had been going around telling people that I had framed him. I had spoken to no one.

But after all this, I had to throw Shibu out of Nrityagram, especially since his behaviour as a guru had become dictatorial. He might have turned out to be a good teacher, but I was more interested in having a good human being.

It had pained me greatly to have forcibly evicted my own guru's son from Nrityagram. But there was only so much I could put up with out of respect for my guru.

I then went through a very difficult period in my relationship with Guruji. I had been his most devoted student for eighteen years, but now he had disowned me because of a son whom he himself knew to be not the best of men.

After the incident, Guruji refused to set foot in Nrityagram. When I went with the students to his house, he did not want to face us. He quickly disappeared from home. What kind of respect were the young girls going to have for a guru who played such games with his students, a guru who was frightened to meet his students who came only to seek his blessings? He would always be my Guruji and I would always love and respect him. I didn't want him to fall in my eyes by choosing wrong and being unjust.

The Shibu affair and Guruji's dealings with Nrityagram also brought to the fore the incredible amount of politics in the dance world. It troubled me that something as divine as our arts should have such a polluted atmosphere. How could the beauty of the arts survive? No one was willing to confront Guru Kelucharan Mahapatra about what they thought was wrong and unjust. How long could we keep muttering behind his back and allow injustice to carry on?

Some dancers like Sanjukta Panigrahi were upset that I had mentioned their names to Guruji as those who had grievances against him and his son. Why didn't they see what I was hoping to achieve? I had a vision where dance was the centre of people's lives, where the divinity of dance would make people good and decent and gentle. How could I close my eyes to the hypocrisy, the cowardice and the politics that had become part and parcel of the dance world? How could I tell the young dancers of tomorrow great things about dance, about its spiritual quality, when I was a part of all that crap?

I had believed that the guru-shishya parampara was a great thing worth preserving and was willing to give up everything which was comfortable in my life to achieve this. I even gave up my own dance for the sake of the younger generation. It was a horrible thing then to have to face such a bad situation with my own guru. It took a lot of courage for me to challenge him. At the risk of Nrityagram closing down, I took it upon myself to make Guruji see the sense of it all. He had to stop being so blind in his love for his son and undermining a noble tradition. Nrityagram almost did close down after that. I had to work very hard to revive it.

I was quite prepared to close Nrityagram, go back to Bombay and leave behind a shattered dream, but I was certainly not prepared to compromise on my principles. I stood firm and let Shibu and Guruji say what they wanted about me. But certain events made me write to Guruji in a very strong way which certainly did hurt him and Guruma. But I knew that Guruji would someday realize the truth. I had full faith in him.

Besides, I had done what I had to. I had no great future in dance to protect. Nor did I feel that odissi would die if Guruji did not teach at Nrityagram. Odissi had been around for centuries and would continue to remain on this planet for a long time to come. It was time to grow out of the shadow of the guru if he was not prepared to give shade.

In many ways, whatever had happened had turned out to be for the best—it made it possible for Nrityagram to have really dynamic teachers: Kumudini Lakhia for kathak, Ranjabati Sircar for creative dance, Kalanidhi Narayanan for abhinaya and Balaji for martial arts and yoga. None of this would have happened if the guru-shishya parampara had been functioning as it was meant to.

O

Murphy's law: If the worst is to happen, it will, and it will choose the worst possible time to do so. My mother had had a major cancer operation. I was with her at Breach Candy Hospital for a whole month, nursing her, and during this time the problems at Nrityagram got worse. There was a nasty campaign launched against me. The *Pioneer* published a half-page report on Nrityagram and me, which was the most vicious and vindictive attack I had ever faced in my colourful life.

Guruji's unhappiness, too, weighed on my mind. I worried constantly about his health. So many times I wanted to phone him, just to hear his voice, but my courage failed me. I knew his anger. But I also knew that he did not carry his anger with him for ever. I had to wait for the bad time to pass. I was certain that he would never find another student like me; I would continue to be his Hanuman all my life.

And to add to it all was the stress of my relationship with Mario which refused to die quietly. It had dragged on for too long already. Even before the Nrityagram project started, the relationship had deteriorated. I had told him that he still meant a lot to me, but nowhere near as much as he used to. After Nrityagram, of course, I had no need for men and romance; there was no room for another passion. I often wished he would just go away to Europe, get out of my life. But I didn't want him to go unhappy, so I left the door open a little.

He, of course, consistently blamed Nrityagram for the shabby condition of our relationship. He never quite saw that it was he who had let me down. Though for that, perhaps, I was the one to blame—I hadn't been sufficiently outraged when I found out that he had tried to get 'funny' with Pooja. He kept making me feel miserable by saying how hurt he was, how unreasonable and selfish I was being.

I had to be brutally honest with him. If it was a question of fault, I wrote to him, I accepted all the faults. Yes, I was to blame, if that was the way he wanted it. What difference did it make to me? 'I became disinterested in your company,' I wrote, 'as I found something more exciting to delve into. This village became my whole life, the students became my family and I feel complete with this new love. I don't need a partner anymore. I can make it on my own. Sounds callous, but isn't this what all of us are doing all the time?' Some months later, I made things even clearer to him: 'The relationship is simply not working. You've tried, I've tried . . . I accept that everything is my fault. It doesn't matter anymore who's to blame. I've lost the will to make it work. I just don't care anymore. Had it not been for my sense of guilt, the relationship would have been over long, long ago. Guilt is a horrible reason to be with someone.'

Mario's response was bitter and brutal:

Dear Protima,

My writing lately does not make for merry reading, it's best kept in the drawer. Love lost is bad; but happens to a great many people—music and literature are thriving on it.

However, the way you explained to me on the occasion of your previous phone call that you had been in love with me because you had nothing else to do—well that carried a special message. I am a prime asshole for having gotten myself to where I am. I am an equally prime asshole for having believed that you and our relationship were the only things of value in my life.

Some wake up at age fifty. Generally, I am OK. Sleep does not come easily though, and is often troubled. Let me share a dream that drove me out of bed last night in a cold sweat. I noted it down.

November Dream, 4 a.m.:

Radiant Kish [Protima] *running towards me, laughing, at Fisherman's Cove. Runs into my arms. I kiss her under her wet hair, on salty lips, and she turns into a giant cockroach dancing on the sand and masturbating, cackling away—'Timepass, timepass!'*

Modi [Mario's new girlfriend] *and Caroline point their fingers at me and chant: 'Told you so, told you so—fool, fool, now marry her!'*

Kabir unwinds a long sky-blue turban and quietly smiles: 'See, pighead, you haven't mastered the art of telling her what she wants to hear, that's your problem. Go away, play in the sand.'

I am OK, really.

It was turning out to be another messy break up, too emotional and full of hurt, like what had happened with Pandit Jasraj. When I heard that Mario had found a Parsi girlfriend, I thought he'd be out of my life for good. But according to him he was having the affair only because it helped to take away the pain I had caused him.

There were times later when I missed Mario, wanted to tell him that I was sorry. I even imagined us looking after Kuteeram resorts together. By then, of course, he had married the Parsi girl.

O

When I took my students to USA on the dance tour in 1993, I had huge problems getting the funds for it. The Indian Council for Cultural Relations gave us the air tickets, but I had almost no money for internal travelling in USA and for the board and lodging for seven people. Wherever possible we stayed with organizers and friends, and despite this we just about managed to break even, which was disappointing, since the idea of the dance tour was to be able to raise some money to support the work I was doing at Nrityagram.

Otherwise, though, it was a very successful tour. In fact the group was so good that we were invited for twenty performances in 1995. The best part was the chance I got to work with Bijayani Satpathy, a student of Guru Gangadhar Pradhan, who had come to our rescue, with her guru's consent, after Guru Kelucharan had refused to let me have any of his students. Bijayani had joined the Nrityagram tour of USA despite many people in Orissa having advised and even warned her against associating with us.

She turned out to be the perfect choice, as she was straightforward, non-gossipy, decent and a very responsible person. The whole group loved her. After the tour she decided to become a part of our performing group ensemble. Ganga bhai had taught her well. I was convinced that if she remained serious about her dance, she could make a very great name for herself. Nrityagram was fortunate to have her.

I returned from USA to unpleasant newspaper reports about Nrityagram. My remarks about the guru-shishya parampara had been printed out of context. I was upset by how my words had been twisted in a manner that implied disrespect to my guru. I could never betray or speak ill of my guru. I did not have good relations with his family, and he was being unfair to me after the Shibu episode, but I could never stop respecting him.

On the following Guru Purnima day I called Bijayani's father in Bhubaneshwar—because Guruji's phone was out of order—and pleaded with him to take an offering of fruits, flowers and coconuts to Guruji's house on our behalf. Poor Mr Satpathy did what we asked of him but Guruji turned him away saying that he was not our guru and would not accept anything from Nrityagram! The students were angry with me as this was the third time Guruji had insulted me. But I couldn't harden my heart towards him. That Guru Purnima day I did his puja and danced especially for him and wept helplessly. For some reason, then, I missed my mother badly. She had spent two weeks with me at Nrityagram and only a week after she returned to Bombay she had died. At least she had given me an opportunity to serve her with love in her last days. Only a mother could truly, really care, no matter what. I felt orphaned. I had lost my mother. I did not want to lose my guru. I waited for him to change his attitude towards me.

Meanwhile, I was becoming extremely respectable. I was invited to become a senior associate at the Indian Institute of Science, Bangalore by the great scientist Dr Raja Ramanna. It was a huge honour. At the same time, prestigious scientific institutions all over the country were inviting me to give lecture-demonstrations and talks on the origin, history, and philosophy of classical dance. I was also appointed on the board of the expert committee for odissi, Department of Culture! I didn't know what to do with all that respect. And what did it do for Nrityagram? In terms of money, virtually nothing. I had applied to the government for salary and construction grants, but got nothing. The state government had not forwarded the papers to the Centre. When I asked the officials about it, they said, 'Because if we recommend the project, then we are asked to fund the project from state money.'

I didn't have the resources to employ a secretary or an accountant and other such people that an organization needs. I did it all by myself. And I was not a business person, so I goofed whenever some interest was shown in my project. I never could figure out how much to ask for and how to present things to business people.

By the time the 1994 Vasantahabba festival came up, I had exhausted my resources completely. Just eighteen days before the event, AT & T, who were going to sponsor the festival, sent a fax saying that they couldn't do it. Pepsi and Coke were of no help either. East West had agreed to be the official carriers, but suddenly changed their minds. So we approached Damania, and they too agreed at first, then backed out. I had never experienced such bad luck.

However, the ultimate optimist, I went ahead with the plan to have the festival for one night only. It was sad that one negative article (in the *Pioneer*) written by a very biased reporter had given people reason to stop supporting a prestigious cultural event. We couldn't afford not to have the Vasantahabba festival that year. The Chief Minister of Karnataka and some Union ministers had all confirmed that they would attend, and we had already spent a lot of money. I was determined to have the festival to make it a huge success. Of course, Nrityagram would be broke after that.

I was tired, very tired of going on and on and on . . . begging, begging and begging. It seemed to me that I had forgotten how to deal straight, to simply pay the price for a thing instead of asking for concessions. I hated what was happening to me. I wanted to be able to look at people just for themselves and not for what I could get from them. There was a limit to how much I could beg and I had reached it. I was not prepared to bash my head over a dream that no one wanted to support anymore. The stress of keeping Nrityagram afloat was almost killing me. There was no more joy left in doing the work I was doing and I often felt that I should simply get up and walk away. It was not difficult for me to return to Bombay and reclaim my cushy existence and my place in the celebrity circuit. At least I had tried. I could give it up with a clear conscience.

I felt bogged down. When would I ever be able to stop all that work and get down to real, creative things, the things I loved and was good at? The office work and fund-raising was draining the joy from my soul and I was afraid of turning ordinary, of losing the spirit within me, of becoming serious about life, of not knowing beauty, love and laughter. I was beginning to wonder whether I had done the right thing in getting so completely involved with this massive Frankenstein that I had created. Sometimes I felt like running into the sunset, screaming, tearing my hair out, and disappearing forever. It would have made a good visual too!

I did not want my faith in life to be undermined. I could not imagine myself as broken, disillusioned and a loser. I did not want to think of money for a year or two.

I had given so much of me to so many people, personally and professionally. Now I wanted 'me' only for myself. I was truly enjoying 'me' very much. I would go for long walks, meditate, work quietly, read, write, and smile a lot. I was sure the phase would pass, but till then I intended to forget everything and reconnect with myself.

There were also family matters to be attended to. Pooja was getting married on 6 May 1994. Her father had absolved himself of all financial responsibilities, which left me to handle everything, as usual. I did my best to see that she had a decent ceremony. I had already missed her engagement because I was on tour in the States at the time. I needed to make up for it. I liked the man she had chosen, Farhan Ebrahim. She deserved happiness and peace. I hadn't been able to relate to my mother, understand her soul. I couldn't afford to have my daughter feel that way about me. I wanted to spend more time with her.

I also wanted to be with my son, Siddharth, whom I was having a difficult time with. He was in Bangalore with me for a while, on holiday from studies in USA, and he was clearly unwell. He would be bright and sunny for days and then suddenly the blackest of clouds would descend and his behaviour would become erratic. I would wake up some nights to find him crying in bed. It broke my heart. I took him to doctors and therapists, and was relieved when they told me that it was probably nothing worse than plain depression. But some of his letters and phone calls from the States after he returned continued to worry me.

Guru Kelucharan Mahapatra had taken to feeding lies to the press. He gave silly reasons for leaving Nrityagram, said that I had accused him of having sexual leanings towards his students. It infuriated me. Why was he doing this? There was a limit to how much bullshit I could take, but I decided not to open my mouth. I could speak to the press too about all kinds of things, but what would the muck-raking achieve? I had enough worries. Soon I would see an ancient woman in the mirror and wonder where I'd been so long? With the full-time responsibilities and worries of Nrityagram, there had been no time for my personal life. I had no home to call my own. I'd also stopped my dance practice and neglected my dance career.

I wanted Nrityagram to be able to run without me. The students had received wonderful reviews during their second tour of USA in 1995. Sheldon Doffer, a very prestigious agent who had also promoted Ravi Shankar at one time, had agreed to become our impresario. Surupa Sen, who had blossomed incredibly and was to me the most perfect, the most complete dancer, had been officially nominated director of the odissi gurukul, which meant that all decisions pertaining to the odissi group would be made by her. She shared my dream and had the guts and the good sense to keep it alive. Lynne Fernandez, our light director, had decided to simply leave Delhi and stay with us doing a whole lot of office work and teaching the girls stagecraft. Financially there was still no answer, but I had always believed that Nrityagram had a life of its own. It would survive. I could let go.

I wanted peace, no more fame and respect and money. I needed very little for myself. I needed change. I went on a pilgrimage to Tirupati and shaved my head.

my flesh and blood

In 1971 I was in the monastery at Rumtek with Ooggee. I was pregnant with Siddharth. I had said to the Karmapa that I wanted a son.

'Then you will have to give him to the monastery,' the Karmapa had said.

'How can I?' I had protested. 'If he wants to, fine, but . . .'

The Karmapa had laughed. 'Try and stop a lama from being one,' he had said to me.

So I had always felt that Siddharth was different. He did all the normal things as a kid, but there was a marked difference. Kids normally lose their sensitivity as they grow older, but his only increased.

In 1996 he was in Bombay. His condition had worsened—the spells of depression that I had first noticed two years ago were much more acute and frequent now and his behaviour was completely unpredictable. He was clearly unhappy, and I was tortured by his unhappiness. I worried about him, but he refused to see me. Kabir and I supported him long distance with money and with the assurance that we were there should he need us.

If I called, Siddharth would say that I was suffocating him with my need for him. He wanted to be left alone. He did not want to be loved by me, he would say; I should set him free. He was pushing me away and out of his life, but my heart told me that in fact he really wanted me to force my affections on him. I had decided to go to Bombay after the Vasantahabba festival and simply be with him at home, no matter what he said and did.

He wanted to return to America, which I thought was not right at the time. But I could not stop him. He went to Canada. It was there that he was diagnosed as suffering from schizophrenia.

Perhaps it was all my fault. I had often felt guilty about not having spent more time with the children. I had wept many times, thinking about Pooja and Siddharth. I would sit and think of what I'd feel if I was on my deathbed. Would I wish that I had loved them more? I could have done so much for them when they were babies which I didn't do. Wasted moments. If only . . . I could have been more caring, more sensitive, more this and more that. And always the old excuses came rushing up—I was too young, too inexperienced, caught up in my own desires and needs.

I loved them both so dearly, and I felt so helpless that I couldn't go back to the past and love them more. Siddharth was unhappy and ill now, and Pooja carried within her so much destructive anger caused by my lack of caring. They would deny it, of course, but I didn't want them to. Anyway, it was too late to change all that, I couldn't repair the past. But that did not mean that I couldn't feel remorse. I could learn from my past and do justice to my present.

'I don't deserve all the care, the love you bestow on me all the time,' I had written to Pooja in one of my letters. 'You give me far too much. You make me feel so guilty, taking such care of me when I didn't do half as much as I could have done.'

I was grateful to Farhan for keeping my daughter happy, and she too had put a huge amount of effort and understanding into her marriage. Siddharth troubled me. Why was he pushing me away? I knew I had to be with him.

O

Motherhood has been the most important aspect of my life. I was happiest when Pooja and Siddharth were little and I spent time playing with them, teaching them the alphabet in the sand on the beach, doing crazy things like mock picnics on the roof of my car. People said that I made the best mother. I didn't merely teach my children, I was constantly learning from them and their unconditioned attitudes to life. I believe a woman is incomplete if she hasn't been a mother. If I became a beautiful person—from within and without—it was all because of my home and my children. I was a hard, bitchy woman without them, but motherhood made me soft and mellow.

At Nrityagram, I was the mother again. Throughout my life I have created and nurtured many relationships. When my creations have appeared self-sufficient, capable of looking after themselves, I have moved on to other things, found someone or something else to 'mother', thereby increasing the number of people and things that I always feel responsible for. Yet, the rewards are unimaginable. What will they ever know, those who do not possess this gift of 'motherhood'? Like jumping into the ocean with one's whole body, one flings oneself one hundred per cent into motherhood. One simply can't help it. One swims or sinks with the love that flows from every pore of one's being. It is a gift of the gods.

When I was busy with Nrityagram, Pooja was a film star and Siddharth a computer wizard in USA. Both were self-sufficient.

I had brought them up to be that way—to be independent and eccentric, for that is the only way to be. And yet, I was 'on call' all the time. Their joys and sorrows affected me doubly—I felt deeply for that part of them which would always be 'me', and because I loved them, I felt for them on their behalf as well. 'When you're happy, I'm happier,' I would say to them.

I tried to be mother, father and God to them when they were growing up. And we didn't leave anything unsaid between us. When my son was six and my daughter eight, I told them the facts of life. They knew everything. I told them about their bodies and about sex, using all the relevant Indian symbolisms—the yoni, the lingum—and it was not at all difficult. When my son had his first erection at a very small age, I knew about it. He used to play with it and say, 'Look, look, look, how it goes up,' and Pooja and I would sit there and watch it and say excitedly, 'Oooh, wonderful, we can't do that!' We never felt shy about things like that.

When Pooja had her periods, I told her about what could happen. 'I'm not saying that sex is good or that it is bad or when you should have it—that's left to you,' I said. 'I just want you to know under what conditions sex is best. But be careful because the result is that you could get pregnant, and then what do you do? It's very romantic to think of having a baby, but remember that it is a whole new responsibility and maybe at fifteen you are not quite ready for it.' And I explained to her all about the pill.

I was constantly encouraging Pooja and Siddharth to go out there and just 'do it'. I supported them fully, in every wild caper till they were four and six years old—visiting a haunted house at midnight, bunking school (favourite pastime), starting a kite-flying business on the beach or a library in the lawns, kissing cops so they wouldn't penalize us for traffic violations . . .

I tried to be my children's anchor, as much a friend as a parent. I tried to do my best.

In the conventional sense, I was not an ideal mother to the

children, the kind who keeps home, cooks and is always around. There have been times when I was sure that many of their problems, especially Pooja's emotional problems as a teenager, were due to my not having spent enough time with them.

Pooja was a lot like me as a young girl. She was quite a little toughie as a young girl—you couldn't bully her, you couldn't put her down. She was indomitable. And she was adamant about doing things her way. She had to have her own answers. So I let her put her fingers into the plug point and get an electric shock. Thereafter, she never did that again. I let her light up and take a few puffs of Papa's cigarettes. She almost choked to death. She was then two years old. She never smoked again.

A minor electric shock or a choking fit cause momentary pain. Unfortunately, emotional and psychological shocks are more difficult to deal with. Pooja has had a few strong 'jolts', but she has emerged from them strong and still indomitable. There is a lot of me in her, though she never sees it—the same stubbornness, the same independence and confidence, the same brutal honesty, the same preference for personal values over established social values.

Pooja had a terrific anger when she was younger, and sometimes she took contrary positions. We went through many strange storms, especially after Mario came into my life. But they were to me petty, idiotic things. We could and we did rise above them.

I never interfered with whatever plans the kids had for themselves, even if I didn't think they were the right plans. I did not want Pooja to be a film actress, but if that was her decision, I respected it and supported her. When she was offered the controversial advertisement for Kamasutra condoms, she was a little unsure and asked me for advice. I told her that I saw no reason why she shouldn't do it. She was being paid a fantastic amount of money, and as far as I was concerned, everyone needed to have an awareness of condoms. If advertisements for cigarettes and liquor and meaningless things like fancy frocks and little cars were okay, why should there be a problem promoting something as important and central to our lives as condoms, especially in the post-AIDS scenario? I told Pooja that as a responsible model and human being, she should promote the use of condoms. 'Will I be known as the Condom Girl?' she asked. 'I guess you will,' I said, 'but you make your decision. Why bother about what people will say?'

After that advertisement the spotlight was constantly on Pooja. There was a lot of unfavourable publicity, but that did not surprise me. It was only to be expected. Society always has problems with anyone who combines courage and curiosity with a strong belief in oneself. Pooja continued to do well professionally as a film and stage actress, as a model, and later as a designer of bedroom accessories.

In 1993, a television company produced a wonderful programme on Nrityagram. Talking about me in the programme, the presenter said that Pooja Bedi was not to be mentioned in my new life, that I blew up whenever anybody mentioned her name. Pooja was a part of my indulgent past, they reported, and I wanted to forget all about it. I had no idea where they had got that from. I was furious when I saw the programme. I called Delhi and fired the producer. He said that one of the students had said it, but they all denied it. It was an unnecessary complication. If I was Pooja, I would have been hurt. But then, I knew that she would let it pass, and she did. I had let her down many times in the past. The incident brought back the old guilt. I couldn't erase the pain of the past, but I was determined to make her the happiest daughter any mother could have. I hoped she could find the grace to understand and forgive me for the mistakes I had made. There were so many things—how I chose to believe Mario and not her, how I mutely allowed Aditya Pancholi to walk in and out of the house when I was there without beating him up for the way he treated her . . . I was completely ashamed of myself.

I missed her engagement to Farhan because I was touring USA with my students at the time, but I made up for it during their wedding. I liked the man she was marrying and his family. Pooja had to convert to Islam for the marriage, and that wasn't pleasant, but as I told her, life was about sharing and for that a few compromises were necessary. Many good people were conservative in their attitudes, one had to respect their feelings. Respect was a very important virtue to have. As a close friend of mine had remarked to me: 'So what's so special about being a liberal? Your broad-minded husband left you and your two kids in a highly insensitive way and re-married not once but twice, without any thought or respect for his wife's feelings! What's the point of being a liberal when you cannot make the world a better place for the ones you care for?'

Sometimes I missed Pooja's company and resented the fact that she never made any effort to come and spend time with me. I did not doubt that she loved me, but why didn't she ever feel like simply being with me? And when she did come, we would hug and kiss and proclaim our love for each other but something was always missing. And again I would feel that it must be my fault.

When she was pregnant and wanted me to be with her, I spent a whole month with her in Bombay. She would give me an opportunity to hold an infant once again in my arms! I was grateful for that.

O

I remember a strange and disturbing dream I had about Siddharth when he was very young, which I have later wondered about a lot. I had the dream shortly after returning from Mahabaleshwar with Pooja, Siddharth and two other children, Rahul and Sonu. We were all tense because we had seen the body of a child killed by a truck lying in the middle of a road. In the dream that night I saw my car very vividly, and I remember every detail as if it is happening before me at this very moment. I am driving, the four children with me. The car crashes into a boulder on a mountainside, and with the impact starts rolling backwards, off the road. I quickly get out of the car and my first thought is to save Rahul and Sonu, for they are not my children. I pull them out through the front window and just about manage to grab Pooja's dress and yank her out before the rear wheels go off the edge of the mountain road and the car keels over. I can see Siddharth, sitting on the far side of the back seat. I see his face clearly. He looks betrayed. And as I look at him helplessly, the car plunges into the ravine.

Many cars stop and many people gather around. I have eyes only for the tiny body lying on a large flat stone thousands of feet below me. I scramble amidst falling rocks, slipping and sliding down the mountainside, and reach Siddharth. I look at his dead face. I stop suddenly just as I am about to touch his body and I control myself. I sit cross-legged, close my eyes and start tuning into his soul. I see him, a little frightened being clinging on to me, not understanding what has happened to him. I tell him that he is dead and cannot be with me any longer in this world. He whimpers, saying that he won't leave me. I try to calm him and start explaining about his journey after physical death and how he must go through it without any fear. He still won't leave and so I tell him that if he really wants to be with me, he must be brave and follow instructions carefully, then on the fortieth day I would give him a chance to be reborn as my child. He seems to get strength of purpose from that and I feel his soul departing. I keep chanting mantras, trying to guide him and give him strength.

After being in continuous touch with Siddharth's soul for thirty-nine days, I remember that I have only one day left in which I must conceive. I break my connection with Siddharth's soul and rush out to the houses of some of my men friends. I tell them that I must have a baby and therefore they must have sex with me. They look at me strangely, as though I have gone mad. No man will have me. Hadn't they all lusted after me just a few days ago? They would have left their wives and children for me. And now here I was offering myself and they didn't want me. 'It's not for myself and my pleasure!' I tell them. 'I must conceive today.' But no one wants me.

I realize that without the special look in the eyes and the whole come-on trip, no one gets turned on. I have to resort to the old ways of seduction to get what I want. I apply my make-up and wear my sexiest clothes. I drive to Centaur Hotel and at the Rotisserie I see a foreigner sitting alone at a table opposite me. I start my seduction routine. All through the small talk, the laughter, the wine and the food my tension builds up because time is running out. All I can think of is Siddharth. I finally get the man to my house and have sex with him. He tries to be loving towards me afterwards, but I speak harshly to him and send him away. I want to be alone with my son's soul.

My stomach starts getting bigger and I know that Siddharth has been successful in his trip. I talk to him continuously all through the nine months of pregnancy. It's now time to deliver and I am in the labour room. Siddharth is born and the moment he comes out, he starts speaking to me, telling me of the wonders and the hazards of the journey. The doctors and the nurses step back, aghast. A psychiatrist is summoned and they declare that my child ought to be put away in the psychiatric ward. To me none of this matters, for all I want is Siddharth and I am happy to be with him wherever it might be.

I tell him that it was my love for him that gave him the strength to complete the arduous journey. On hearing this, he gives me a horrible and strange look. He stares at me with venom in his eyes and says, 'You are the most self-centred woman alive. You are so bloody immersed in yourself, so much in love with yourself that you've blinded yourself to the world. How you pretend to be good and pure, to the extent that even you believe it to be true! Don't give me this shit! You did all this only for yourself. *You needed me, and not I, you.* You brainwashed me to go through the Bardo. "Come to me, come to me, come to me," you carried on, wishing me, pulling me back into this life. Don't think you've done me any favour—coming here and being your son is a regression for me. Had you not selfishly called me back, I would have gone higher and higher and found my nirvana!' So saying he walks out of my life.

My body convulses involuntarily. Shocked, I open my eyes. I stare out at the sea for a long, long time.

Was it a warning notice? Was it a flash, a glimpse of the future? Was it just another story in my head? The dream left me feeling very uneasy.

As a little boy Siddharth was extremely sensitive and gentle and very attached to me. When I first sent Pooja and him to boarding school, he was unhappy because he only wanted to be with me.

One day we read in the papers about a terrible plane crash. An Air-India Jumbo had crashed into the sea and all aboard had died. Siddharth was deeply concerned. He kept thinking and talking about the crash.

'But they could have just jumped out with their parachutes, no?' he said. I told him that there had been no time for that.

'But when the plane crashed, they could have just opened the windows and started swimming quickly.' There was no time for that either, I said. After going through all the possible ways in which the people in the plane could have saved themselves, when he realized that there really had been no chance of their surviving, he asked, 'But does it hurt?'

I realized that he was taking the episode personally, identifying with the crash victims and feeling their agony and pain. I told him that there probably wouldn't have been time for them even to feel any pain. Death must have been instantaneous.

He listened attentively. I saw a far-off look in his eyes. He asked no more questions that day. The next day he questioned me about the *Tibetan Book of the Dead*.

'What do those people do with the dead bodies, those who have not read the *Dead Book*?' I told him that people had their own particular customs and prayers for their dead.

'But which is the best one?'

I told him that the Tibetan way was the most convincing. I had already explained to him about the different phases of the journey after death. To make it lighter, I now laughed and said to him that he should not allow anybody to cry over my body when I died, for it would be hard for my soul. I was charging him with personally guiding my soul on its journey through the seven planes.

Two weeks later, I was flying to Goa to shoot for a Thums-Up ad. It was early morning and I was packing. Siddharth ran into my room, very concerned, sat on the bed, watching me pack, and anxiously asked what would happen if my plane crashed. I said that I would die.

'Don't go, Caco,' he said. I explained that when the call of death came, I could be sitting talking to him and the roof would fall on my head, killing me instantly. Hundreds of planes flew every day and only one crashed sometimes, I said, just like a car accident. Did it mean that I should stop driving?

'Suppose your plane crashes, how will we know that it has happened?' he then asked.

Guli and Shakti uncle and Leela would know of it immediately from the airline office and they would inform him, I said.

'But how will we get your body?' I asked him why he was interested in my body and he said that it was necessary to sit near my body in order to recite the prayers from the *Tibetan Book of the Dead*.

'Oh! Don't worry, they will fish out my body from the sea and hand it over to you.'

I was amused and touched by his concern for his duty and his love for me. I continued packing, and a few minutes later he asked, 'Caco, what's this word? How do you say it?'

He was holding a small version of the *Tibetan Book of the Dead.*

'Tri-kaya,' I said, looking in the book, 'it means the three bodies.'

'It is written that the book must be buried with the body, so every one should have their own book. So if we bury this book with your body, then who will buy books for us?' he said. I told him that he could buy one for himself when he grew up. And if my plane did not crash, which was more than possible, then I would buy one for him. In any case, I did not think that there was too much need for him to start reading the book immediately.

'No, Caco, I am only looking for difficult words which I can't understand. Otherwise how can I read it nicely for you?'

Just then Pooja rushed in, and standing in front of my open cupboard, looking at all my clothes, she asked sweetly, 'Caco, when you die, can I have all your clothes and jewels?' I laughed and told them both that I wasn't going to die, I'd be back as soon as the ad was done.

Siddharth continued to be very attached to me till he left for USA to study computers. He wrote to me regularly. He was a wonderful boy. There wasn't a single person among those we knew both in India and USA who didn't sing his praises. Pooja had problems adjusting to the new conditions in America, to Kabir and his wife, but Siddharth adjusted himself to the situation very well. Though for him it must have been more difficult. Kabir hadn't let the Fred Kinzel episode influence his attitude towards Siddharth, but he had still never felt naturally loving towards his son. It was Pooja who was the apple of his eye.

I was proud of Siddharth's brilliant record in college, and he had his priorities worked out clearly. He wanted to do well as a professional—'I'll be a good manager,' he wrote once, 'I can sense that I'd be a good "goat-herder"—but was worried that he might get caught up in the corporate world and find himself 'chained to my executive seat in a suit and tie'. He didn't want to suddenly wake up when he was forty-five and realize that he'd been living a lie. He really didn't care about making millions. As long as he could do something he enjoyed, could live comfortably, and as long as he was surrounded by wonderful people, he said, he'd be happy. And he was quite certain that his happiness lay in India, not in America.

When he turned twenty, he wrote: 'I'm now a strapping twenty-year-old youth. Ugh! Life is going by too quickly. Sometimes I wonder if I'm making the most of it. I guess I'm filling my head with knowledge which is good for my profession and will help me earn a living anywhere in the world. This knowledge will make my "timepass" more enjoyable. At least it'll add some jazz, mirch-masala and curiosity to my years of "timepass". Good concept this "timepass"—it exonerates you of any guilt you might feel for not doing anything truly "meaningful" in your life.'

His resolution that year, he wrote, was 'not to look at myself in the mirror as much as I do. It's a disease. Of course now and then I can't control the urge to stare at my handsome self. God, vanity runs in the family!'

He often wrote about death and dying. Writing to me about how secure he felt knowing that if everything should go wrong in his life he always had his parents to turn to, he added, 'Maybe that's the hardest part of your parents dying (there I go with that death thing again). The realization that you don't have that kind of security anymore and that you are the one that people are going to run to and depend on when they're down and out. Well, Deek, ya know my home (wherever it's going to be) will always be wide open, so if you find yourself down in the dumps and life is giving ya a bum deal, ya can always come and stay with me. I don't care what my wife thinks about mother-in-law living with us.'

When he thought he was in love, he wrote to me about it, asking for advice on 'the ways of women, relationships and the rest of the hodge-podge'. He was dating an English girl in college, a little older than him. He'd had three relationships already ('Amy—22, Chinese American, quiet, too timid for me; Cynthia—36, outgoing, raunchy, American, too old for me; Christie—22, manic depressive, on lithium, made a few jokes about chopping my head off with a butcher's knife') and this one seemed perfect. But she was afraid of getting too close because he was shifting to the University of North Carolina soon.

He wanted badly to fall in love. 'I've reached a final conclusion about myself. I'm a hopeless romantic. No matter how much you might talk about the untactful ways in which I put things, I'm a complete sucker for dim lights, slow music, and a long wet kiss. I'm not much of a sweet-talk person though.' He would enquire about my romantic life. When I told him that I did not need anybody, that I was content lying under the stars at Nrityagram, reading a book and listening to music, he warned me to watch out—'Don't you ever get lonely, Deekoo? And I don't mean lust, I mean the desire for a constant companion to hug and squeeze and maybe tickle.'

But even in such letters sometimes he'd reflect on death: 'My good friend George's father died a week ago . . . Boy, life really gives you the upper-cut sometimes. It's strange to think that just about all of us have to go through it someday. Just like you have to go through Nani's death, I will have to go through your death and Pa's. I know you feel I'm preoccupied with death sometimes but it's really amazing how fragile life is. One wrong step here, I could be dead. Pa, you, or Booie could die tomorrow. Absolutely nothing stopping it. I'm not sure how I'd react if anything like that happened. I think I'd take it pretty well. But still Deek . . .

I'd miss you guys a whole bunch were anything to happen. Family is just such a great thing to have.'

In mid-1992, he moved from Pittsburgh to North Carolina and took up a summer job. He and a couple of friends had found a place of their own on rent, got themselves a car and tried hard to impress the pretty girls who were their neighbours. He was enjoying his job, the freedom of it. He still missed India but didn't dislike America or feel alienated, in fact he was quite tuned into what was going on in that country. The presidential elections were happening that year and he liked Clinton. If he had to cast in his lot, he said, it would be for Clinton. 'He admits to having smoked marijuana, he appears on TV playing the saxophone, and has also admitted to cheating on his wife. Finally an honest candidate!'

Pooja visited him around this time and he wrote to me that 'she seems to be slowly calming down'. Pooja and he were close, but very different temperamentally. He liked the fact that she was more in control now because it made his interactions with her easier for him. 'I don't know if being a calm person is a good thing or a bad thing,' he wrote. 'When I talk about calmness I'm referring to a certain quality about someone. Some people have a "calmness of the soul" about them, a deep-seated maturity. Booie throws calmness to the winds. There are always major earthquakes happening in her soul. She quietens down for a little while and just when you think it's safe to touch her, she'll come up with a little aftershock, a shudder. I'm not saying that these earthquakes and shudders are bad, they might be completely good-natured shrieks, but they're still shudders. She's completely capricious, unpredictable. When I approach her, it's with the same gait as a person going to pet a dog that he's not sure about. Is it tame, will it growl, will it bite his hand off? But from what I see, she's slowly but surely calming down.'

When he came to India for his holidays, he'd stay in Bombay or Bangalore and visit me at Nrityagram. He was perfectly normal then. He would keep talking of coming back. On one occasion he wondered if it would be a good idea for him to live in Kuteeram with me, commuting to work in Bangalore from there, and helping me finance the building of the resort with what he earned. My tight financial situation concerned him. In one letter he wrote, 'In a few years, I'll be working at a job. If ya ever, ever need moolah, just you ask! I know you've got that whole pride thing, but please try to get over that. If I have moolah lying around it's yours. If I don't, I'll tell you, it's that simple. I would never start resenting you or anything like that, my head and my thinking are much too simple and straightforward for any of those twisted complications.'

It worried me sometimes that he thought so much about his future professional career. His anxieties about ending up hopelessly caught up in the corporate world and about not being able to return to India had suddenly become quite frequent.

In August 1992 I wrote to him about this.

Dear, dear, Shone,

You just do what's good for you. Do what you FEEL you want to do. Don't get cerebral about it. You've got the best of both worlds in your parents. Pa's good head-sense and Ma's good, time-tested heart-sense. A sort of midway between the two sounds ideal.

Go with the flow, don't always think of India = house = happy. Just enjoy yourself, Shonoo boy. Be American, be a mongoose, be a stupid boy, be Indian, be anything, it don't matter.

But over the next two years his worries and anxieties got worse. In his letters and phone calls I sensed his confusion. He had even started talking of going to the monastery in Sikkim. He was depressed and totally at sea now. There were times when he even refused to speak to me on the phone. It was too sudden. I did not understand it. In January 1994, I wrote him a long letter about how I saw his condition.

Dear Shone Boy,

The Karmapa had said to me, a long time ago, 'Try and stop a lama from being one,' when I had protested to him that I couldn't give you to the monastery and intended to bring you up in a normal way. You have never really been normal. You did all the usual things like any kid, yet . . . there was a marked difference. You did them in a very special way and instead of losing your sensitivity as kids normally do as they get older, yours increased. I think the time is up for you to get away from yourself in a deep sort of way. You have to get back in touch with yourself, find out who you really are and what it is that you are here to do.

You may remember you have said to all of us on many occasions, 'So, I'll get a job, I'll do well in the corporate world, and then I will marry and have kids and then retire, it's all so done. So I knew that like Siddhartha the seed of discontent had been sown in your mind and you were looking for answers that were not of this world. You have to come on those answers yourself and not have someone else tell them to you. The journey is very painful and takes a lot of courage and patience. I have to give you this hint as I can't bear to see you suffer.

You may be an incarnate lama but for me you will always be my sweet sensitive little boy. I see no reason why a lama in today's world cannot be a professional person earning his own keep and living with worldly possessions. But then again, that world is so utterly different, the perspectives of this world and that are diametrically opposite, and I wonder whether it is not just my pipe dream. My terrifying dream comes back to me about you being 'killed' in the car accident and me going into a deep frenzy to get you back and doing the craziest things to keep you with me, until you at the end of it all said, 'If it weren't for you, imagine which world I would have been part of! You have dragged me back to this wretchedness whereas I could have been with the gods!' Do you remember me telling you about this dream? Every time you said to me, 'I have to take the key from under your pillow,' I trembled. I knew what it was that you had to get away from and get to, and I was never going to stop you. I said, 'I am throwing the key at you but you don't want it.' Well, it is here right now. The key is to the door to your inner self tucked away amidst terrific confusion and noise in the material world.

Strange things are said and remembered and they all have a bearing somehow. Right from the time you were a kid, I had constantly said, 'Hey guys, just know that there will always be a roof over your heads and food to eat. That much I promise you. Be anyone, anything you want to be. It's not important that you earn money. Be a philosopher, a poet, a loafer, a thinker, anything.' Booie feels very close to me today because she remembers these words. Think of them objectively, like reading them in a book. There is deep meaning in them. The freedom was given to you a long time ago. A secure future was being provided so that when you went through the storms of becoming, you wouldn't have these superfluous insecurities getting in your way. The whole stage was set up long, long ago.

It's not my business to tell you how to go about (finding yourself), simply because I don't know and I don't want to bullshit to sound smart. It's also not my business to try and channel you in a particular way because Life knows its job and does not need me to orchestrate or supervise. I happen to be your mother, a person who has been fortunate enough to get a chance to nurture you and love you. That's all I have to do. I may point out a way but it is not my business to see that you take it. Life has shown me that it knows best. And funnily enough, when the going gets real bad is when all the great and the good changes happen. This is in retrospect, of course. Though even if you are aware of this beforehand, it does not stop you from feeling the pain and the searing aloneness. So, as a mother I can only stand here and watch and pray that you don't suffer too much and can fight all the demons in your way and come out victorious. I can only be here and give you love and care whenever you need it from me. That you have. UNCONDITIONALLY. ALWAYS.

The best thing for you right now would be a break from your studies.

The world has woken up around me and my deep connection with you starts to get interrupted. So many sleeping giants and monsters and terrifying doors to open! But eventually it is always all right. That's the relief! And in any case, IT'S ONLY LIFE!

You know that I love you. Perhaps no one can ever love you as deeply as I do, as there are too many connections between us, unknown.

Loves you,

Kish

A couple of months later Siddharth came to India. He was suffering from major mood shifts and spells of depression and his behaviour was very erratic. He complained constantly of a buzzing in his ears. I was with him, driving him every other day to the doctor for treatment of a sinus infection. It seemed to be working at first. He felt better but not completely okay. The infection apparently had been around so long that it would take a few more courses of antibiotics.

Meanwhile Siddharth was being exceedingly crabby and nasty to me, which I guessed was the only release he had available to him. I would cook him soup and spaghetti, make salads and nurse him. I was available for his every passing whim and fancy, like being woken up at 2.30 a.m. to talk to him because he couldn't sleep, and thereafter playing carrom till 4 a.m. so he could beat me at the game and feel good about something.

Over the next two months he assumed top priority in my life as his condition didn't seem to improve. I took him to neurologists, determined to get to the bottom of his illness and relieve him of his problem. He would cry with great racking sobs in bed late at night and I would wake up to hear him pretending that it was just a stuffed nose and a bad cough. My heart broke watching him so miserable. I had not been able to do a shred of office work for Nrityagram for three months. But all of that could wait for the well-being of my son.

Kabir said he'd pay all the medical bills under his insurance and I thought how easy it was to simply fork out the money (which in turn would be repaid by insurance agencies) instead of changing your life to make yourself available full-time for your children with no thought of self and work-security.

After all the tests had been done, it was a relief to find that there was nothing physically wrong with Siddharth. It could be clinical depression, at worst, and Siddharth had decided to check that out at NIMHANS (The National Institute for Mental Health and Neuro Sciences, Bangalore) on his own.

Back in USA, he started seeing a therapist. I did not want him to become completely dependent on therapists. It was more important that he help himself. He had given me a copy of a book called *The Road Less Travelled* which he said he was influenced by greatly and which he wanted me to read. The book irritated me. It was definitely not the kind of book he should have been reading, given his state of mind. I gave him the reasons in a long letter.

Dear Shone,

Just finished reading The Road Less Travelled. The lesser travelled the better. In sheer disgust I wanted to put down the book a couple of times but carried on regardless to inform myself on what you were impressed by. Books have a way of insidiously transforming thought patterns. They can make you agree with them if you are of the same mind and they can make you think anew too. Some books play on the basic insecurities that all human beings grow up with—and most grow out of as they grow up. These sort of books are dangerous and use emotional hang-ups to make a point.

It is an outright, insidious Christian book. I know you are going to wince at that statement but for those who are not taken in by the man's cleverness it is very easy to see this. All missionaries use the same tactics to convert people. They first debunk or brush aside all reference to God. Then they appeal to you with their sensitivity to your problems. You get hooked to them and invest trust in them and then Whammo! comes the real message. This time I was lucky that I partially read his second book first and saw it to be exactly what it was.

Next I read his first book and I see his maneouvres and his sly and dirty methods of earning trust.

Every child is fearful of being abandoned. Every child believes that he is not loved as much as he would like to be, every child believes that his parents have no time for him. Every child doubts his capabilities and fears the future. Every child needs reassurance that he is OKAY. These hang-ups usually drop off somewhere along the way of GROWING UP.

Writers like Mr Scott Peck—or whatever his name is—cleverly use the innocent mind of the adolescent, his childhood fears, his traumas and his weaknesses. And the youngster thinks, 'This man really understands and knows. This man knows what suffering is all about. I am not alone in this world . . .' and he actually starts to believe that he has a problem and needs psychotherapy or God. Bullshit.

All your fears, your worries are normal ones. You do not need someone fooling around with your head. The more you get into psychology/psychoanalysis/therapy and all those mental gymnastics which do not allow you to ever see and experience things just as they are and instead put all kinds of meanings into everything, the more screwed up you get.

You should have been banned from reading all this a long time ago. I think you probably started getting good doses of all this too early in life. Lectures about perspectives and understanding from ME!

Life is NOT a serious business and Life is certainly NOT about suffering, nor is it difficult, as Mr Scott would have you think. It's one of the easiest things you could ask for. It's simple and uncomplicated and fun and remarkable. There's so much bounty and so much experience waiting to be had. You choose what you want or if you are lucky you just allow life to do its bit. It knows what it's all about and you need to concentrate on just letting go, which means investing in trust of some sort.

There is no good and there is no bad. Just human rules for human good as a whole. Nature has its own laws and some of us are lucky to have discovered this secret and gone with it.

Yes, we kept saying to you when you were a tot that you thought too much. I should have been able to transform that quality outwardly instead of allowing you to take it inwards. But then I was not knowledgeable at that time and did what I knew best. I too can see all the things that went wrong in my childhood according to me, which could have been avoided by the elders. But then, in the process of growing up one simply lets go of the bad memories and gets on with living and healing the wounds. Some of them keep hurting all one's life as and when you remember them.

I am sure that your anti-depressant pills will balance out your energy flow to being fifty per cent outside and fifty per cent inside. It should do the trick. You say that I do not know you as a person, that I am not informed of all that you have done and achieved and experienced in the past six years or so. Perhaps you are right. But I know your soul. I know the quality of the stuff that has gone into your foundation and nobody can know you better than that. The rest I will catch up on sometime sooner or later.

It's easy to think I am anti-Christian or anti-Muslim from all my remarks. But I am much too tuned into Nature to be anti something which is positive, constructive or harmonious. I am definitely anti anything which is restrictive and ugly and unhappy. There are many situations in both the religions which are anti-Life and I definitely am against those thoughts. Therefore I keep saying to you, Read the Gita. It is certainly one of the best positive manuals on trust in LIFE. Its perspectives are mind-boggling and it never gets down to petty levels of one against the other. There is no suffering and no sin and no difficulties and no Dukha.

Also, not all information is good for all people at all times. There is a time and an age for different things. Reading psychology and getting perspectives at a young age will screw up things. Having sex as a ten-year-old is meaningless and frightening. It ruins things for you.

If you are enjoying the sessions of therapy then treat it as an experience to go through. Perhaps it will help you see things and tidy up. However, if you have the strength of mind and the will to tidy up on your own, then nothing like it.

Perhaps Pa or I or Booie may not spend much time with you giving love and doing the things that show love, but if deep inside you know that we will always be there for you then it is proof enough that the right thing is being done. I may stand in the kitchen for hours cooking a meal for you, or drive around the city taking you to doctors or seeing that your clothes are washed and you are well fed, etc. But the times are such that you will not see all these things as a sign of love.

You would probably feel loved if one spent most of the day playing chess and scrabble with you, or going for long silent walks, or just being together doing small things. This is according to me your idea of love. It is also valid.

Shone boy, I am so pissed off with this Scott fellow. I know you were terribly impressed with his commiserations. Chirag and I had a long discussion on the book. He too said that it was an attractive trap and he thought it was next to God when he read it at the time he was depressed and he thought it was the real thing. And now he can see it for what it is—a foul Christian trap.

Soon Siddharth started saying plainly that he did not like receiving my phone calls. He wanted to be left alone, he said. By not letting him be, I was suffocating him. I was horribly depressed. I had no idea that my being the way I was caused him distress. But I could not change the way I was, I told him, and did not even feel the necessity to do so. I was a success in my work, with my friends and with my colleagues. I didn't think it was right for me to pretend that I was someone else just to make him feel comfortable. He would have to just accept me the way I was.

I wanted him to know that I would go out of my way to help him. I only wanted him to tell me how. I promised him that I wouldn't call, that whenever he felt that he could take some affection and love from me, he was welcome to call me and ask me to call him back. I would do that immediately. I wanted him to be happy and to somehow, anyhow know from deep inside that his mother loved him. There was no way I could prove this to him from such a distance except to tell it to him. I hoped it helped. If it didn't, I asked him to let me know and I would stop saying it.

Wanting to ensure that there should be no distance between us, and to put the bits and pieces he knew about me and his father and the circumstances of his birth in perspective, I wrote Siddharth a letter telling him everything about my affair with Fred Kinzel and the uncertainty for some years about who his father was. I wrote the letter because I thought that it would perhaps help him sort out some of the queries that occupied his mind.

I admitted to him that perhaps I had been uncaring and too self-centred. And I also told him how I admired Kabir for always loving him for who he was and not for his antecedents. Kabir had loved him, I wrote, in the best way he could with all his failings and shortcomings.

Everything I had, I wrote to Siddharth, was his and Pooja's. I had achieved a lot, much more than I had ever thought it possible for me to achieve, and now I had nowhere to go to, nothing to excel in, no name to make or preserve, no attachments which were greater to me than him or which demanded more time than what I wanted to give him.

I asked for his forgiveness. Even if I had made mistakes, was it very difficult for him to accept my love for him? Pooja had told me that he was going to Trivandrum. Couldn't he come and be with me for a while at Kuteeram or in Bombay? Couldn't he empty himself of the anger he felt against me for some reason? I was not his enemy.

Kabir was angry that I had written that letter to Siddharth, but I knew he had his own problems with that and let it be. I had done what I felt was right.

Siddharth did come to Bombay and was staying in my empty apartment. Pooja and I paid the rent and all his bills, paid for his transport in the city, for his food and the servants. He was nasty to both Pooja and me. He had categorically told me many a time that he had no desire to see me or to talk to me. But at least he accepted all the things we did for him.

He was seeing a therapist in the city, though he refused to divulge any information on that to any of us. He had been wanting to do yoga courses and asked me to find out all the details in various cities, which I did and which he thanked me for. He sat or lay around at home all day long, playing his guitar and listening to music or sleeping. I went through agony wondering how I could help.

I was in a dilemma. If I kept supporting him and he sat doing nothing, I thought, it might not be good for him in the future at all. But if I gave him a time limit and thereafter stopped supporting him, he could get worse, since it was clear that he could not get on in the real world! I went through a terrible time, until I realized that I had to do only that which made my heart feel happy. So I decided to support him till I could. Only he was responsible for not taking care of himself. I felt that I owed myself the feeling that I had done all that I possibly could . . . The rest I left to the Maker as only He knew the whys and the wherefores of things he had created. I could only pray now.

Pooja was a tremendous source of strength and joy to me through all this. I adored her. I was in constant touch with Bijoy (Siddharth's friend) as Siddharth called him regularly. Couldn't help it . . . I was a mother, I had to know. Bijoy said the same thing time and again to me: 'Let him go, leave him alone, it's not your responsibility. He'll be okay! He'll be okay, he'll be okay!' I also heard that Siddharth was desperate to do LSD and had been calling Bijoy to get him to do it together. Bijoy wasn't going to do it, but he had promised to be with Siddharth should he want to do the trip himself! It worried me no end. However, after I spoke to Kabir, I felt a bit better about leaving Siddharth alone to sort out his life.

I could understand what Kabir must have been feeling. I too was part of the sadness and could not escape the pain both for myself and on his behalf. It was a cruel and a terrible situation. It seemed the right time to practise my non-attachment—all the lessons of Vipassana as well as all that Ooggee had taught me. It felt good to detach.

I was hoping to do the same with Nrityagram. Perhaps, like my children, it too had grown up and needed to have its own life, to develop as it wanted to . . .

Siddharth's condition deteriorated. He was with me in Bangalore for three days and I tried my best to get help for him. He insisted he had to go back to America. It was very hard for me to let him go, but I had to. He went. Fifteen days later the Canadian police picked him up on the streets of Montreal and he was in the state hospital for days. They diagnosed his illness as schizophrenia. Kabir finally traced him and brought him to Los Angeles. He was admitted to the UCLA psychiatry ward.

I went crazy wondering what to do. The pain of being a mother! I needed help. I needed to know how I could help. He obviously had to be on medication every day, but he refused to accept that he needed it. He hated me and didn't trust me, so he wouldn't come to India to be taken care of by me. Kabir couldn't keep him at his house in Los Angeles as he disrupted Kabir's life with Nikki and would not agree to a contract about his medicines or therapy. I felt helpless. He was such a wonderful, beautiful person. How did it all go wrong? I was ready to go to USA and give him all my time and energy if it would help him. But he wouldn't have me near him. Why did he hate me?

I felt very stressed being needed by people around me and not being able to do anything. I looked for freedom and my own space, but events never turned out that way. I needed my solitude desperately. I needed to know that all was well with the people I loved.

Siddharth committed suicide in Los Angeles on 19 July 1997.

His suicide note read:

Well, this is it.

Please don't feel any 'guilt' at this. It's my way of taking control and opting out and, strange as it may seem, I'm going happy, not sad.

I did not get to explore the other side. If there is a rebirth, I hope I come back with the faculties to be a technical genius. The times that we live in are so exciting.

I'm sure there'll be some anger on your sides . . . but I hope it passes soon.

Booie, keep smiling . . . huska huska huska . . . good luck with the baby.

Mum, I love you the most of all . . . big kisses on your fat cheeks . . . please don't be angry.

Love to all.

Siddharth

Technicalities:

There's a check for $1,000 for death-related expenses.

I don't want to be buried in India—bury me here, cremate me here or cremate me in India but don't bury me in India. Something in my sensibility doesn't want my body to be lying in India.

Siddharth had gone away. And I could only weep. No one could take the pain away. The devastation I had suffered made me numb with pain. Why? Why? What for? Where were we all going, what was it all about? So many questions raged within. If only . . . I should have . . . I could have . . . and it went on and on. The guilt of not knowing my son—what made his heart beat faster, what his aims, his dreams were all about. How could I explain my feelings to anyone? I cried alone, I died every moment in flashback.

I carried my grief to the San Francisco mountains, to the Yuba river, where I went back to my original hippie self. I lived like a gypsy, close to nature, with the Indians who lived there with the legacy of their ancestors. The sun, the waters, the land rich with sentiment. Siddharth had brought me here.

Oh! I went through that sad journey of guilt at not having done more, done right, done best. There were only regrets. I cried with the sadness only a mother can know. Had I been such a negligent mother? Had I put too much energy into loving men, when I should have given it to my children? The guilt was immense. I had learnt not to be judgmental about people. Could I not apply the same to myself? What happened simply happened. Whether I did right or wrong hardly mattered. It just was. That was the way it was. We all had our experiences and were transformed. Nature looked after everything. Some died, some survived. But my mind came in the way of my peace. I could not run away from my mind.

How I had meditated every morning, forcing an image of Siddharth dancing, being happy, months before he died! Such positive thought and energy had not been successful. Perhaps, by going away, he had found the dance and the joy. I had to free myself from narrow, limited human thinking in material terms and let in the concept of limitless possibilities. He could never have been that happy person that I created in my mind, not in the body frame he was in. I had willed happiness on him. My positive energies had driven him out of his body, so his soul, his spirit could dance with the wind. 'God,' I prayed, 'if you are there, open up my mind and let me believe, let me see, let me experience his happiness. Let me not dwell on the sadness and sorrow. Let me just plain accept it all.'

Doing a Vipassana course months after Siddharth went away, on a day of silence I spotted a young man who looked exactly like Siddharth from behind. The same body, hair, walk. My heart suffered a slow, fierce crunch. Was that my Shone? How alive he was in my memory! He *had* to be alive, in the wind, the sunshine, the mountain, the fragrance of the flowers. He lived.

If I believed that I had been mountains, rivers, trees, fossils, animals and would continue to be, then the same applied to him. I shut my eyes at the sun and the wind caressed my eyelids. 'Shone, Shone, Shonoo boy, is that you? The gentle warmth of the sun on my cheeks, is that you? What was it that made you go away? What was your destiny, and what is it now? Every time I love, will it be you? Every time a happy thought, a happy feeling possesses me within, shall it be you? What is you? I yearn for your known form, unhappy as you were in it. Just to hold it, caress it, love it.'

Yet, when he was alive, I didn't fly into his arms, hold him to my breast and give him the love I carried within. Why, why? Do we all believe we are immortal and therefore neglect each other in form? Do we wait to become formless so we can love deeply? Does the form create an ego which creates a separation between beings? Is it the form that distances us from the Essence?

Sometimes I was close to ending my life. The despair was great. But I neither had the courage nor the conviction for such a deed. There was still some optimism—there would be greater things . . . I was resting my energies, or at least trying to do that. I would be a grandmother soon. I hoped with all my heart that the child and mother remained safe and normal. I had such a deep fear within me. Couldn't explain it.

sanyas

By 1996, I had begun to feel that I had to move on from Nrityagram to other things. Once I had got Kuteeram going and bringing in profits which would enable me to get a right price for it, I would sell it and move right out. I was determined to break all my bonds with earthly things and fly into the realm of finer and more satisfying experiences. I was tired of matters of property, of attachments to people and wanting something in return from them. I could not bear to think that I would have to remain enslaved to Kuteeram and Nrityagram till I had made enough money to pay off my debts, and then be free some day in the future to enjoy the fruits of all my labours. I wanted the time and the energy now, to read poetry, to teach dance, to watch sunsets, to reflect, to simply be . . . I wanted to move to higher planes and destinations and experience other things.

They were small desires, simple targets.

When I shaved my head at Tirupati, it was to begin a new life. I had given all my waking energies to the Nrityagram project, and yet there had been moments of great restlessness and loneliness. After Siddharth's illness and his death, the loneliness and the feeling of being at a loss in the kind of life I had been living became overwhelming. There was no joy of success or fame that could help me cope with it. I even thought of half-baked measures, impossible ones, of going back to Kabir, to Mario, to Jasraj!

I went on pilgrimages, sought peace and purpose in meditation and spirituality. I was disassociating myself from Nrityagram. Pooja said to me at one point, 'Why are you always running away? You ran away from your mother and father, you ran away from your husband, then you ran away from us, your children, and now you're running away from Nrityagram. Why?' I told her that her perspective was wrong. I was not running away from anything, I was always running towards something. My work at Nrityagram was over, it was running well. The Taj group had bought Kuteeram resorts on a lease, so there was no anxiety about money. The girls would manage Nrityagram.

Ambition, security, love, affection, care—they were all part of the great illusion. Eventually you died and left it all behind. All the things one craved for, one worked for, one slaved for . . . where was the point in them? All that mattered was the present. You were here and the world was here and everything was in the 'now', to be lived and enjoyed simply. Life was a great gift to have. What more could anyone want? What did life mean? You knew if you had lost someone you adored and loved. All you wanted was to bring that one person back to life, regardless of whether he would love you back or not, be of some use or none at all. You wanted only that he be alive, reclaim the gift of life.

I had to connect with life, with my inner self, and live simply. I did not want to think about how I looked, about what I had and what I needed. I wanted no mental activity.

o

All through those restless years I had overlooked and then underestimated another beautiful beginning happening right under my nose. It had started out in 1995 as an innocent fling, a passing attraction, but was growing into a deep bond. The man clung to every word I spoke, listening closely to each anecdote from my past. He came to know of my past lovers and my life with them—he saw my life through my eyes. He stood like a rock behind me through the most painful and difficult moments at Nrityagram—the troubles with Shibu and Uday, the break-up with my guru (the most traumatic event for both the students and for me), the many financial crises, the departure of trusted colleagues and friends like Balaji, Siddhu and John Devraj. He was there all along, on call, every minute, every day.

In our dance, we learn from poetry that when Krishna plays his flute, the gopis slip away from their homes, uncaring of their husbands, their in-laws and their society, for they cannot ignore a call from their beloved. This man, Harish Futnani, had prayed to all his gods and goddesses for years for me. In fact, he said I was a living incarnation of his Goddess, the fruit of all his meditation. He was totally and irrevocably committed to my happiness and well-being. It was his sacred duty to serve me.

For a while I was amused, then irritated, then angered. I tried every trick I knew to shake him off, to humiliate him, to hurt him . . . but he held his ground. I promised him nothing. I never swore that I loved him, never hinted at any future together. I had his company whenever I needed it, not the other way around. His brothers talked to him in vain and they approached me to do my bit in ending the whole thing because it caused great hurt to his wife, his mother, his entire family. I went away to Kottakkal in Kerala, feigning illness. The stay there would also help me get back in touch with myself, I felt, after all the worries of Nrityagram and Siddharth's (then) inexplicable illness. But there was no way I could get rid of him, no way his wife could make him forget me. His mother was deeply distressed and asked him whether he loved me so much that he would give up his wife and children for me, to which he answered, 'If I have to, I will.' I couldn't help admiring him for standing firm and refusing to let anyone bulldoze him on moral grounds. He said he was aware that he was in the wrong as far as the world was concerned. He didn't mind being thought badly of. He wanted to be happy without taking away the happiness of his family. If his wife's happiness depended on his being faithful to her, then it was she who had to re-think her idea of happiness and accept him for what he was willing to give her, which was everything that she had always had, except that he had now added an extra emotional happiness to his life. He was willing to let her walk out of his life, even though I had made no promises.

I was in the ashram at Kottakkal for over a month. I hoped to shake Harish off, though when I needed some company, I missed him. But I had decided that I was going to be firm and leave him. He would survive. I had to let go. When he called the ashram, I refused to speak to him, but he wouldn't give up. Each time the phone rang, I knew it was Harish. Why did he call? 'Please God,' I prayed, 'give him the common sense to stop. I don't want to hurt him.' What did I have to do to make him understand that I neither needed nor wanted this relationship? I had to tell him that I only wanted to be with myself, that I didn't want to be swamped by his love and he should take it somewhere else because it came in my way.

One night he kept calling till the operator, whom I had asked not to let any calls through, gave up. I took the call.

'You shouldn't have called. I don't want you to call me. I'm finding myself here and I need my privacy and my space. Please don't trouble me,' I said.

'Okay,' he said. 'If that is what you want.'

I hung up. I felt rotten. Not him! I couldn't do this to him. What if I was in his place? The least I would expect would be some explanation. I called him at the office the next morning and apologized. I tried to explain. I wanted him to understand that it had nothing to do with him. He would always be my best friend, if he could only understand. I needed space. He called again that night. We spoke for almost an hour. I did most of the speaking. It sounded horrid to my ears, but I was committed to doing it. This had to come to an end. And this was the nicest, easiest way to let it happen.

'Be a good human being,' I said to him. 'Let everyone know what a good guy you are.'

He said, 'I'm only committed to you. If you want it this way, I'll do my best.'

He broke my heart. How could I not want to hug and hold this man? How could I not love him, for better or for worse? He was totally committed to me and I was turning him away. Who knows why we do what we do. And why things choose to happen the way they do.

I read out a poem from Bhartrihari:

'When dark passion wove a web of ignorance about me, then a Man seemed to fill the world's expanse. But now that I am favoured with keener discernment, my tranquil sight sees Brahma throughout the Universe.'

I changed Brahma to Shiva when I repeated the lines to Harish. 'Who is Shiva here?' he asked.

'Not you,' I said. 'My Shiva is beautiful and serene and fills the universe.'

'You are my universe and I dwell on you,' he said. Of course I was thrilled with such a response. I wished he would continue to say those things. In spite of my telling him to go his way and live a proper family life, I knew I would have been disappointed had he tried to be a good husband. Because it would be forced for him. I wanted him to control his need for sex. He couldn't have it with me, but he shouldn't want it with or give it out of a sense of duty to anyone else. If he did, I'd turn him away for good. No excuse would be good enough. Yes, that was it! I'd have a solid reason to turn him away. I'd deny him my body. If he slipped and gave in to husbandly duties, he could continue with that and there would be no guilt from my side. I felt rotten, egotistical, self-centred, and utterly selfish! But it seemed a reasonable plan.

'I don't know why I'm saying this to you, but I don't mean to let you have sex with me in future. It's ridiculous—I don't want it, but I won't let you have it elsewhere either,' I said to Harish when he called next.

He laughed! 'Baby, there's no way that can happen. In fact I've been thinking of what you said about us being spiritual friends. You're right. I had lost my spiritual path, but now I'm back with a vengeance. We'll do this together, don't you worry!'

'Actually, Tiger, I'm terribly confused,' I said. 'I have these two philosophies which are diametrically opposite. The first one is to do with Maya—everything is illusion. Everything passes. Nothing is forever. So everything loses value and meaning and I feel a certain detachment. All striving is for the spiritual self, which is the only thing that endures. Then there is the other theory, that there is only one life and it is short. Do what you must, get your pleasures, there is no tomorrow.'

He laughed again. 'Champu, I'm quite happy as I am but I have decided to change to become the man you have always longed to have. A spiritual partner. And I will give up whatever you feel is not desirable. Don't worry, I'll be whoever you want me to be. I'll do my best.'

'I'm so self-centred, Tiger. I know that I'm here only because you love me. If it wasn't for you, I'd float off and attach myself to another thing. You ground me, like a string on a gas balloon!'

'So how's the gas?' he guffawed.

'Still farting uncontrollably. I've read an article on menopause which says that gas, strange mind patterns, weight are all symptoms of menopause.'

He chuckled, and I wished I was back at Nrityagram, with

him rubbing oil into my feet and adoring me. I wondered at myself and asked myself again for the 600th time, 'What do I really want?' I didn't want to hurt him and lose him for ever. I also didn't want the guilt of ruining his home. Actually, I wanted to have my cake and eat it too.

I imagined him dying and my life completely empty without his presence, his total love, his laughter, his care and single-mindedness. The thought was unbearable. Tears came to my eyes just thinking about the loss. Maybe I didn't know it, perhaps I wouldn't ever accept it, but could it be that I loved this man as deeply as he loved me?

I saw a very ill old man in Kottakkal, a victim of paralysis. What would I do if that kind of thing happened to me, I thought. I knew I'd only have Harish. How long could the students serve me? My son and daughter would never stay month after month looking after me. They would certainly pay my bills and phone every once in a while to find out how I was. They might even come for one or two weekends and keep a nurse to look after me. It was sad, but then I would probably have done the same with my mother. I had not stayed with her throughout her illness. Nor had I shown great love, patience or tolerance when she visited me. It hurt to remember my insensitivity, my lack of care. No, I couldn't expect my children to be different from me. I did have expectations from my students, but Harish was the only one I could be absolutely certain about. He reminded me so much of Mario's good ways in the care, the time, the attention he gave me, despite how I treated him: 'I'll never marry you, never live with you,' I'd say; I wouldn't allow him to visit me on a regular basis; he couldn't just drop by whenever he wanted to be with me. That was just the way I was. Nrityagram was my first priority and I was a fickle creature. 'I could get attracted to someone else,' I would tell him, 'and then feel guilty and miserable about you being there, so will you *please* release me?'

Then, sometime in 1996, he left his home so that whenever

I called he would be free without hassles to come to my aid. I was in Bombay for a fortnight and on my return I found that he had taken a room on rent in town. He had left his wife and children! I was furious. How dare he make me feel guilty about another break-up! He calmly said that it was not for me but for himself that he had done this. He wanted to free himself from his wretched family life and find himself! I refused to let him visit me at Nrityagram. It could not be home. I would not be a substitute wife or a mistress either. I forbade him to call me. If I wanted to speak to him, if I wanted to get in touch, I'd call. He agreed. He said he would wait. And he did. I called him over for his birthday, made dinner, brought out the drinks. I allowed him to worship me. The devotion of that man was great. It humbled me, it humiliated me. 'Don't love me so much,' I cried, 'I don't deserve any of this. It's too much for me. Find yourself someone more deserving.'

'You are my Goddess,' he repeated for the millionth time. 'I have meditated all these years to find you. There's not a single moment when you don't exist in my mind!'

Does anyone know how it feels to be worshipped by a man? Forget the moments when you are irritated by his stupidity, his lack of knowledge and sophistication. Forget that he doesn't woo you in ordinary ways, doesn't try to impress you, doesn't pretend to be other than himself. Just imagine how it is to be the centre of a man's universe. The idea that he breathes only for you! Sounds fantastic, and one could say that it's always like this in the beginning of any romance. True. But this had been going on for three years already.

I had high blood pressure and my heart was skipping a beat and the doctor had said that I had to watch out for heart damage. When I came back from hospital, Harish called to say that I should come with him for a holiday, I needed a break. 'I'm tired,' I said, 'I just want to sleep.' So he asked me to put the receiver next to my pillow and go to sleep. He wanted to hear me breathe, snore, shuffle, everything. I left the phone close to my head and fell asleep. At 2 a.m. I awoke and whispered 'Tiger'. Immediately he answered. I sighed and went back to sleep. I awoke again at 4 a.m. and spoke into the phone: 'Are you still there?' 'Yes!' he said. 'I'm here, listening to your breath and your dogs barking in the distance.' At 8 a.m. he was still on the phone: 'Good morning, Champ. Time for tea.'

It was crazy. The man was a raving romantic. What a magnificent obsession. What a feeling to be wanted so intensely. To mean so much to someone! If only I could feel like that.

My office tensions and personal worries took their toll and I had a minor heart attack on 16 December and another one on 4 January. I was told to rest for six months! Pooja came to the hospital and took me back with her to Bombay for three weeks. I had to return for the Vasantahabba festival. It was a raging success as usual. Lynne had taken care of everything. She could take charge of Nrityagram. I had a man devoted to me, who gave me security. It was time, perhaps, to give up the old things and go in search of more meaningful things.

O

Till Siddharth died, I continued to treat Harish as a significant but temporary feature in my life. He was someone who was filling my days till the real thing claimed me. After the tragedy, I asked him whether he could give me a full twenty days of his life—I wanted him to travel with me to Kullu-Manali. That changed everything, both for him and for me.

So far, we would make a quick getaway whenever we could to Nagarhole or Mudumalai sanctuary near Mysore for two or three days at the most. He had business to attend to and a wife to answer to. He had freed himself of the daily problems of having to lie, to quarrel, to fight with his wife by simply moving out on his own, but he still had to continue attending to his business and supporting his family. Now I was asking for twenty whole days. His business would not survive that. He hesitated, said he'd let me know.

He had been feeling already that he had failed in his duty towards me. I had seen the pain in his eyes when he saw me cry uncontrollably after Siddharth's death. I remember the night in the amphitheatre when I had wailed and howled for hours into the night. He had stood there looking completely defeated. He could do nothing to ease my pain, undo my loss. He felt he had failed. What use was his life, his fortune, if he couldn't make me happy? I had asked for something now—his company for twenty days in the Himalayas. Of course he couldn't but say yes.

His hesitation lasted one full day. The turmoil in his mind must have been great, for he took hard decisions that day which would change his life completely. And for what? A mere twenty days that I would allow him? I think I would have forgiven him if he had been unable to say yes to my request. But life goes by its own laws. He had prayed to his gods to give him a few moments with his beloved one, and now I was asking him for twenty full days of togetherness, to share my loss and pain and to be of some help. Suddenly it was crystal clear to him—the gods had heard his prayers, they were offering him the chance of a lifetime and he was not going to throw it away. That was when he decided to give up all his worldly possessions, his attachment to his children, just to be with the woman he thought he was born to serve.

It would be wrong of me not to stress his attachment to his children. He missed them deeply, he suffered within, but he had to live with that torment because nothing was more important than me. He would have no ambition, no pride, no ego, no values, no attachment, no desire. When I had my heart attacks, he suffered more than I did, not being allowed to be near me all the time. He prayed, meditated non-stop. When I went through a tough time deciding to hand over Nrityagram, he stood behind me like a rock, never disapproving or approving, only supporting me. He was ready to take me away to safety in some Himalayan cave or temple or, if necessary, to start a business again, no matter how small, to keep me supplied with all my needs. He gave me the courage and the will to hang in there.

Where others said, 'Don't hesitate, just let us know when you need something' or 'Remember that we're always there for you', he said nothing. He just made himself available for anything. He knew what I needed, before I needed it. He didn't say, 'Take your medicine,' he brought it, placed it in my mouth and handed me the glass of water. He made my bed tea and pressed my feet every night. Every whim of mine was attended to. I became a child once again. I had learnt to trust fully again.

Somewhere I carried a guilt that I had not been fair to him, not loved him back, not cared for him. True to character, I had been self-centred and selfish. But his faith was contagious, I was learning, slowly, how to let go of my own insecurities and fears.

Instead of Kullu-Manali, I went with him to Tapovan in Badrinath, Kedarnath, Kalisaur and Hemkund. Without my knowing it, I had started Harish on an action plan. Thus far, for years he had meditated on Shiva-Shakti, going from one astrologer to another, believing he had a spiritual calling and knowing that he was meant for other things, but he was trapped in family life and business. Chance remarks from me over the past four years had strengthened his spiritual urge and he had moved away from his wife and family. In his small rented room, he was trying to live the life of a sadhu, but was still attending to his business. He wanted nothing for himself. My ill health, my loss, my unhappiness at the events in my life caused him great pain. Strange urgings rose within him and he decided to abandon all that he knew and take sanyas. He asked me about it. 'So much courage. Where do you get it from?' I said. That was all he needed to hear. His mind was made up. He wrote letters to his mother and wife, handing over to them his business and all his belongings.

We had a strange and wonderful time for three weeks, driving, walking, trekking in the Garhwal Himalayas, camping by the Ganga, cuddling in our tent, unafraid, free and happy.

In the mountains I saw proof of what I already knew, that he was a good human being. He was kind to all animals (he regularly bought special food to feed birds and dogs). He would have handed over his last currency note to anyone more desperately in need of it than him. Even his one and only blanket, which was his protection from the cold Himalayan winds, was given to an old woman who did not have enough warm clothes. He had great respect for all the sadhus and various gurus of ashrams. He was living the life of a true sadhu, unlike those others who smoked charas, huddled in groups, enticed foreign women, and sometimes cheated people of their money. He bathed regularly in the Ganga, sat by her banks for six to eight hours in meditation, minded his own business, spoke very little, asked for nothing and always seemed content and happy.

On my return to Bangalore, I cleaned out his rented room and handed over his belongings to Jay Kumar, his friend. It felt like disposing off the belongings of a dead person. Exactly what I had done three months ago for Siddharth. It seemed to be a year of departures, for the end of various attachments—Nrityagram, Kuteeram, Siddharth, Harish. But I knew that new blades of grass would shoot out from under the snow after winter and a new life would begin. My grandchild was to be born and with it would come a whole new energy for doing more and better things. New horizons would open up and I would be whole again.

I wrote to Harish every day, letters c/o Postmaster Rishikesh. I sent him a telegram wanting to know if he was safe and okay. I, who fell asleep even before hitting the pillow, could not sleep. I would pace and prowl around the empty kathak gurukul, wander outside, sit in meditation and try desperately to connect, to get onto his wavelength. But where was he? I had a horrible gut feeling about him not being okay. What if he died? I had never been loved in that way, so obsessively, so completely. What if he should discover such a deep oneness with his spiritual self that he needed me no longer? The thought frightened me. And yet how wonderful it would be for him.

Harish phoned, saying he was okay. I said we could go to Kullu-Manali after I returned from USA where I was going for the birth of Pooja's child. That made him happy.

I returned from the US, healed by the miracle of my granddaughter's birth. She had brought hope into my life. In Manali I sat on a huge boulder one afternoon with the river Beas rushing and frothing below. I was trying to commune with my son, who had loved me beyond words and whom I still loved with all my being, and I went into a trance. I closed my eyes and asked for a direction, a meaning, a purpose, a deliverance from my loss, an understanding, a freedom from my petty and restricted self, and the answer came like lightning and with amazing clarity—'Give to this man all that you wish you had given your son. Learn the language of love, service and caring in its true meaning. Have faith and trust.'

Before I could turn around to signal to Harish to come to me, I felt his arms around me, his face resting at the nape of my neck. Exactly as Shone used to do. I heard Shone's voice, full of love and embarrassment, saying 'Deekoo' again and again and I understood then that Shone boy would always be near me. I had seen his face in the faces of so many young men, including Farhan, my son-in-law. My son would always live for me.

Even after that I gave no assurance to Bheeshma (he had changed his name and was no longer Harish) that we would live together in the future. He had no clue that I had already made my will. All I had told him was that he was to deal with my mortal remains after my death. We lived one day at a time.

In 'The Valley of the Gods', I would spend my time walking

in the mountains, by the riverside, cooking exotic food with him, discovering new places, playing cards, reading, writing, listening to old sentimental Hindi songs, and watching the light change in the early mornings and in the evenings. I lazed in bed, fussed and cribbed just to feel like a spoilt brat. I received a lot of love, physical and emotional, from him. I had become a child once again. I laughed a lot, because I was treated like a child. My shoelaces were untied for me, my socks were removed, I was given baths—'Shut your eyes now,' he would say, 'I'm going to soap your face.' I was spoon-fed, my clothes were washed and folded away, my bed was made for me. I hoped I would never grow up again. I had found the perfect Mother/Protector/ Devotee.

o

February 1998, Dhammagiri Vipassana Centre

There always must be a lesson in every experience. I think about my life and where it is going and realize that once again time is running out. Perhaps Harish will die too and I will be left without his love. If he should die, I will sink in regret and guilt. There would be too much grief and suffering because I would know that I hadn't really loved him back. Please, please let him be alive and well. I will find him wherever he is, in Assam or Rishikesh, and give him the joy and happiness he always dreams of. Let me make up for not having loved my mother and son. I let them go without showing them that I loved them deeply. Harish always says to me, 'If you die, or if you leave me for someone else, I won't feel unhappy, because I've given you my best. I haven't wasted a single moment of my life. You have been in every breath, my every moment is full of you and when you are with me I take all that I can from you. Yes! I've truly enjoyed you, loved you one hundred per cent.'

And he's right. He's lucky he lives so well. I've caught him staring at me in my sleep, massaging my feet, caressing me with his looks. 'Can't lose a moment,' he says. 'I have to get my fill of you.' O Lord! To love like that! What a great feeling it must be for him to love like that.

Many are the times when I think that he's certainly more 'there' than I can ever hope to be. He's aware, he's in the 'present' at all times, he's positive, he's active, he's smiling and he's always ready for anything and everything. He's amazing! How can I, a wretched, ignorant woman, unenlightened, crabby and limited that I am, how can I continue to be blind, to have so many chances and yet screw up? I'm not going to continue my old patterns. I'm going to find my Tigerman and live with him, enjoying every moment of our togetherness. I'm going to encourage his meditation and growth, and who knows, he may even succeed in teleporting himself, as he believes he can, and do 'astral-travel'. Let me not close my mind to his dreams. He just may be more right than me!

How long must the land lie fallow to regain its strength? It's been a few years now. Three heart attacks, much travel, the giving up of Nrityagram and Kuteeram, Siddharth's loss, and becoming a grandmother! So much has happened. What is my future? I want to buy a Tempo traveller and put all my belongings in it and roam around India as a gypsy, dispensing compassion, learning, care, and medicines to the needy. My money will be well spent.

There is such a quickening of the pulse when I think of my future. Something great, something grand is in store for me. I can sense it, but what can it be? The temptation to peek into the future is overpowering.

Where is life taking me? Am I to have an enlightened death? I dream of my death often. I hope I go courageously, with an aware and equanimous mind.

[*Shortly afterwards, Protima left on a pilgrimage to Kailash-Mansarovar. She died on the way, on 17 August 1998, in a landslide.*]

afterword

(by pooja bedi ebrahim)

Birth, according to my mother, was not the beginning, and death was not the end. 'To fear death is to fear life itself,' she would say, 'it's all part of the karmic cycle. The body may age and eventually perish, but the soul is eternal. If you take an empty closed jar and break it, the air within the jar merges with the air around it. It's the same with us. Once our bodies are no more, the soul merges with the universal energies, so we must ensure that the energy that is our soul remains vibrant, pure and good . . . Our bodies are merely jars that contain the soul. I'm just a soul having a human experience.'

And what a fabulous experience she had. She would breeze in and fill your life with light, energy, love and joy. She enriched many lives. No matter how much you took of her love and generosity, there was plenty remaining for everyone else. Life was to be shared and experienced. She would raise her tattooed eyebrows in mock despair and exclaim, 'How *boring* people are!

They form narrow little social units and meander aimlessly through life, so afraid of change. What a waste of this glorious gift called life.'

She firmly believed that life's experiences could and should make one better, not bitter. Even before Siddharth's suicide, which was a shattering blow, she had started on a path to personal transformation, both external and internal. She would waste no time and attention on her external self and wanted to make it insignificant in her interactions with people, so she shaved her head and donned blue robes. Her overwhelming desire was to establish a deeper connection with nature and be better attuned to God and the universe. She had become very interested in religion and spiritualism.

She realized that in her new quest she had to cut herself loose from everything that bound her materially and physically. She had to give up Nrityagram, Kuteeram, even her dance.

Dissociating herself from the day-to-day administration of Nrityagram was easy. But letting go of her dream project entirely was hard. There were too many emotions involved. Nrityagram was her baby. She had started it and had remained in control throughout. Everybody there needed her and looked up to her; it was enough to make anyone in her position feel proud and terribly attached to the place. There were times when she would yell at herself: 'No attachments!'

Fortunately for her, she found in Surupa Sen, Nrityagram's star dancer, someone who shared her spirit and her vision. She was entirely convinced that Surupa would preserve what she had created. More importantly, in Lynne Fernandez she found someone practical who could take Nrityagram to greater heights. Lynne became her right arm—her 'olde doggee-faced darling, capable and trusted'. 'She's doing a better job than I ever could,' she told me. The board of trustees was reconstituted to ensure that Lynne would have the support necessary for the continued success of Nrityagram.

Finally the handing over of Nrityagram happened to her satisfaction. It had established itself firmly on the country's cultural map and the dance ensemble was earning rave reviews at home and abroad. Now it had been handed over to people who had given the best years of their lives to it.

The process of giving up Kuteeram proved more difficult. The pressures of the loans she had taken to set it up were mounting, and then Rahul and Malini Akerkar, who were managing the resort for her, decided to return to Bombay. Finally the Taj group entered the scene and she felt relieved. But as with any big enterprise, they took their time, tying up loose ends and working out endless formalities. She began to despair. She had to be free, and soon. Siddharth's death took a huge toll on her. She could wait no longer and went to Mr Krishna Kumar's office at Taj and broke down. She wanted all material responsibilities to end. She could not have any more bonds, dues or liabilities. The memorandum of agreement was signed soon afterwards and she made plans to go off to the Himalayas.

She had decided to live the life of a sanyasin, wandering from ashram to ashram, bathing in the Ganga, going on pilgrimages. She was also concentrating on sorting out her personal life, clearing out the old cobwebs and leaving good feelings behind. She had always maintained that my dad and she would be together in their old age, sitting around the fireplace with their children and grandchildren and reminiscing about their lives. After Aalia's birth, when the family was together at my dad's Santa Monica home for Christmas, she said to me, 'Remember that vision I always had? It's happened, even if not exactly as I wanted it. Kabir, me, Farhan, you, Aalia, Nikki, Susan and Adam—all of us eating and drinking around the fireplace. So much love and laughter and good cheer!'

The way she went about things, it was almost as if she had made up her mind not to return from the Himalayas. She made out her will, handed over all her jewellery to me and informed me of all her investments and life insurance policies. She spent hours crooning to Aalia. Then, with the clanging of the lift doors, she was gone. That was the last time I saw her.

I have wondered about this often. It was too neat, too perfect. Could she have known? She had turned deeply spiritual and had become practically a vegetarian. She had made trips to Hemkund Sahib, Gangotri, Rishikesh, Tirupati and to monasteries in Ladakh. Before embarking on the pilgrimage to Kailash-Mansarovar, she wrote to practically everyone she loved and cared for, even to eight-month-old Aalia. All the letters had an air of finality about them.

In her long letter to me she summed up her entire life. She wrote of her childhood and adolescence, her insecurities as an adult and how she had come to terms with them, and the immense joy she had found with her soul mate, Bheeshma (Harish). 'I'm having a very happy, contented time,' she wrote. 'I have become a child once again. I laugh a lot because I'm treated like a child . . . I hope I never grow up again. I wish you some of the joy and contentment I feel these days. I'm definitely in heaven. Kullu means 'The Valley of the Gods'; may all the gods and goddesses know of my gratitude.'

The Kailash-Mansarovar yatra is an arduous pilgrimage and despite my valiant attempts to deter her (she had already had three heart attacks), she went ahead. But then, nothing had ever daunted her. She knew no fear. No challenge was too great, no task too arduous, no mission impossible. On the night of 17 August her group camped at Malpa, Pithoragarh in the Garhwal Himalayas. It was raining heavily and the landslide occurred very late at night. They were all asleep. Death was instantaneous. There were no survivors. The weather conditions made rescue operations practically impossible. While my mother's belongings, including her passport, were recovered, her body never was. She had always wanted to die one with nature and used to wince at the thought of dying a common, painful death and being burned in some soulless crematorium. Well, I guess she had her way even in death.

It is said that those who die on the Kailash-Mansarovar pilgrimage attain moksha. That is small consolation for those who get left behind. But then mourning is such a selfish thing. We cry and grieve because *we* are unhappy, *we* miss the dead and feel alone and abandoned. We cry for ourselves, not for the person who has moved on. I think the biggest gift is to have the good fortune of dying happy. My mother died a happy human being.

Protima may not be with us physically, but her essence cannot die. She lives on. In everyone and everything that she touched with her love, generosity, wit, compassion and courage. She lives through me, Aalia, Nrityagram and Kuteeram.

source notes

Apart from the incomplete manuscript of Protima Bedi's autobiography, *Timepass* has been derived from the following sources:

prologue

p.1-2 'I am told . . .', Journal, undated

my first death

p.3-5 'I should start with . . .', Journal, undated

p.5-8 'On 12 October 1949 . . .', Journal, 1970; Journal, August 1977

the early years

p.9-18 'When I was about . . .', Journal, undated; *Savvy*, April 1985

p.18-20 'Being a good girl . . .', Journal, August 1977; *Bombay*, 7-21 November 1979

first loves

p.21-29 'In the second year . . .', Journal, undated

meeting kabir

p.30-42 'It was September 1968 . . .', Journal, undated; Journal, 1970

p.42-45 'Kabir and I moved . . .', Journal, undated; *Savvy*, April 1985

marriage

p.46-47 'We married, Kabir and I . . .', Journal, undated

p.47-53 'Less than a year . . .', Journal, 1970; Journal, undated

p.53-59 'Early in 1971 . . .', Journal, February 1971

p.59-60 'I knew I had . . .', Letter to Siddharth Bedi, 16 December 1996; Journal, undated

p.60-61 'After I had my . . .', Journal, April 1991

p.61-63 'After the success of . . .', Journal, January 1973; Journal, February 1973; Journal, July 1973

p.66-67 'Meanwhile the problems . . .', Journal, 18 August 1976

p.67-68 'One ocassion when he . . .', Journal, July 1973

p.68-70 'My reactions to . . .', Journal, October, 1973

p.70-71 'Some months later . . .', Journal, January 1974

europe

p.72-79 'In May 1974 . . .', Journal, undated; Letter to Kabir Bedi, 25 May 1974

p.79-80 'But not every . . .', Journal, undated; Letter to Kabir Bedi, 3 June 1974

p.80-81 'I wanted to extend . . .', Journal, undated; Letter to Kabir Bedi, 15 August 1974

p.81-82 'But I had a . . .', Journal, undated; Letter to Kabir Bedi, 17 July 1974

p.82 'I left Europe . . .', Journal, August 1974

p.82-83 'And it has always . . .', Journal, undated

p.83-85 'Shortly after I returned . . .', Journal, undated; *Savvy*, April 1985

finding a purpose

p.86-87 'I was a product of . . .', Journal, March 1975; *Gentleman*, August 1981

p.87-94 'And then one day . . .', Journal, July 1975; Journal, May 1987; *Savvy*, April 1985 p.94-96 'Guruji told me . . .', Journal, undated; Journal, May 1987; *Gentleman*, August 1981

p.96-98 'Even in those early . . .', Journal, 23 November 1976

p.98 'When I came back . . .', Journal, July 1975; *Bombay*, 7-21 November 1979

the split

p.99-102 'I returned from Orissa . . .', Journal, August 1975; Journal, December 1975

p.102-05 'Parveen had been . . .', Journal, August 1975; Journal, undated; *Stardust*, September 1977

p.105-07 'Soon after I had . . .', Journal, December 1975; Journal, undated

p.107 'Actually, everything had . . .', Journal, January 1976

p.107-09 'Parveen did not bother . . .', Journal, undated

p.109 'Kabir insisted on . . .', Journal, 20 January 1976

p.109-12 'Parveen and I never . . .', Journal, undated; Journal, 5 February 1976

p.112-13 'When Kabir rang up . . .', Journal, 20 February 1976

p.113-14 'The divorce finally . . .', Journal, undated

p.114-16 'After the divorce . . .', Journal, undated; Journal, 10 February 1984

p.116-18 'Kabir and I remain . . .', Journal, March 1979; *Stardust*, February 1976

p.118 'It is peculiar that . . .', Journal, undated; *Stardust*, September 1977

a new direction

p.119-23 'The time Kabir left . . .', Journal, March 1977; Journal, 1983; Journal, undated

p.123-26 'In Bombay my first . . .', Journal, undated

p.126-31 'After the separation . . .', Letters to Pandit Jasraj, 1 April 1980, 14 May 1981; Journal, November 1987

finding a balance

p.132-34 'Kabir is getting married . . .', Journal, January 1979; Journal, February 1979 p.134-35 'The Odissi Dance Centre . . .', Journal, February 1979; Journal, May 1987

p.135-39 'Kabir and Susan arrived . . .', Journal, March 1979

p.139-40 'My dance had become . . .', Journal, July 1979; Journal, undated

p.140-42 'Through 1980 I lived . . .' Journal, undated; Letter to Pooja and Siddharth Bedi, 20 March 1980; Letter to Pooja Bedi, 25 March 1980

p.142-44 'Pooja and Siddharth went . . .', Journal, undated; Letter to Kabir Bedi, 29 October 1980

p.144 'Only when I was . . .', Journal, February 1981

a beautiful relationship

p.145-47 'I was living in with . . .', Letter to Amit Patel, 11 October 1996; Journal, undated

p.147-49 'I gave up a lot . . .', Journal, undated; *Celebrity*, July 1984; *Savvy*, April 1985

p.149-51 'Even when Rajni . . .', Journal, 27 April 1982

p.151-53 'I will never forget . . .', Journal, undated; Letter to Amit Patel, 11 October 1996

p.153-56 'Rajni and I used to . . .', Journal, undated; Letter to Amit Patel, 11 October 1996; Journal, 27 April 1982

p.156-58 'I was working . . .', Journal, 26 June 1982; *Femina*, October 1982

p.158-59 'Russi Karanjia wrote . . .', Journal, 30 June 1982

p.159-63 'In September 1982 . . .', Journal, 24 September 1982; Journal, 26 September 1982

p.163-64 'I remember a party . . .', Journal, 24 November 1982

p.164-65 'I kept Rajni's letters . . .', Journal, undated; Letter to Amit Patel, 11 October 1996

moving on

p.166-73 'In the winter of 1982 . . .', Journal, October 1982

p.173-76 'I did not seriously . . .', Journal, 12 November 1982

p.176-77 'Perhaps I was . . .', Journal, undated

p.178-80 'The year 1982 was . . .', Journal, 16 December 1982

p.180-83 'In those heady days . . .', Journal, 14 January 1983 p.183-88 'In Jan 1983, Kabir . . .', Journal, 25 January 1983; Journal, 30 Jan 1983; Journal, 1 February 1983

p.188-89 'After Kabir and Susan . . .', Journal, 31 March 1983

p.189-92 'In April 1983 . . .', Journal, 7 April 1983; Journal, May 1983

blind date

p.193-97 'The year following . . .', Journal, undated; Journal, November 1983

p.197 'Manu had a . . .', Journal, July 1983

p.197-200 'Mario Kropf, the blind . . .', Journal, November 1983; Journal, 4 January 1984

p.201-09 'Mario left for . . .', Journal, 23 January 1984; Journal, 27 January 1984; Journal, 30 January 1984; Journal, 10 February 1984

p.209-14 'In March 1984 . . .', Journal, 6 March 1984; Journal, 13 March 1984; Journal, 22 March 1984

p.214-16 'One night there was . . .', Journal, 24 April 1984

p.216-17 'I had lunch with . . .', Journal, undated

p.217-22 'Mario and I went . . .', Journal, June 1984

p.222-23 'In 1985, I was . . .', Journal, undated; Letter to Pooja Bedi, 7 August 1985; Journal, November 1987

a dream come true

p.224-25 'When I was in . . .', Journal, August 1985

p.225-29 'In 1987 I was in . . .', Journal, 27 March 1987; Letter to Pooja Bedi, 3 September, 1987; Letter to Pooja Bedi, 22 September 1987

p.229 'Kabir was back . . .', Letter to Pooja Bedi, 15 May 1988

p.229-32 'One day in March . . .', Journal, undated; Letter to Martand Singh, 16 May 1989

p.232 'One acre of land . . .', Journal, undated; *City Tab*, February 1990; Letter to Vijaypat Singhania, 24 November 1996; Letter to Martand Singh, 7 December 1989

p.232-34 'Sometime in January . . .', Journal, undated; *City Tab*, February 1990; Journal, 17 November 1989; Letter to Martand Singh, 4 March 1990

p.234-35 'When some of the . . .', Journal, undated; Letter to Martand Singh, 3 October 1989 p.235-36 'When I first arrived . . .', Journal, undated

p.236-37 'I wanted Nrityagram to . . .', Journal, August 1989; *City Tab*, February 1990; Letter to Martand Singh, 29 June 1989; Letter to Martand Singh, 30 October 1989

p.237 'But the dejection . . .', Letter to Martand Singh, 8 August 1989

p.237-38 'During the election . . .', Journal, 17 November 1989; Letter to Martand Singh, 7 December 1989.

p.238-40 'Six months after . . .', Journal, May 1990; Letter to Martand Singh, 16 May 1990

p.240-41 'We had chosen Gauri . . .', Journal, August 1989; Interview in 'From the Horse's Mouth', Doordarshan.

p.241-42 'I did wonder at . . .', Journal, undated; Letter to Martand Singh, 3 May 1990

p.242-43 'At night, when . . .', Journal, May 1990

p.243-47 'A month after . . .', Journal, 31 August 1990; Letter to Martand Singh, 20 June 1990

p.247-48 'That night the moon . . .', Journal, 5 September 1990

p.248-50 'By September 1990 . . .', Letter to Siddharth Bedi, 21 September 1990; Letter to Mario Kropf, 15 September 1990

p.250 'Despite my disappointment . . .', Journal, undated

shaping nrityagram

p.252-53 'Nrityagram won the . . .', Letter to Nilima, 20 March 1991; Journal, undated

p.253 'I did pujas . . .', Journal, June 1992; Letter to Pooja Bedi, 17 June 1992

p.253-54 'All the tension of . . .', Journal, 20 August 1992

p.254-56 'It was easier to . . .', Journal, 9 August 1992; Journal, 13 August 1992

p.256 'Collecting funds had to . . .', Journal, 9 August 1992; Letter to Kumudini Lakhia, 5 November 1992

p.257-59 'Guru Kelucharan had . . .', Journal, November 1992; Letter to Guru Kelucharan Mahapatra, 23 May 1992; Letter to Pattabhi Raman, 17 July 1993

p.259-60 'I was taking the . . .', Journal, December 1993; Letter to Bijaya Das, 2 December 1993

p.260-62 'None of us at . . .', Journal, December 1993; Letter to

Ratikant Mahapatra, 23 July 1993; Letter to Pattabhi Raman, 17 July 1993; Letter to Guru Kelucharan Mahapatra, 17 July 1993; Letter to Sanjukta Panigrahi, 15 April 1994

p.262-63 'Murphy's law: If . . .', Journal, undated; Letter to Guru Kelucharan Mahapatra, 12 March 1994

p.263-65 'And to add to . . .', Journal, undated; Letters to Mario Kropf, 27 June 1989, 24 August 1991, 31 March 1995; Letters from Mario to Protima, 19 November 1992, 1 December 1992

p.265-66 'When I took my . . .', Journal, November 1993; Letter to Guru Kelucharan Mahapatra, 24 November 1993; Letter to Bijaya Das, 2 December 1993; Letter to Cornelia Besie, 29 July 1993

p.266 'I returned from USA . . .', Letter to Guru Kelucharan Mahapatra, 24 November 1993; Journal, 24 July 1994

p.266-67 'Meanwhile, I was . . .', Letter to Cornelia Besie, 29 July 1993; Letter to Kapil Dev, 17 July 1993; Letter to Ramesh Morarka, 17 March 1993

p.267 'By the time . . .', Journal, February 1994; Letter to Ramakrishna Hegde, 26 January 1994; Letter to Lynne Fernandez, 22 March 1993; Letter to Margaret Leung, 12 January 1994

p.267-68 'I was tired . . .', Journal, February 1994; Letter to Vijaypat Singhania, 1 February 1994; Letter to Gerard da Cunha, 1 February 1994

p.268-69 'There were also . . .', Letter to Vijaypat Singhania, 16 February 1994; Letter to Pooja Bedi, 6 June 1994

p.269 'Guru Kelucharan Mahapatra . . .', Journal, 12 September 1994

p.269-70 'I wanted Nrityagram . . .', Journal, January 1995; Letter to Arjun Sajnani, 9 January 1995

my flesh and blood

p.271-72 'In 1971 I was . . .', Journal, undated; Letters to Siddharth Bedi, 12 January 1994, 16 December 1996; Letter to Pooja Bedi, 6 June 1994

p.272-73 'I don't deserve . . .', Letter to Pooja Bedi, 18 June 1995

p.273-74 'Motherhood has been . . .', Journal, April 1991

p.274-75 'I tried to be . . .', Journal, undated; *Savvy*, April 1985 p.275-76 'I never interfered . . .', Journal, undated; Protima Bedi's rejoinder to Dom Moraes' article in *Mid-Day*, 6 October 1991

p.277-82 'I remember a strange . . .', Journal, 3 January 1978

p.282-83 'Siddharth continued to . . .', Journal, undated; Letter to Pooja Bedi, October 1987

p.283-85 'When he turned . . .', Letters from Siddharth Bedi to Protima Bedi, 6 December 1991, 16 January 1992, 11 June 1992; Journal, undated

p.285-86 'When he came to . . .', Journal, undated; Letter from Siddharth Bedi to Protima Bedi,—August 1992

p.286-88 'It worried me . . .', Journal, undated; Letter to Siddharth Bedi, 12 January 1994

p.289-90 'A couple of months . . .', Journal, undated; Letter to Pooja Bedi, 6 June 1994

p.290-93 'Back in USA . . .', Journal, undated; Letter to Siddharth Bedi, 29 June 1994

p.293-94 'Soon Siddharth started . . .', Journal, undated; Letters to Siddharth Bedi, 14 December 1995, 16 December 1996; Letter to Kabir Bedi,—December 1996

p.294-96 'Siddharth did come . . .', Journal, undated; Letter to Cornelia Besie, 18 January 1997; Letters to Kabir Bedi, 12 December 1996, 1 April 1997

p.296 'Siddharth committed suicide . . .', Journal, undated; Siddharth's suicide note, 19 July 1997

p.297-99 'Siddharth had gone . . .', Journal, undated; Journal, 14 November 1997

sanyas

p.300-02 'By 1996, I had . . .', Journal, June 1996; Letter to Rajiv Agarwal, 13 August 1996; Letter to Pooja Bedi,—July 1998

p.302-07 'All through those . . .', Journal, June 1995; Journal, December 1995; Journal, February 1996; Letter to Pooja Bedi,—July 1998

p.308-11 'Till Siddharth died . . .', Journal, October 1997

p.311-12 'I returned from . . .', Journal, October 1997; Journal, February 1998

p.313-15 'There always must be . . .', Journal, February 1998

index